HTML5 Game Development HOTSH⊕T

Build interactive games with HTML, DOM, and the CreateJS game library

Makzan

BIRMINGHAM - MUMBAI

HTML5 Game Development HOTSHOT

First published: July 2014

Production reference: 1010714

Published by Packt Publishing Ltd.
Livery Place
35 Livery Street
Birmingham B3 2PB, UK.

ISBN 978-1-84969-546-6

www.packtpub.com

Cover image by Thomas Mak (mak@makzan.net)

Credits

Author
Makzan

Reviewers
Maxime AILLOUD

Hatem Alimam

Othree Kao

Willian "PotHix" Molinari

Kevin Roast

Tim Severien

Roberto Ulloa

Commissioning Editor
Erol Staveley

Acquisition Editors
Saleem Ahmed

Antony Lowe

Rebecca Pedley

Luke Presland

Content Development Editor
Amey Varangaonkar

Technical Editors
Mrunmayee Patil

Aman Preet Singh

Copy Editors
Gladson Monteiro

Adithi Shetty

Project Coordinator
Shiksha Chaturvedi

Proofreaders
Simran Bhogal

Maria Gould

Paul Hindle

Indexers
Mehreen Deshmukh

Rekha Nair

Graphics
Abhinash Sahu

Production Coordinator
Manu Joseph

Cover Work
Manu Joseph

About the Author

Makzan focuses on web development and game design. He has over 14 years of experience in building digital products. He has worked on real-time multiplayer interaction games, iOS applications, and rich interactive websites.

He has written two books and one video course on building a Flash virtual world and creating games with HTML5 and the latest web standards. He is currently teaching courses in Hong Kong and Macao SAR.

I would like to thank my wife, Candy Wong, for supporting all my writings. A book is not a one-man effort. This book wouldn't have happened without the help of the Packt Publishing team and the reviewers. Thanks to all the editors and technical reviewers for improving the book and making sure it happened.

About the Reviewers

Maxime AILLOUD was always involved in game development along with his study from the time he was a child. He wasn't aware of web development at first, but it wasn't so far along the road as some of his colleagues created an association in Lyon to promote game development. Organizing a game jam, 48h of game creation, was one of their goals. It was enough for him to get into game development. For now, it's just a hobby, but maybe one day, it'll be a part of his job.

> Big thanks to Packt Publishing for letting me help them review this book; hope it suits their needs.

Hatem Alimam is a senior developer at Engineering Ingegneria Informatica. He has been involved in making the "today" website since he was 16. He has reviewed several books based on various web technologies, and he's also interested in open source projects. In his free time, you will find him on `http://stackoverflow.com/`. You can find more details about him at `http://hatemalimam.com/`.

Othree Kao is a frontend engineer at HTC, Taiwan. He has played with and studied web standards for more than 10 years. He has developed several Vim plugins such as `vim` and `javascript-libraries-syntax.vim`, which has made an F2E's life happier. He is also a very active web standards evangelist in Taiwan. He has given speeches at COSCUP, OSDC, and JSDC. Besides this, he has also worked as a volunteer photographer at these conferences.

Willian Molinari, also known as PotHix, is a Brazilian developer who works with languages such as Ruby, Python, a bit of Go, and some others that may appear as the correct tool for the job.

He is one of the main organizers of Sao Paulo Ruby Users Group (Guru-SP), created in 2008. In his free time, he likes to play with different things, such as game development with JavaScript and HTML5 and quantitative finance with Python. He has developed a game called Skeleton Jigsaw that is open source, and the code for this is available on the Plaev GitHub account (`http://github.com/plaev`).

Tim Severien is an ambitious frontend developer from the Netherlands. In his spare time, he assists his fellow developers and writes and fiddles with the newest features available. Occasionally, he writes for `flippinawesome.org`.

Roberto Ulloa has a diverse academic record in multiple disciplines within the field of computer science. He obtained an MSc from the University of Costa Rica and has also taught programming and computer networking there. He then spent two years doing PhD-level research on cultural complexity at the CulturePlex Lab of the University of Western Ontario.

He loves travelling and enjoys an itinerant life, living among different cultures and environments. He loves nature and has spent many months volunteering in Central and South America. Currently, he can be found somewhere in South East Asia, wandering in a new place or settling down for a few weeks in a comfortable town to get some work done. Indeed, at one of his stops, he wrote the book *Kivy: Interactive Applications in Python*, *Packt Publishing*, which was published in 2013, for which he is very grateful.

He earns his living as a web developer in Python/Django and PHP/Wordpress. Also, he tries to have as much free time as possible to collaborate with different research colleagues; work on his own projects, which includes his blog (`http://robertour.com`); or acquire new knowledge through reading books or online courses. He constantly worries that the Internet has already become aware of itself, and we are not able to communicate with it because of the improbability of it being able to provide information in Spanish or any of the 6,000 odd human languages that exist on the planet.

www.PacktPub.com

Support files, eBooks, discount offers, and more

You might want to visit www.PacktPub.com for support files and downloads related to your book.

Did you know that Packt offers eBook versions of every book published, with PDF and ePub files available? You can upgrade to the eBook version at www.PacktPub.com and as a print book customer, you are entitled to a discount on the eBook copy. Get in touch with us at service@packtpub.com for more details.

At www.PacktPub.com, you can also read a collection of free technical articles, sign up for a range of free newsletters and receive exclusive discounts and offers on Packt books and eBooks.

http://PacktLib.PacktPub.com

Do you need instant solutions to your IT questions? PacktLib is Packt's online digital book library. Here, you can access, read and search across Packt's entire library of books.

Why subscribe?

- ▸ Fully searchable across every book published by Packt
- ▸ Copy and paste, print and bookmark content
- ▸ On demand and accessible via web browser

Free access for Packt account holders

If you have an account with Packt at www.PacktPub.com, you can use this to access PacktLib today and view nine entirely free books. Simply use your login credentials for immediate access.

Table of Contents

Preface

HTML5 Game Development Hotshot combines the two latest hot topics: HTML5 and game development, and aims to showcase how we can build interactive games on the Web following the latest standards.

HTML5 has been widely adopted recently. It has become popular thanks to the widespread usage of modern web browsers in both desktops and mobile devices. The JavaScript and rendering performance has also improved. The nature of the web standards makes game development shine on web browsers.

We demonstrate two common approaches to build an HTML5 game. They are Document Object Model (DOM) elements with CSS and the canvas tag. The new properties in CSS3 provide convenient and high performance animation and transform control. On the other hand, the canvas tag along with the CreateJS library provide solid game-object management.

What this book covers

The following is a list of what we are going to build in this book. There are eight projects with eight different types of HTML5 games. Each project makes use of the knowledge learned in previous projects and introduces new techniques.

Project 1, *Building a CSS Quest Game*, starts with building a DOM element-based game. The game requires a player to choose the correct pattern sequence to complete the level.

Project 2, *Card Battle!*, deals with creating a card battle game that makes use of the CSS transform transition. We also learn the 3D-flipping effect.

Project 3, *Space Runner*, deals with building a running game that makes use of keyboard controls and frame-based animation in CSS.

Project 4, Multiply Defense, teaches us how to use the canvas tag and CreateJS game library to build an HTML5 game.

Project 5, Building an Isometric City Game, deals with constructing an isometric city-building game. We learn how we can store data locally and grow the city.

Project 6, Space Defenders, deals with creating a defending game. We learn how we can create animations easily in the CreateJS suite.

Project 7, A Ball-shooting Machine with Physics Engine, deals with creating a ball-throwing game by making use of the popular Box2D physics engine.

Project 8, Creating a Sushi Shop Game with Device Scaling, deals with making use of the media query to create a responsive game that works on mobiles or desktops. We also learned how to add sound effects.

After reading through all the projects, we should know how to build production-ready games and deploy them on the server to allow others to play them. The games may combine different web technologies and we learn the flexibility to choose the right technique for a specific type of game.

What you need for this book

In order to follow most of the game examples in this book, you need to have a modern web browser and a code editor. You may install Google Chrome, Mozilla Firefox, or Internet Explorer 10. The default Safari browser from Mac OS X also works like a charm.

In some projects, we used Adobe Flash to create graphics assets and animations. The graphics are exported into image files and a file named assets.js. Adobe Flash is not required to go through these projects. However, if you need to modify the source graphics, you will need Flash CC.

Ideally, we prefer a web server to host the game project. We do not use any server-side logic in this book. Any static web server should work. Optionally, opening the game HTML file directly from the filesystem will work.

Who this book is for

Whether you are familiar with the basics of object-oriented programming concepts, new to HTML game development, or familiar with just web designing, this project-based book will get you up and running in no time. It will teach and inspire you to create great interactive content on the Web.

Sections

A Hotshot book has the following sections:

Mission briefing

This section explains what you will build, with screenshots of the completed project.

Why is it awesome?

This section explains why the project is cool, unique, exciting, and interesting. It describes the advantages the project will give you.

Your Hotshot objectives

This section explains the major tasks required to complete your project, which are as follows:

- Task 1
- Task 2
- Task 3
- Task 4, and so on

Mission checklist

This section mentions prerequisites for the project (if any), such as resources or libraries that need to be downloaded.

Each **task** is explained using the following sections:

Task 1

Prepare for lift off

This section explains any preliminary work that you may need to do before beginning work on the task. This is a mandatory section.

Engage thrusters

This section lists the steps required in order to complete the task. This is a mandatory section.

Objective complete – mini debriefing

This section explains how the steps performed in the previous section (*Engage thrusters*) allow us to complete the task.

Classified intel

This section provides extra information that is relevant to the task.

After all the tasks are completed, the following sections should appear:

Mission accomplished

This section explains the task we accomplished in the project. This is mandatory and should occur after all the tasks in the project are completed.

A Hotshot challenge / Hotshot challenges

This section explains things to be done or tasks to be performed using the concepts explained in this project.

Conventions

In this book, you will find a number of text styles that distinguish between different kinds of information. Here are some examples of these styles and an explanation of their meaning.

Code words in text, database table names, folder names, filenames, file extensions, pathnames, dummy URLs, user input, and Twitter handles are shown as follows: "We will enter the following HTML code in the index.html file."

A block of code is set as follows:

```
<!DOCTYPE html>
<html lang='en'>
<head>
  <meta charset='utf-8'>
  <title>Color Quest</title>
  <link rel="stylesheet" href="game.css">
</head>
```

```
<body>
  <!-- game content here -->
  <script src='js/game.js'></script>
</body>
</html>
```

When we wish to draw your attention to a particular part of a code block, the relevant lines or items are set in bold:

```
startLevel: function() {
  game.quest = new game.Quest(this.currentLevel);
  game.compositionSeq = [];
  game.composition = new game.Composition();
  game.gameScene.visualize(game.quest);
  game.gameScene.handleInput();
},
```

New terms and **important words** are shown in bold. Words that you see on the screen, in menus or dialog boxes for example, appear in the text like this: "Click on the **Compress JavaScript** button and the tool generates the compressed code into the text area of the result."

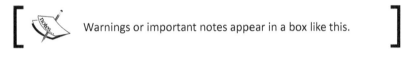

Warnings or important notes appear in a box like this.

Tips and tricks appear like this.

Reader feedback

Feedback from our readers is always welcome. Let us know what you think about this book—what you liked or may have disliked. Reader feedback is important for us to develop titles that you really get the most out of.

To send us general feedback, simply send an e-mail to feedback@packtpub.com, and mention the book title via the subject of your message.

If there is a topic that you have expertise in and you are interested in either writing or contributing to a book, see our author guide on www.packtpub.com/authors.

Customer support

Now that you are the proud owner of a Packt book, we have a number of things to help you to get the most from your purchase.

Downloading the example code

You can download the example code files for all Packt books you have purchased from your account at http://www.packtpub.com. If you purchased this book elsewhere, you can visit http://www.packtpub.com/support and register to have the files e-mailed directly to you.

Errata

Although we have taken every care to ensure the accuracy of our content, mistakes do happen. If you find a mistake in one of our books—maybe a mistake in the text or the code—we would be grateful if you would report this to us. By doing so, you can save other readers from frustration and help us improve subsequent versions of this book. If you find any errata, please report them by visiting http://www.packtpub.com/submit-errata, selecting your book, clicking on the **errata submission form** link, and entering the details of your errata. Once your errata are verified, your submission will be accepted and the errata will be uploaded on our website, or added to any list of existing errata, under the Errata section of that title. Any existing errata can be viewed by selecting your title from http://www.packtpub.com/support.

Piracy

Piracy of copyright material on the Internet is an ongoing problem across all media. At Packt, we take the protection of our copyright and licenses very seriously. If you come across any illegal copies of our works, in any form, on the Internet, please provide us with the location address or website name immediately so that we can pursue a remedy.

Please contact us at copyright@packtpub.com with a link to the suspected pirated material.

We appreciate your help in protecting our authors, and our ability to bring you valuable content.

Questions

You can contact us at questions@packtpub.com if you are having a problem with any aspect of the book, and we will do our best to address it.

Project 1

Building a CSS Quest Game

In this project, we are going to build a card quest game using HTML elements and CSS styling. We will also learn how to separate JavaScript logic into modules for clarity. We will build the game from scratch with a basic HTML layout and then represent the composition of the pattern in logic and CSS.

Mission briefing

We are going to create a matching game. This game presents a combination of patterns to the player, and some of these patterns overlap each other. Players analyze the patterns and then select them in the correct sequence so that the composition matches the provided one. You may visit the URL `http://makzan.net/html5-games/color-quest/` to play the example game in order to have a better understanding of what we will build throughout this project.

The following screenshot shows the final result of this project. The upper part is a timer, the part to the left shows the quest, the right part is the composition of the player, and the lower part is the deck of patterns.

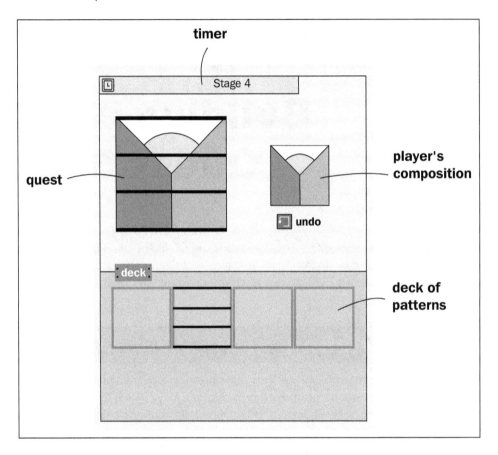

Why is it awesome?

A simple matching game like this is a perfect way to get you warmed up with the HTML5 games' development rhythm. What we will learn in this project is the foundation to build more complicated games later in this book.

This game uses what we are familiar with: HTML element interaction and styling in CSS. What's new, is JavaScript logic. This project will show us how to convert the game rule into code. We will also learn how to separate logic into different parts with different responsibilities.

Your Hotshot objectives

We'll perform the following tasks in this project:

- ► Creating the HTML structure
- ► Managing the game scenes
- ► Representing the quest pattern composition
- ► Placing the patterns on the deck
- ► Selecting the pattern
- ► Comparing players and compositions of the quest
- ► Showing different quests
- ► Counting down the game

Mission checklist

In this game, we are going to stick to plain JavaScript without using a library. This will help us get started with a basic foundation in JavaScript.

Note that writing JavaScript for games is a little bit different from writing it for a web page. Game logic requires well-structured code to ensure the logic is easy to read and maintained. The following essays provide an in-depth discussion on writing JavaScript in the right way:

- ► *JavaScript best practices*:
  `http://www.thinkful.com/learn/javascript-best-practices-1/`
- ► *JavaScript the right way*: `http://www.jstherightway.org`

Creating the HTML structure

In this task, we are going to kick-start the project by creating the file structure, ensuring that the essential files are ready.

Prepare for lift off

We need several things to get started. First, we will create an empty project directory. Then, we will create an `index.html` file, a folder where we will put the CSS styling files, and a folder to put the JavaScript logic files in.

During the missions, we need several graphics files, including the background and buttons; you can find the graphics from the sample code. Put all the images into a directory named `images`. The created file structure is shown in the following screenshot:

Engage thrusters

Use the following steps to create the basic game structure:

1. We will enter the following HTML code in the `index.html` file. It is a basic HTML structure that includes the CSS file in the head and the script tag at the bottom:

```
<!DOCTYPE html>
<html lang='en'>
<head>
  <meta charset='utf-8'>
  <title>Color Quest</title>
  <link rel="stylesheet" href="game.css">
</head>
<body>
  <!-- game content here -->
  <script src='js/game.js'></script>
</body>
</html>
```

2. Right after the opening of the `<body>` tag and before our `<script>` tag, we add the following HTML code for the game page. The content is divided into four parts: header, game section, the how-to-play section, and footer. The game section is where all the game logic happens. The `#element-template` is the template of game elements that will be used for cloning later:

```
<header>
  <div class="row">
    <h1>Color Quest</h1>
  </div>
</header>
```

```
<section id="game">
</section>
<section class='how-to-play'>
  <div class="row">
    <h2>How to Play?</h2>
    <p>Composite your card to match the given
      pattern.</p>
  </div>
</section>
<footer>
  <div class="row">
    <p>This game is an example for the HTML5 Games
      Hotshot book. Free for personal and commerical
      use.</p>
  </div>
</footer>
<div id='element-template'>
</div>
```

3. Add the following JavaScript to the game.js file. It acts as the entry point of the game logic:

```
(function(){
  // Entry Point
  var init = function() {
  };

  init(); // start the game
})(); // self-executing function.
```

Downloading the example code

You can download the example code files for all Packt books you have purchased from your account at http://www.packtpub.com. If you purchased this book elsewhere, you can visit http://www.packtpub.com/support and register to have the files e-mailed directly to you.

Objective complete – mini debriefing

We have created a very basic structure of the game. The following sections explain what we have done.

HTML structure

The header, section, and footer arrangement follows a simple HTML5 content structure. We will put the game elements inside this structure, attached to the game. The following screenshot shows the HTML structure:

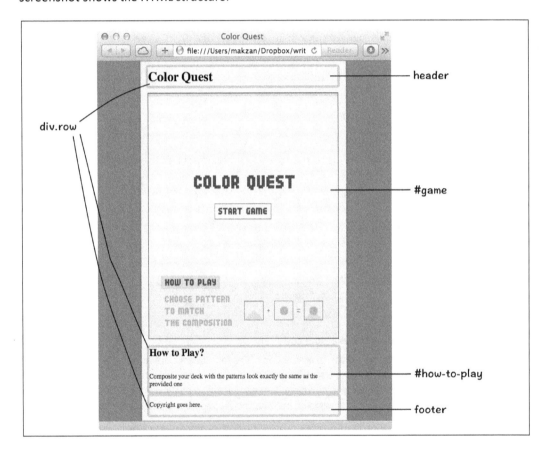

Modularizing the logic

We separate the JavaScript logic into modules, and each separated file encapsulates one module. This allows us to tackle each part individually. The first JavaScript file we have is the game.js file. It is in charge of controlling the game flow. There are other different parts in this game, and for these parts, we are going to create different files with the purpose of using them for future tasks.

Variable scope in JavaScript

In JavaScript, we want to have as few global variables as possible. Variables are global when they are attached to the highest scope of the runtime environment. In a web browser, this refers to a variable that is attached to a `window` scope. A variable that is created with the `var` keyword lives inside the scope of the function that encloses it.

This is why we put all the logic inside a self-executing anonymous function. This ensures that by default, we will not pollute the global scope with our game logic variables. The following code block shows how to create each module with one global game variable and one local game variable inside a self-executing-anonymous function:

```
(function(){
  var game  = this.colorQuestGame = this.colorQuestGame || {};
})();
```

We will intentionally create one global variable named `colorQuestGame` to act as the namespace. In the later sections, we will put different logic modules into different files under the same global object.

The `this.colorQuestGame || {};` declaration means that, by default, it will use the existing `colorQuestGame` variable if it was already declared previously. Otherwise, it will be a new empty object. We will put this line of declaration into every file.

This scoping feature is also useful when we need to encapsulate logic into private functions. For example, the following code shows how we can create private functions that are only accessible inside a specific scope to help extract the code:

```
Composition.createFromSequence = function(sequence) {
  // helper functions
  var privateHelperA = function() {}
  var privateHelperB = function() {}
  // end helper functions

  // use your private helper functions here.
}
```

Inside any method, we can declare local scoped functions to help extract the logic and to make the code more readable.

Classified intel

For performance, we usually place scripts at the end of **Document Object Model (DOM)** and just before the closing of the `</body>` tag. This is because script loading may block the loading of DOM and cause the webpage to load slower. For more details, please have a look at the Yahoo performance rule, *Put Scripts at the Bottom*, at `http://developer.yahoo. com/performance/rules.html#js_bottom`.

Managing the game scene

In this task, we create four scenes and display different scenes based on the game flow.

Prepare for lift off

The following figure is our planning of the four scenes and the flow, showing on how they should link together:

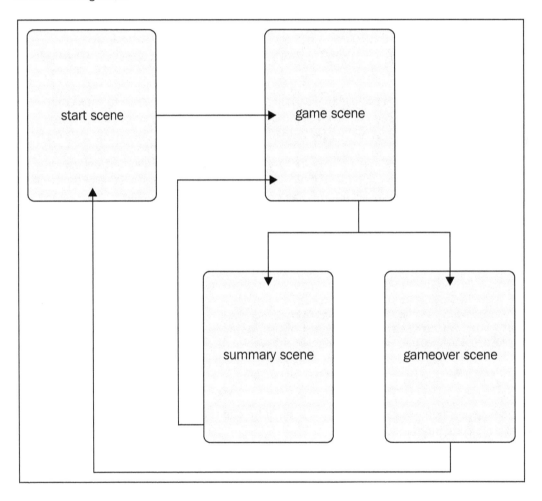

The following figure shows three scenes of what we will create in this task:

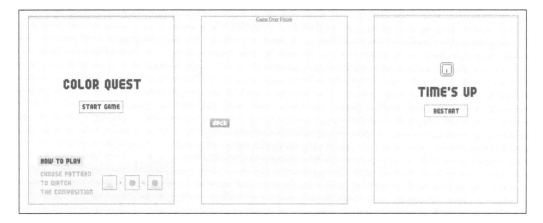

Engage thrusters

We code the management part of the scene via the following steps:

1. The scenes are DOM elements, so we will have the following HTML elements defined inside the tag with the game ID:

    ```
    <div id="game-scene" class="scene out">
      <a href="#" id="gameover-btn">Game Over</a>
      <a href="#" id="finish-btn">Finish</a>
    </div>
    <div id="start-scene" class="scene">
      <a href="#" id="start-btn" class="button">
        Start Game</a>
    </div>
    <div id="summary-scene" class="scene out">
      <a href="#" id="next-level-button"
         class="button">Next</a>
    </div>
    <div id="gameover-scene" class="scene out">
      <a href="#" id="back-to-menu-button"
         class="button">Back to menu</a>
    </div>
    ```

2. Now, we need to import our newly created scenes.js file into the HTML file, before the game.js file:

    ```
    <script src='js/scenes.js'></script>
    <script src='js/game.js'></script>
    </body>
    ```

3. In the `scene.js` file, we add the following code to define the scene's object and its instances:

```
(function() {
  var game = this.colorQuestGame = this.colorQuestGame ||
    {};
  // put common scene logic into 'scene' object.
  var scene = {
    node: document.querySelector('.scene'),
    show: function() {
      this.node.classList.remove('out');
      this.node.classList.add('in');
    },
    hide: function() {
      this.node.classList.remove('in');
      this.node.classList.add('out');
    }
  };

  // scene instances code to go here.
)();
```

4. Then, we create an instance of the game scene. Put the following code right after the `scene` object code. The following code creates two temporary links to finish the level and complete the game:

```
var gameScene = game.gameScene = Object.create(scene);
gameScene.node = document.getElementById('game-scene');
gameScene.handleInput = function() {
  document.getElementById('finish-btn').onclick =  function() {
    game.flow.finishLevel();
  };
  document.getElementById('gameover-btn').onclick = function() {
    game.flow.gameOver();
  };
};
```

5. The start scene instance comes after the game scene code. The following code handles the clicking of the start button that links to the game scene:

```
var startScene = game.startScene = Object.create(scene);
startScene.node = document.getElementById('start-scene');
startScene.handleInput = function() {
  document.getElementById('start-btn').onclick =    function() {
    game.flow.nextLevel();
  };
};
```

6. Then, we have the summary scene. The summary scene has a button that links to the game scene again to show the next level:

```
var summaryScene = game.summaryScene =
  Object.create(scene);
summaryScene.node = document.getElementById('summary-
    scene');
summaryScene.handleInput = function() {
document.getElementById('next-level-button')
  .onclick =  function() {
    game.flow.nextLevel();
  };
};
```

7. At last, we add the game over scene code to the scenes.js file. When the game is over, we bring the player back to the menu scene after the back button is clicked:

```
var gameoverScene = game.gameoverScene = Object.create(scene);
gameoverScene.node = document.getElementById('gameover-scene');
gameoverScene.handleInput = function() {
  var scene = this;
  document.getElementById('back-to-menu-button').onclick =
function() {
    game.flow.startOver();
  };
};
```

8. Now, we will define a game flow in the game.js file that will help us control how to show and hide the scenes:

```
// Main Game Logic
game.flow = {
  startOver: function() {
    game.startScene.hide();
    game.summaryScene.hide();
    game.gameoverScene.hide();
    game.gameScene.hide();
    game.startScene.show();
  },
  gameWin: function() {
    game.gameScene.hide();
    game.summaryScene.show();
  },
  gameOver: function() {
    game.startScene.show();
    game.gameScene.hide();
    game.gameoverScene.show();
  },
```

```
      nextLevel: function() {
        game.startScene.hide();
        game.summaryScene.hide();
        game.gameScene.show();
      },
      finishLevel: function() {
        game.gameScene.hide();
        game.summaryScene.show();
      },
    }
```

9. The `init` function is the entry point of the game. Inside this function, we will register the click input listeners:

```
var init = function() {
  game.startScene.handleInput();
  game.summaryScene.handleInput();
  game.gameoverScene.handleInput();
  game.gameScene.handleInput();
}
```

10. At last, we need some styling for the scenes to make them work. Put the following CSS rules at the end of the `game.css` file:

```
#game {
  width: 480px;
  height: 600px;
  margin: 0 auto;
  border: 1px solid #333;
  text-align: center;
  position: relative;
  overflow: hidden;
}

.scene {
  background: white;
  width: 100%;
  height: 100%;
  position: absolute;
  transition: all .4s ease-out;
}
.scene.out {top: -150%;}
.scene.in {top: 0;}

.button {
  width: 145px;
```

```css
  height: 39px;
  display: block;
  margin: auto;
  text-indent: 120%;
  white-space: nowrap;
  overflow: hidden;
  background-repeat: no-repeat;
}
.button:hover {
  background-position: 0 -39px;
}
.button:active {
  background-position: 0 0;
}

#start-scene {background: url(images/menu_bg.png);}

#start-btn {
  background-image: url(images/start_btn.png);
  margin-top: 270px;
}

#game-scene {background: url(images/game_bg.png);}

#game-scene.out {
  opacity: 0;
  top: 0;
  transition-delay: .5s;
}

#summary-scene {background: url(images/summary_bg.png);}

next-level-button {
  background-image: url(images/next_btn.png);
  margin-top: 370px;
}
#summary-scene.in {
  transition-delay: .5s;
}
#gameover-scene {
  background: url(images/gameover_bg.png);
}
#back-to-menu-button {
  background-image: url(images/restart_btn.png);
  margin-top: 270px;
}
```

Objective complete – mini debriefing

We have created scenes in this task. Now let's take a closer look at each block of code to see how they work together.

Creating buttons

Each button is of 145 pixels by 39 pixels in size and has two states: a normal and a hover state. Both states are combined in one image and thus the final image is of 78 pixels in height. The bottom part contains the hover state. We switch these states by setting the background's *y* position to 0 pixel for the normal state and -39 pixel for the hover state, as shown in the following screenshot:

Placing the scene logic and the namespace

We encapsulated the scene's management code in a file named scene.js. Similar to the game.js file, we start every logic file with a self-invoked anonymous function. Inside the function, we use the same namespace: colorQuestGame.

The transition between scenes

We use CSS to control the visibility of the scenes. The .in and .out CSS properties that apply to all the scenes have different top values. One is -150% to ensure it is not visible, and the other is top: 0; therefore, it is visible in the game element.

Then, we toggle each scene between the .in and .out class to control the visibility. In addition, we add transition to these CSS rules so changing the value from 0 to -150 percent and vice-versa becomes a smooth animation.

The scene object inheritance

There are four scenes in this game: the pregame start scene, game scene, game over scene, and level-completed summary scene. Each scene shares certain common logic; this includes showing and hiding themselves. In JavaScript, we can use object inheritance to share common logic. The scene is an object with default show-and-hide behaviors. It also defines a dummy sceneElement property that points to the DOM element of that scene.

A game scene is another object. However, we do not create it as a normal object. We use the `Object.create` method with this scene as the argument. The `Object.create` method will chain the argument as the new object's prototype. This is known as a *prototype chain*.

What if we want to show a different effect for hiding a game scene? It depends on whether your effects are done in CSS or JavaScript. If it is a CSS-only effect, you can just add rules to the `#game-scene.out` scene. In the management part of the scene, `.in` is to display the scene and `.out` is for rules that hide the scene.

For the CSS approach, assume that we want a fade-out effect; we can do so using the following CSS rule:

```
#game-scene.out {
    opacity: 0;
    top: 0;
}
```

Prototype chaining

JavaScript is an object-oriented programming language without the requirement of a class definition. It uses a prototype chain for object inheritance. Each object comes with a special `prototype` property. The prototype defines what this object is based on; you can think of it as inheritance in traditional object-oriented languages.

Let's take a look at how JavaScript accesses object properties. When we call `Scene.show()`, it takes a look at the property list and finds a property named `show`, which is of the type `function`.

Imagine now that the `show` method is not there. The JavaScript runtime looks it up in the prototype. If it is found inside the prototype, it returns the method. Otherwise, it keeps looking up prototype's prototype until it reaches a generic object.

This is the meaning of prototype chaining. We build an object based on another object by putting the other object into the prototype. The following screenshot shows the `startScene` property and the properties in its prototype (`scene`):

```
> colorQuestGame.startScene
< ▼ Object
      ▶ handleInput: function () {
      ▶ node: div#start-scene.scene
      ▼ __proto__: Object
        ▶ hide: function () {
        ▶ node: div#game-scene.scene out
        ▶ show: function () {
        ▶ __proto__: Object
```

In order to attach the object to prototype, we use `Object.create`. The original object's prototype is attached to the new object. It allows us to directly inherit an object's instance into a new object without going through the traditional abstract class definition.

Another approach to put a different object into the prototype is using the `Function` and `new` approaches. When we define a function, we can use `new` to create an object from the function. For example, observe the following function:

```
function Scene() {}
Scene.prototype.show = function() {}
Scene.prototype.hide = function() {}
```

Now, when we create a scene object instance by using `new Scene()`, the instance has the method `show` and `hide`. If we want to have a `GameScene` definition based on the `Scene`, we can do that:

```
function GameScene() {}
GameScene.prototype = new Scene();
```

In this function, we have added an instance of `Scene` into `GameScene`. Therefore, the `GameScene` instance now has all the functionalities of `Scene`.

More explanation on the difference between the new instance approach and the `Object.create` approach can be found in the following link to a post from the Mozilla Developer Network:

```
https://developer.mozilla.org/en-US/docs/Web/
JavaScript/Reference/Global_Objects/Object/create
```

Classified intel

Besides changing the CSS `.in` and `.out` classes of the scenes, we can also add extra animation or logic when the scene shows and hides. Instead of the plain scene movement, we can further enhance the transition by defining the game objects `in` and `out` of the CSS rule. For example, we can make the buttons fade out during the transition, or we can drop the quest element to the bottom to create an illusion of it being unlocked; this can be done using the following code:

```
// an example of custom hide function
gameScene.hide = function() {
  // invoke the hide function inside the prototype chain.
  // (aka. super.hide())
  Object.getPrototypeOf(this).hide.call(this);
```

```
    /* extra */
    // add the class for the out effect
    var questView = document.getElementById('quest');
    questView.classList.add('out');
    /* end extra */
}
```

Since, we have overridden the `hide` method from the scene object, we need to call the prototype's hide using the scope of `gameScene`. Then, we add our extra logic to add the `out` class to the quest DOM element.

We define the dropping effect with CSS transform and transition:

```
#quest.out {
  transition: all .8s ease-out;
  transform: translateY(800px) rotate(50deg);
}
```

The `out` object of the game scene is a delayed fading out transition:

```
#game-scene.out, #summary-scene.in {
  transition-delay: .5s;

}
```

In addition, we used the transition delay to make sure that the drop animation is displayed before the scene goes out and the next scene goes in.

Some new properties of CSS are not stable yet. When a vendor adds support to these styles, they add a vendor-prefix to the property. The vendor prefix indicates that the user should use that property with caution.

In this project, we will omit all the vendor-prefixes for clarity when showing the code in the book. In order to make sure that the code works in a browser, we may need to add the following vendor prefixes: `-webkit-` (for Chrome and Safari), `-moz-` (for Mozilla Firefox), `-o-` (for Opera), and `-ms-` (for Internet Explorer).

If you find adding prefixes troublesome, you may use some tools for help. The tool *prefix-free* (`http://leaverou.github.io/prefixfree/`) is one that can help. Compile tools will add these prefixes for you, such as CSS preprocess compilers.

Representing the quest composition

In this task, we declare the quest level and then display the level in the quest composition view.

Prepare for lift off

We will need three more JavaScript files in this task, so let's create them. These files are as follows:

- **patch.js**: This file is used for adding methods to existing built-in objects to enhance convenience
- **composition.js**: We use this file for logic that represents the composition
- **quest.js**: These files represent the data of a quest, including the level and quest data manipulating methods

At the end of this task, we should be able to create a composition of patterns according to our level. For example, the following quest composition is composed of four patterns: a circle, the left and right trapezoid, and lines, as shown in the following screenshot:

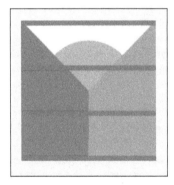

Engage thrusters

We put patterns into composition using the following steps:

1. To start with, in HTML, we want to remove the dummy `gameover` link and the finish link from the game scene. As we are now putting real content in the game scene, these two links may affect the placement of our game elements:

```
<div id="game-scene" class="scene out">
  <div id="stage">Stage 1</div>
  <div id='quest' class="quest">
    <div id="quest-composition"
      class="composition"></div>
```

```
      </div>
    </div>

    <div id='element-template'>
      <!-- for composition view -->
      <div class="pattern" data-pattern='1'></div>
    </div>
```

2. We will import the three files at the end of HTML file. They are `patch.js`, `composition.js`, and `quest.js`:

    ```
    <script src='js/patch.js'></script>
    <script src='js/composition.js'></script>
    <script src='js/quest.js'></script>
    <script src='js/scenes.js'></script>
    <script src='js/game.js'></script>
    ```

3. We want to make it easy to remove all the DOM elements from the quest view. This is why we have a patch file. Put the following code in the `patch.js` file to add the `removeAllChildren` method to all the DOM nodes:

    ```
    // add removeAllChildren to Node object.
    Node.prototype.removeAllChildren = function() {
      while(this.firstChild) {
        this.removeChild(this.firstChild);
      }
    };
    ```

4. Then, we add a basic skeleton to the `composition.js` file:

    ```
    (function(){
      var game  = this.colorQuestGame = this.colorQuestGame || {};

      // composition model definition
      // composition is a deck of pattern put together
      var Composition = game.Composition = (function(){
        function Composition(){
          this.data = [];
        }

        return Composition;
      })();
    })();
    ```

5. In the `quest.js` file, we represent the level of data in arrays. The number is the pattern. We will discuss how we come up with this special array structure later:

```
(function(){
  var game  = this.colorQuestGame = this.colorQuestGame || {};

  // level data
  var questLevels = [
    [ [5, 6], [3] ],
    [ [6], [1, 2]],
    [ [5, 6] ],
    [ [3], [1, 2], [4] ],
    [ [1, 2], [3], [4], [5, 6]],
  ];

  // quest model definition
  // quest is a kind of composition, the difference is that
  quest is specifically used as the question for player to give the
  answer.
  // so it comes with comparing logic.
  var Quest = game.Quest = (function(){
    function Quest(level){
      var questData = questLevels[level];
      this.data = questData;
    }
    Quest.prototype = new game.Composition();
    // extends the Quest prototype from Composition.
    return Quest;
  })();
})();
```

6. Since we have removed the dummy `gameover` and have finished with the link of the game scene, now, from the `scenes.js` file, we will also remove the `onclick` event for these two links inside the `handleInput` method.

7. We add a new method to the `gameScene` instance that displays the data in the game scene. This method creates the patterns in the quest area of the game according to the given data:

```
gameScene.visualize = function(quest) {
  var questData = quest.data;
  var patternsToShow = [];
  for (var i in questData) {
    for (var j in questData[i]) {
      patternsToShow.push(questData[i][j]);
    }
  }
```

```
    // Quest
    // visualize the quest composition view:
    var questCompositionNode = document.getElementById('quest-
composition');

    // empty the DOM view
questCompositionNode.removeAllChildren();

    // visualize the pattern view:
    for (var i in patternsToShow) {
      var patternNode = document.querySelector('#element-template
.pattern').cloneNode(/*clone children=*/true);
      patternNode.setAttribute('data-pattern',   patternsToShow[i]);
      questCompositionNode.appendChild(patternNode);
    }
};
```

8. We need to modify the game flow in the `game.js` file to show the quest:

```
game.flow = {
  currentLevel: 3,
  startLevel: function() {
    game.quest = new game.Quest(this.currentLevel);
    game.gameScene.visualize(game.quest);
  },
  ...
}

var init = function() {
  ...
  game.flow.startLevel();
}
```

9. Finally, we will create the view of the patterns and the quest in CSS:

```
#stage {
  position: absolute;
  width: 100%;
  height: 30px;
  line-height: 30px;
}

/* Template */
#element-template {display: none;}

/* quest */
#quest {
```

```
    width: 200px;
    height: 200px;
    position: absolute;
    left: 30px;
    top: 70px;
}

/* individual pattern */
.pattern {
    width: 200px;
    height: 200px;
    background-size: contain;
}
.pattern[data-pattern='1'] {
    background-image: url(images/pattern1.png);
}
/* pattern 2-5 puts here */
.pattern[data-pattern='6'] {
    background-image: url(images/pattern6.png);
}
.composition {
    position: relative;
    height: 200px;
    background: white;
}
.composition > .pattern {
    position: absolute;
}
```

Objective complete – mini debriefing

We created the visual and data composition of a quest. Let's go in detail on what we have done in this task.

Separating the data and view

While designing games, we usually want to separate the logic of manipulating data and the logic of displaying and drawing elements. In our logic, the composition and quest are data. The scenes are for displaying. That's why we use the gameScene.visualize method to display data into the DOM element once we declare the quest composition data.

We need to dynamically create elements to represent the pattern in the quest DOM node. Sometimes we create HTML directly in JavaScript and append it to the node. A better approach is to have the HTML placed inside, well, HTML. That's why we have the template element for JavaScript to clone it and put it back into the quest node.

Using the data-* attribute

It is often useful to use the `data-*` attribute to embed extra information when we use DOM elements to represent game objects. Take the card as an instance. We can define `data-pattern='3'` to indicate that element is a visual of pattern number 3. We can define whatever we like as long as it begins with `data-`. Then, we can use the `getAttribute` method to access it and use the `setAttribute` method to update it. Alternatively, we can use the `dataset` method to access the `data-*` attribute.

Visualizing the quest patterns

A pattern is a stack of background-transparent cards. We can represent each card as a DIV and overlay them together in one container. In the composition node, we overlap the pattern by setting the position to absolute, top-left position to 0.

Whenever we use absolute elements, we want to make sure that we have control of the reference point of the top and left properties; this means controlling where the top 0 and left 0 positions are.

Elements that are positioned at the absolute point reference the top-left point in the following way:

▸ They find the first parent with a position and set it as absolute or relative

▸ They use the body's top-left point if no parents are found with the position's setting

Therefore, what we need to do is set a position that is relative to the container, namely, `.composition`.

The position styling for the quest and pattern has been defined in the CSS. What we need to do is append the newly created HTML node to the quest node from the `gameScene.visualize` method. The pattern HTML nodes are created from the template and with the class defined that match the CSS rules.

Quest level

In this game, we require the player to select the pattern in the correct sequence to match the quest. However, some patterns are not overlapped with other patterns. In this case, we will put the two non-overlapped pairs together so that the order of choosing among these patterns will not be treated in the wrong order.

We would like to come up with an approach to compare the player's composition with the quest's composition.

The quest is composited by a sequence of patterns. A straightforward approach is to store the pattern sequence in an array. Then, all we need to do is compare whether the player's sequence is exactly the same as the given one.

Sounds good, but it fails in one case. In our patterns, there are some patterns that don't overlap with the others. Take the following pattern shown in the screenshot as an example:

The trapezoids to the left and right fit together without overlapping. We require the player to match the pattern visually so the sequence of these two selections does not change the effect, as shown in the following screenshot:

However, in the following pattern, the circle does overlap with the triangle:

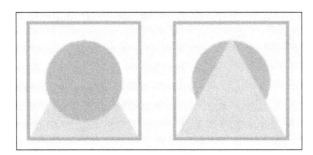

Therefore, a simple sequence array does not work. Let's improve how we store the patterns in an array. How about using a 2-dimensional array?

The first dimension is the *z* index of the patterns, which is the sequence that players must match.

In order to represent the same level of relationship between the two trapezoids, we put them into one slot inside our array; thus, the array inside the code becomes the following:

```
[ [Left Trapezoid, Right Trapezoid], [Triangle] ]
```

To make the array item type consistent, we can force a single item to be wrapped inside the group too. Let's call each group of non-overlapped pattern *layer*.

Now, the final data array will be as follows:

```
[ [Left Trapezoid, Right Trapezoid], [Triangle] ]
```

Here, each array inside the quest level represents one layer with patterns that are interchangeable. Any overlapping pattern will be another new layer. Moreover, we put all the levels into an array to represent all the levels.

Composition and quest modules

The composition module contains only a data instance variable in the current task. The data has the same format as the multilayered patterns. Quest modules inherit the composition with logic that is related to the quest levels.

In future tasks, we are going to add more logic to the composition and quest modules to help in manipulating the format of a multilayer pattern.

Placing the patterns on the deck

In this task, we are going to list the pattern in the deck. Later, we will let the player select patterns from this deck.

Prepare for lift off

We are going to need a new module to handle the display of the composition. Let's create a new empty JavaScript file named `composition-view.js`.

We need to import the file into the `index.html` file, as follows:

```
<script src='js/composition-view.js'></script>
```

Engage thrusters

Let's work on the pattern with the following steps:

1. In the game scene of the `index.html` file, we add two DOM elements, namely, `#your-composition` and `#deck`:

    ```
    <div id="game-scene" class="scene out">

      . . .

      <div id="your-composition"></div>
      <div id="deck" class="deck"></div>
    </div>
    ```

2. In the template element, we add the template for the pattern's slot:

    ```
    <div id="element-template">
      <!-- for deck view -->
      <div class="pattern-slot">
        <div class="pattern" data-pattern="1"></div>
      </div>
      . . .
    </div>
    ```

3. The following is our `composition-view.js` file:

    ```
    (function(){
      var game  = this.colorQuestGame =
        this.colorQuestGame || {};

      // composition module
      game.compositionView = {
        node: document.getElementById('your-composition'),
      };
    })();
    ```

4. Before the end of the `gameScene.visualize` method, we add the visualization logic for the player's composition:

    ```
    // randomize the patterns array
    patternsToShow.sort(function(a, b){
      return Math.random() - 0.5;
    });

    // empty the current deck view
    var deckNode = document.getElementById('deck');
    deckNode.removeAllChildren();

    // add the pattern to the deck view
    ```

```
for (var i in patternsToShow) {
  var patternSlotNode = document.querySelector
    ('#element-template .pattern-slot').cloneNode
    (/*clone children=*/true);
  patternSlotNode.querySelector('.pattern')
    .setAttribute('data-pattern', patternsToShow[i]);
  deckNode.appendChild(patternSlotNode);
}
```

5. From the `game.js` file, we remove all the selected patterns before starting a new level:

```
nextLevel: function() {
  ...
  game.compositionView.node.removeAllChildren();
  this.startLevel();
},
```

6. We need the following CSS style for the composition and patterns:

```
/* player's composition and pattern */
#your-composition {
  position: absolute;
  width: 100px;
  height: 100px;
  right: 65px;
  top: 120px;
  border: 3px solid #999;
}
#your-composition > .pattern {
  width: 100px;
  height: 100px;
  position: absolute;
}

/* deck and pattern */
  .deck { position: absolute;
  top: 360px;
  left: 20px;
}
.pattern-slot {
  width: 100px;
  height: 100px;
  outline: 4px solid #BC7702;
  float: left;
  border-radius: 3px;
  margin: 10px 0 0 10px;
}
```

```
.deck .pattern {
  width: 100%;
  height: 100%;
}
```

We should have the following screenshot once this task is completed. The deck shows the patterns that a player needs to compose the quest:

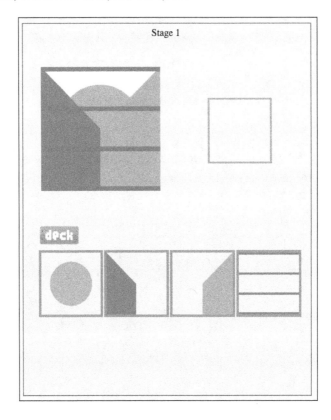

Objective complete – mini debriefing

JavaScript comes with a `sort` method for the array. Normally, we compare the given two array elements and return `+1` or `-1` to control elements' swapping.

We can randomize an array by randomly returning either `+1` or `-1`:

```
patternsToShow.sort(function(a, b){
  return Math.random() - 0.5;
});
```

After we randomize the patterns, we clone each pattern from the template and append them to the deck element.

Selecting the pattern

In this task, we allow players to select the pattern from their decks and display the sequence of the selection in the composition view.

Engage thrusters

Perform the following steps to add user interaction to our game:

1. We allow players to undo their selection, so we need to add an undo button to the index.html file:

```
<a href="#" id="undo-button" class="button">Undo</a>
```

2. When starting a level in the game.js file, we store the player's selection sequence and register the clicking event by adding the following highlighted code:

```
startLevel: function() {
  game.quest = new game.Quest(this.currentLevel);
  game.compositionSeq = [];
  game.composition = new game.Composition();
  game.gameScene.visualize(game.quest);
  game.gameScene.handleInput();
},
```

3. In the patch.js file, we need to add forEach to the NodeList and HTMLCollection objects using the following code:

```
NodeList.prototype.forEach = Array.prototype.forEach;
HTMLCollection.prototype.forEach =
  Array.prototype.forEach;
```

4. In the composition-view.js file, we need the following methods to display the pattern selection in the composition's DOM element:

```
game.compositionView = {
  node: document.getElementById('your-composition'),
  pushPattern: function(patternId) {
    var newChild = document.createElement('div');
    newChild.classList.add('pattern');
    newChild.setAttribute('data-pattern', patternId);
    this.node.appendChild(newChild);
  },
  pullPattern: function() {
    var lastChild = this.node.querySelector
      ('.pattern:last-child');
```

```
        if (lastChild) {
          // find the pattern in the deck and make it visible
          var deckNode = document.getElementById('deck');
          var resumePattern = deckNode.querySelector
            ('[data-pattern="' + lastChild.getAttribute
            ('data-pattern') + '"]');
          resumePattern.style.display = 'block';

          // remove the current pattern
          this.node.removeChild(lastChild);
        }
      },
      selectPattern: function(pattern) {
        this.pushPattern(pattern);
        game.compositionSeq.push(pattern);
      },
      undo: function() {
        this.pullPattern();
        game.compositionSeq.pop();
      },
    };
```

5. Then, we need the mouse event to invoke our selection logic. In the `scenes.js` file, we add the following clicking event to the `gameScene`:

```
gameScene.handleInput = function() {
  document.querySelectorAll("#deck .pattern").
forEach(function(elm){
    elm.onclick=  function(){
      var pattern = elm.getAttribute('data-pattern');
      elm.style.display = 'none';
      game.compositionView.selectPattern(pattern);
    };
  });

  var undoBtn = document.getElementById('undo-button');
  undoBtn.onclick = function(e){
    game.compositionView.undo();
    e.preventDefault();
  };
};
```

6. Let's move to styling. We have a new undo button, so we need the following CSS rules to place it in the right position with the image:

```
#undo-button {
  position: absolute;
  right: 70px;
```

```
    top: 240px;
    z-index: 999;
    background: url(images/undo_btn.png) no-repeat;
    width: 90px;
    height: 26px;
}
#undo-button:hover {background-position: 0 -26px;}
```

7. Also, we add mouse-related styling to the pattern's slot:

```
.pattern-slot:hover{outline-color: #D68700;}
.pattern-slot:active {outline-color: #BC7702;}
```

Objective complete – mini debriefing

The selection is done by the click event on the pattern. Basically, we get the pattern ID from the `data-` attribute. Once the pattern ID is known, it triggers the following method:

```
game.compositionView.selectPattern(pattern);
```

Then, the composition pushes the selection into an array.

Undo the player composition

We trigger the undo logic by listening to the undo button's click event. Then, the undo logic removes the last pattern from the array. At the same time, we find the last pattern element in the composition view and move this element to the pattern deck.

Comparing the player and compositions of the quest

In this task, we create logic to make multilayered pattern compositions from player's selection and then compare it with the quest pattern's composition.

Prepare for lift off

We need a way to represent the pattern overlapping and non-overlapping relationships.

Representing a pattern overlapping relationship

We will use the data structure of this section to remember the overlapping relationship. Most patterns will overlap others, so we would need to think the other way round. So, we store those patterns that do not overlap together.

The pattern is a two-dimensional (2D) array. The first dimension contains every pattern. Each pattern is a list of the other patterns that do not overlay with it.

For example, the following A pattern does not overlap with the C and D shapes. We represent it with the ensuing equation:

array['A'] = ['C', 'D'];

For a pattern that always overlaps with the others, an empty array will be assigned.

Engage thrusters

In the following steps, we code the logic that allows us to compare two given quest compositions:

1. In the composition.js file, we have the following class variable to represent the relationship of the overlapping patterns. It indicates the pattern that overlaps with other patterns. The index of the nonOverlappedPattern array is the pattern ID, and the corresponding array value is the list of patterns that do not overlap with that pattern:

    ```
    // static variable. available as only one copy among all
    composition instances.
    Composition.nonOverlappedPattern = [
      [], // pattern 0
      [2], // pattern 1, doesn't overlap with pattern 2.
      [1], // pattern 2, doesn't overlap with pattern 1.
      [], // pattern 3
      [], // pattern 4
      [6], // pattern 5, doesn't overlap with pattern 6.
      [5], // pattern 6, doesn't overlap with pattern 5.
     ];
    ```

2. We create the following new method in the Composition method that can turn a composition back to a one-dimension array:

    ```
    Composition.prototype.toSequence = function() {
      var seq = [];
      for (var i=0; i < this.data.length; i++) {
        for (var j=0; j <this.data[i].length; j++ ) {
          seq.push(this.data[i][j]);
        }
      }
      return seq;
    }
    ```

3. Then, we create the `createFromSequence` method with the following code that turns a sequence back to a composition:

```
Composition.createFromSequence = function(sequence) {
  // function to determine if 2 given patterns overlap.
  var allowPatternsInSameLevel =
    function(patternA, patternB) {
      // iterate the array to see if current pattern overlaps the
      var nonOverlappedPattern = Composition.
nonOverlappedPattern[patternA]
      var len = nonOverlappedPattern.length;
      for (var i=0; i<len; i++) {
        if (nonOverlappedPattern[i] === parseInt(patternB)) {
          return true;
        }
      }
      return false;
    };
  // layer is an array that contains existing pattern
  var layerAllowsPattern = function(layer, pattern) {
    for (var i=0, len=layer.length; i<len; i++) {
      if (!allowPatternsInSameLevel(layer[i], pattern)) {
        return false;
      }
    }
    return true;
  };
  // end helper functions

  var newComposition = new Composition();
  var layer = [];
  for (var i=0, len=sequence.length; i<len; i++) {
    if (layerAllowsPattern(layer, sequence[i])) {
      // we are still in same layer.
      layer.push(sequence[i]);
    } else {
      // two patterns overlapped,
      // we push the current layer to composition
      // and use a new layer for the current pattern.
      newComposition.data.push(layer);
      layer = []; // new array instance to prevent browser using
the same array and crashes the data.
      layer.push(sequence[i]);
    }
```

```
    }
    // for the last layer
    if (layer.length> 0) newComposition.data.push(layer);
    return newComposition;
}
```

4. We add a new method to the `Quest` method that can compare two multilayered pattern compositions and check whether they are equal to each other:

```
Quest.prototype.isEqualToComposition = function(composition) {
  var a = this.data;
  var b = composition.data;

  // sort each level in both array
  for (var i=0, len=a.length; i<len; i++) {
    a[i].sort();
  }
  for (var i=0, len=b.length; i<len; i++) {
    b[i].sort();
  }
  // flatten both compositions into sequence.
  a = this.toSequence();
  b = composition.toSequence();

  if (a.length !== b.length) return false;
  for (var i=0, len=a.length; i<len; i++) {
    if (parseInt(a[i]) !== parseInt(b[i])) return false;
  }
  return true;
}
```

5. In the `composition-view.js` file, we check whether the player's latest selection matches the quest level. Therefore, in both the `selectPattern` and `undo` methods, we keep a composition from the sequence and check it with the quest level:

```
selectPattern: function(pattern) {
  ...
  game.composition = game.Composition.createFromSequence(game.
compositionSeq);
  if (game.quest.isEqualToComposition(game.composition)){
    game.flow.gameWin();
  }
},
undo: function() {
  ...
  game.composition =   game.Composition.createFromSequence(game.
compositionSeq);
```

```
      if (game.quest.isEqualToComposition(game.composition))
      {
        game.flow.gameWin();
      }
    },
```

Objective complete – mini debriefing

The comparison requires us to create a multilayered pattern composition from the selection sequence. Then, we compare the player's one with that of the quest level.

Composition is a two-dimensional array that we need to compare between the quest and the player's selection. However, the player's selection is a sequence that does not reflect our layer's structure. This is the reason why we need a conversion between the composition and the sequence. Moreover, we need to keep a copy of the player's sequence because we need that information for the undo feature.

Comparing players and compositions of the quest

In our `createFromSequence` method, we created two helper functions to manipulate multilayered patterns. The `allowPatternsInSameLevel` function checks whether the given two patterns can be overlapped together by looking up the non-overlapped pattern table. The `layerAllowsPattern` function makes use of the previous function and checks whether the given pattern fits all other patterns inside the given layer, which is an array of all non-overlapped patterns put together.

The `createFromSequence` method makes use of the function to scan the selection array in a sequence and then put each pattern into either the same layer (without overlapping) or a new layer.

Finally, we have the `isEqualToComposition` method in the quest instance to compare the player's selection composition with the quest level's one. This method sorts all the layers in both the compositions into the same order and then converts the composition back to a one-dimension array using the `toSequence` method.

This ensures the player's selection can match our defined level of data on non-overlapping patterns, regardless of the order of selection.

Classified intel

We attach the relationship of non-overlapping patterns directly to the composition object because they are the same, regardless of each instance. Attaching it to the composition instead of the instance's prototype prevents this block of data from being copied to each instance.

Showing different quests

In this task, we are going to show how to advance to the next level when the player's composition matches that of the quest compositions in the current level.

Engage thrusters

This time, we need quest-level data in the `quest.js` file to be accessible from another file, so we need to attach the `questLevels` and `questData` methods to the game scope rather than the original local scope:

1. In the `quest.js` file, we change the `questLevels` declaration from `var questLevels` to `game.questLevels`.

2. We apply the same to `questData`:

```
// from
var questData = questLevels[level];
// to
var questData = game.questLevels[level];
```

3. In the `scenes.js` file, we display the level with the following function:

```
gameScene.updateLevelInfo = function(level) {
  document.getElementById('stage').textContent = "Stage "
    + level;
};
```

4. At last, we modify the game flow in the `game.js` file to count the level:

```
game.flow = {
  currentLevel: -1,
  maxLevel: game.questLevels.length - 1,
  startOver: function() {
    ...
    this.currentLevel = -1;
  },
  nextLevel: function() {
    this.currentLevel+=1;
    if (this.currentLevel>= this.maxLevel) this.currentLevel =
this.maxLevel;

    game.gameScene.updateLevelInfo(this.currentLevel+1);
    // when displaying level, we start from 1 instead of 0, so +1
here.
    ...
  },
  ...
}
```

Objective complete – mini debriefing

The level up is done by counting the current level and selecting the level from the questLevels array. The nextLevel method is used to increase the currentLevel counter. Moreover, this method is called once startButton is clicked from the menu. Therefore, it will increase the currentLevel counter at the beginning. This is why we set the initial value of currentLevel to -1. This will ensure that it selects the first level once the game starts that is at index 0 of the level array. We reset currentLevel in the startOver method once the game is over. On the other hand, we display the current level at the top of the game inside the #stage element. Therefore, we also update that wording every time the level is up.

Adding a countdown timer to the game

In this task, we are going to give a final touch to the game by adding a countdown timer. With the timer, the players are not only challenged to select the correct sequence but also restricted in terms of time in order to make the game more exciting for the player.

Prepare for lift off

We will need a new file for the timer. Let's create a new empty file and name it timer.js. With the new file, we also need to import it in the index.html file, which is done using the following code:

```
<script src='js/timer.js'></script>
```

The timer would be a horizontal bar at the top of the game. Its width decreases when you count down the time.

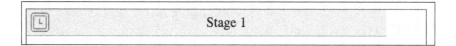

Engage thrusters

Let's count down the game with the following steps:

1. In the index.html file, we need to add a div method for the timer. Add the following code to the HTML inside #game:

    ```
    <div id="timer"></div>
    ```

2. Let's move to the `game.js` file to add the timer control to the game flow:

```
gameWin: function() {
    ...
  game.timer.stop();
},
gameOver: function() {
    ...
  game.timer.stop();
},
startLevel: function() {
    ...
  game.timer.restart();
},
```

3. We remove the following code from the `init` method in order to prevent the timer from starting during the menu scene:

```
var init = function() {
  game.flow.startLevel();    <<<<< Delete this line.
}
```

4. The timer is something that can be reused in other games, so it is worth creating a dedicated file named `timer.js`. Let's put the following timer code into the newly created `timer.js` file:

```
(function(){
  var game = this.colorQuestGame = this.colorQuestGame || {};

  game.timer = {
    interval: undefined,
    countFrom: 60, // second
    count: this.countFrom,
    progressView: document.getElementById('timer'),
    restart: function() {
      if (this.interval) {
        clearInterval(this.interval);
      }
      this.count = this.countFrom;
      this.interval = setInterval((this.tick).bind(this), 1000);
    },
    stop: function() {
      clearInterval(this.interval);
    },
    tick: function() {
      this.count -= 1;
```

```
      if (this.count<= 0) {
        this.count = 0;
        clearInterval(this.interval);
        game.flow.gameOver();
       }
      // update the view
      var progress = this.count / this.countFrom * 100;
      this.progressView.style.width = progress + "%";
    }
  }
})();
```

5. Now, it is time for styling. Let's append the following CSS rules to the `game.css` file:

```
#timer {
  position: absolute;
  top: 0;
  left: 0;
  height: 30px;
  width: 100%;
  background: #7ADAF6 url(images/timer_symbol.png) no-  repeat 5px
50%;
  border-bottom: 1px solid #4F8EA1;
  transition: all .3s ease-out;
}
```

Objective complete – mini debriefing

A simple way to count down is to use the `setInterval` or `setTimeout` methods. However, for games, we usually want a global timer to act as the world clock. This way, all the elements will listen for the tick of the timer. When the world clock pauses, all game elements stop, when it resumes, all resume. That's why we have a separate timer object.

The timer has its own interval managed. All we need to do is start and stop the timer and it will run the `setInterval` and `clearInterval` methods for us.

By default, the tick function checks whether the time is up and also updates the visual timer DOM node with a width that reflects the countdown.

Mission accomplished

We created our first playable game. We learned how to separate data manipulation and visual presentation. We also learned how to manage the game scenes and create logic for each state.

There are many ways to create games with web standard. We explored how to create the game with HTML DOM elements, CSS properties, and JavaScript. There are other approaches such as using canvas-drawing APIs and even with some third-party game libraries. In later projects, we will explore these different approaches.

There are some approaches though, such as WebGL, which we will not discuss in this book. The programming of WebGL requires a different kind of programming skills that is not quite related to traditional web designing skills.

In the next project, we will create a card game that uses flipping and CSS animation techniques.

Hotshot challenges

There are always improvements in game development. The following sections act as suggestions that can further enhance the game.

Storing the data in local storage

Currently, the game restarts every time a page is refreshed. We can keep progress by saving the completed level locally. Furthermore, we can store the current level that is in progress so a player resumes at the exact point they left the game. We are going to discuss local storage in *Project 5*, *Building an Isometric City Game*, when creating the isometric city-building game.

Collecting stars

A level-unlocking game usually works better with stars collection. In each quest level, we can define three levels of achievement. Each achievement rewards the player with one star. For example, completion of a quest can be worth the first star, no-undo is worth the second star, and the final star is awarded only when a player completes the level very fast.

Then, we may have a total count of all the collected stars, and it can be used to unlock new quests or even unlocking new abilities to help player advances.

Project 2

Card Battle!

In this project, we are going to create a playing card game with the heavy use of CSS transition and animation. The player selects a card out of the three choices given to him/her and tries to beat the opponent's card until either side runs out of health points.

Mission briefing

This is a fighting game between a player and the computer, using battle cards.

Technically, the game contains four cards; three for the player to choose and one for the opponent. On each card, there is a random number representing the power. The battle begins by comparing the cards of both the player and the opponent. The difference between the power values acts as damage to the weaker side. The game is over when either side dies with no more health points left. You may visit `http://makzan.net/html5-games/card-battle/` to play the example game in order to have better understanding on what we will build throughout this project.

The following is a screenshot showing the battle in the middle of the fight:

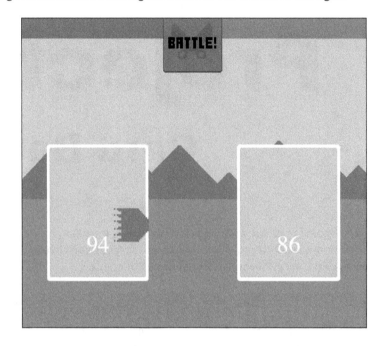

Why is it awesome?

This game showcases how we can put CSS3 transition and animation together to create different effects, including sliding and 3D flipping. The animation-sequence script shows us how we can stack the animation one-by-one. After creating this game, we can use a similar approach to create most of the animation sequences for game objects.

Your Hotshot objectives

We are going to divide our mission into eight objectives, shown as follows:

- ▶ Creating the game scenes
- ▶ Creating a 3D card-flipping effect
- ▶ Selecting a card
- ▶ Adding a power value to the cards
- ▶ Creating the opponent's card
- ▶ Building the battle animation
- ▶ Adding health points to the game
- ▶ Restarting the game for the next round of the battle

Mission checklist

We have a very similar project in *Project 1*, *Building a CSS Quest Game*, with similar HTML layout and scenes management logic.

Creating the game scenes

In this task, we kick-start the project with game scenes such as the menu, game, and game-over condition, defined in a game-flow logic. We will also get these scenes linked together.

Prepare for lift off

We need to create a new directory for our new game project. Inside the project folder, we have the following:

- An `index.html` file for the view
- A `game.css` file for the styling
- A directory named `js` for all the logic files
- A directory named `images` for all the game graphics
- Lastly, we need the following four images placed in the `images` folder:

Engage thrusters

First of all, we start at where the web browser begins loading our game, that is, the `index.html` file, and perform the steps given as follows:

1. Put the following HTML code in the `index.html` file. Most of the tags and layout codes are similar to the ones we saw in *Project 1*, *Building a CSS Quest Game*:

```
<!DOCTYPE html>
<html lang='en'>
```

```
<head>
  <meta charset='utf-8'>
  <title>Card Battle</title>
  <link rel="stylesheet" href="game.css">
</head>
<body>
  <header>
    <div class="row">
      <h1>Card Battle!</h1>
    </div>
  </header>
  <section id="game" class="row"> <!-- The game section starts -->
    <div id="start-scene" class="scene">
      <a href="#" id="start-btn" class="button"></a>
    </div>
    <div id="game-scene" class="scene out"></div>
    <div id="gameover-scene" class="scene out won loss">
      <p><a href="#" id="back-to-menu-button" class="button"></a></p>
    </div>
  </section> <!-- The game section ends -->
  <section class='how-to-play row'>
    <h2>How to Play?</h2>
    <p>Pick one card and watch the battle result. Beat opponent before you run out of HP.</p>
  </section>
  <footer>
    <div class="row">
      <p>Copyright goes here.</p>
    </div>
  </footer>
  <!-- Loading all the JS logics -->
  <script src='js/patch.js'></script>
  <script src='js/scenes.js'></script>
  <script src='js/game-scene.js'></script>
  <script src='js/game.js'></script>
</body>
</html>
```

2. The HTML only defines how the content and game elements are grouped and organized. The styling is always done in CSS. So, we have the following style rules defined in the game.css file:

```
#game {
  width: 480px;
```

```
  height: 600px;
  border-radius: 8px;
  overflow: hidden;
}
.scene {
  width: 100%;
  height: 100%;
  position: absolute;
  overflow: hidden;
  border-radius: 8px;
  transition: all .3s ease-out;
}
.scene.out {
  transform: translate3d(100%, 0, 0);
}
.scene.in {
  transform: translate3d(0, 0, 0);
}

.button {
  position: absolute;
  width: 100%;
  height: 100%;
  top: 0;
  left: 0;
}
#start-scene { background: url(images/start-scene-
  bg.png);}
#game-scene { background: url(images/battle-bg.png);}
#gameover-scene.won { background: url(images/you-
  won.png);}
#gameover-scene.loss { background: url(images/you-
  loss.png);}
```

3. Now, we have the game elements and their styles defined. The next thing is the logic of toggling the different states of the game elements. This is the job of JavaScript. There are many different components in a game, and we will divide them into individual files for easier code readability. The following code controls the game flow and is placed in the game.js file:

```
;(function(){
  var game = this.cardBattleGame = this.cardBattleGame
    || {};

  // Main Game Flow
```

```
game.flow = {
  startOver: function() {
    game.startScene.show();
    game.gameScene.hide();
    game.gameOverScene.hide();
  },
  startGame: function() {
    game.startScene.hide();
    game.gameScene.show();
    game.gameOverScene.hide();
  },
  gameOver: function() {
    game.startScene.hide();
    game.gameScene.hide();
    game.gameOverScene.show();
  }
}

// Entry Point
var init = function() {
  game.startScene.setup();
  game.gameScene.setup();
  game.gameOverScene.setup();
}
init();
})();
```

4. Then, we move to define how each scene should behave. Scene management is a major component worth a dedicated file. We put the following code in the scenes.js file:

```
;(function(){
  var game = this.cardBattleGame = this.cardBattleGame
    || {};

  // Generic Scene object.
  var scene = game.scene = {
    node: document.querySelector('.scene'),
    setup: function(){},
    onShow: function(){}, // hook for child objects to
      use.
    show: function() {
      this.node.classList.remove('out');
      this.node.classList.add('in');
      this.onShow();
```

```
    },
    hide: function() {
      this.node.classList.remove('in');
      this.node.classList.add('out');
    }
  };

  // Start Scene
  var startScene = game.startScene =
    Object.create(scene);
  startScene.node = document.getElementById('start-
    scene');
  startScene.setup = function() {
    document.getElementById('start-btn').onclick =
      function(){
      game.flow.startGame();
      return false;
    };
  };

  // Gameover Scene
  var gameOverScene = game.gameOverScene =
    Object.create(scene);
  gameOverScene.node = document.getElementById('gameover-
    scene');
  gameOverScene.setup = function() {
    document.getElementById('back-to-menu-
      button').onclick = function() {
      game.flow.startOver();
    };
  };
})();
```

5. We just created the starting menu and the game-over scene. But where is the major game scene? This time the game scene will grow into a large block of code. In order to make it easier to maintain, we put the code into a new file named game-scene.js shown as follows:

```
// game scene module
;(function(){
  var game = this.cardBattleGame = this.cardBattleGame
    || {};

  var gameScene = game.gameScene =
    Object.create(game.scene);
```

```
        gameScene.node = document.getElementById('game-scene');
        gameScene.onShow = function() {
            setTimeout(game.flow.gameOver, 3000);
        }
    })();
```

That's all the code that we need to complete the objective of creating the game scenes.

Objective complete – mini debriefing

We have set up the HTML structure and game scenes as explained in the following sections.

HTML structure for scenes

The #game element is the key element. Inside the game, we have scenes that contain game objects. We have three scenes in this game. The major scene is game-scene which contains most of the card-battle objects. The following is the structure of the HTML nodes in our game:

```
#game
  #start-scene
    //Start button
  #game-scene
    //Game elements to be added later
  #gameover-scene
    //Startover button
```

HTML structure for game objects

In a **Document Object Model (DOM)**-based HTML game, we define game objects by using DOM elements.

Logic modules

There are several core modules in our game, such as game flow, scene, game scene, battle animation, and health point. In this task, we define the game flow module and the structure of the scenes module. In the future tasks, we are going to refine each module to make them work together.

Game flow

The game flow logic is heavily inspired from the CSS matching game in *Project 1, Building a CSS Quest Game*. But in this game, we simplified the flow to have only three states: start over, start game, and game over. When each flow is toggled, the corresponding scene is displayed and all other scenes are hidden.

Scenes' methods

Some of the commonly defined methods are the `setup` and `onShow` methods. The `setup` method is used for a specific scene to initialize and the `onShow` method is called every time the scene is shown by its `show` method. It is provided as a hook for each scene to have logic every time the scene is displayed. For example, in the later stage, our `game-over` scene will change between the win and loss screen during the `onShow` method.

Creating a 3D card-flipping effect

In this task, we will take a look at how to create a 3D card-flipping effect. This effect will be used in our playing card element.

Prepare for lift off

We will need to prepare card graphics for this task. They are `front-face.png` and `back-face-pattern.png`.

Engage thrusters

We will start by defining the game elements in HTML, as we have done in the previous section:

1. Inside `#game-scene`, we create two card elements with front and back faces:

```html
<div id="game-scene" class="scene out">
  <div class="card a">
    <div class="front face"></div>
    <div class="back face"></div>
  </div>
  <div class="card b flipped">
    <div class="front face"></div>
    <div class="back face"></div>
  </div>
</div>
```

2. The core part in this section is the CSS styling. In the `game.css` file, we append the following styling to the card container for its front and back faces, flipped state, and the in-between transition:

```css
/* Card */
.card {
  width: 140px;
  height: 180px;
  perspective: 700;
  transition: all .3s ease-out;
```

```
}
/* card flipping related */
.card > .face {
  position: absolute;
  top: 0;
  left: 0;
  width: 100%;
  height: 100%;
  border-radius: 4px;
  backface-visibility: hidden;
  transition: all 0.3s ease-out;
}
.card > .face.front {
  background: #81d1e9 url(images/front-face.png);
  transform: rotate3d(0, 1, 0, 0deg);
}
.card > .face.back {
  background: #4474b5 url(images/back-face-pattern.png);
  transform: rotate3d(0, 1, 0, 180deg);
  border: 3px solid white;
}
.card.flipped > .face.front {
  transform: rotate3d(0, 1, 0, -180deg);
}
.card.flipped > .face.back {
  transform: rotate3d(0, 1, 0, 0deg);
}
```

3. The card-flipping effect requires only the HTML and CSS part. We use JavaScript just to trigger the flipped state. We define the following JavaScript in the gameScene.onShow function, which is called when the scene appears:

```
gameScene.onShow = function() {
  setTimeout(function() {
    var cardA = document.querySelector('.card.a');
    cardA.classList.add('flipped');
    var cardB = document.querySelector('.card.b');
    cardB.classList.remove('flipped');
  }, 1000);
};
```

Keep in mind that the JavaScript we just added to this task in step 3 is to test the card-flipping effect. We will be changing it in the next task.

Objective complete – mini debriefing

We have created a 3D card-flipping effect. Let's discuss how we built this effect.

3D transform

Transform applies position movement, rotation, and scaling to the elements. Moreover, it can transform in either a 2D or 3D space. The element is still 2D but it is put into a 3D space using the z-axis, as shown in the following figure:

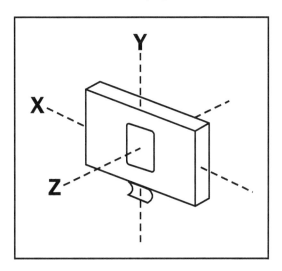

The card-flipping effect

The DOM element is always a 2D pane with only one face. In reality, a card contains two faces—the front and back. So, in HTML, we create two faces inside each card element. We overlap them together and use the rotation transform to create the back and front faces.

The **back face visibility** is a key property to make the effect work. It hides the back face visibility when it is rotated to the back; or else, the rotated back face will still be there.

Another key property is the **perspective**. It is defined in the container of the 3D transformed elements. The higher a perspective value is, the more distortion it creates when it is rotated. The following figure shows how a card rotated in 45 degrees is displayed in different perspectives. A suitable perspective value creates a realistic 3D illusion. The distortion looks strange when the value is too low. The effect looks flat when the value is too high.

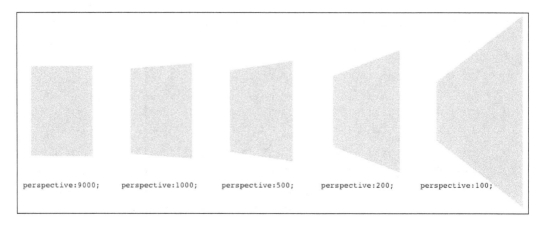

perspective:9000;   perspective:1000;   perspective:500;   perspective:200;   perspective:100;

Toggling the flipping state

In this CSS-driven game, we use many CSS classes to act as a state. Take the flipping effect as an example; we add a "flipped" state to the card, and at the same time, the newly enabled CSS style defined in the .flipped rules is applied to the card to create a flipping animation. It is actually more than just a styling. In the later tasks, we will query the cards with specific classes to perform actions, such as selecting the flipped player's cards or the selected player's card.

Also, the beauty of using separated classes such as card and flipped is the ability to extract common styles for each class category. In future tasks, we are going to have more classes applied to the card, including the player, opponent, and selected classes.

Classified intel

We used the y-axis to rotate the card. Another effect is rotating it on the x-axis. Furthermore, the rotation doesn't necessarily happen at the center point. The rotation origin can be set by the transform-origin property. The following two URLs link to examples that make use of 3D transform properties to create different effects:

- `http://jsfiddle.net/makzan/N7UnH/`
- `http://jsfiddle.net/makzan/QMQLQ/`

The following screenshot shows the rotation effect:

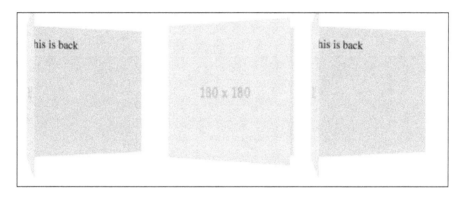

Microsoft created an interactive tool to play with a combination of transform-related properties, which can be found at `http://ie.microsoft.com/testdrive/graphics/hands-on-css3/hands-on_3d-transforms.htm`.

David DaSandro wrote a detailed tutorial on how to make use of the 3D transform to create different effects, which can be found at `http://desandro.github.io/3dtransforms/`.

Selecting a card

To select a card, we will make use of the cards and their flipping effects to let the player select one card among the choices.

Prepare for lift off

The previous task focuses on defining the card style. In this task, we let the player choose one card in each round of battle. The following screenshot shows our planning. We show three cards as a deck at the bottom of the screen. When the player selects one card, we flip the selected card and put it at the center-right side of the screen. The other non-selected cards will hide at the bottom.

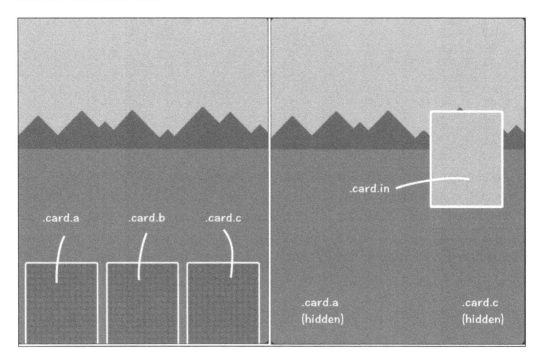

Now, in the `index.html` file, we change the card elements inside `game-scene` into three cards for the player, as shown in the following code:

```
<div id="game-scene" class="scene out">
  <div class="card player a flipped out">
    <div class="front face"></div>
    <div class="back face"></div>
  </div>
```

```
<div class="card player b flipped out">
  <div class="front face"></div>
  <div class="back face"></div>
</div>
<div class="card player c flipped out">
  <div class="front face"></div>
  <div class="back face"></div>
</div>
</div>
```

Engage thrusters

Let's create the card-selecting logic by following the given steps:

1. We want to place the player's cards at the bottom. We will use the absolute
    position for that, as shown in the following code:

```
.card {
  position: absolute;
  bottom: -30px;
  /* rest of .card styles here */
}
.card.a { left: 15px; }
.card.b { left: 170px; }
.card.c { left: 325px; }

.card.player.out {
  transform: translate3d(0, 150%, 0);
}
.card.player.in {
  transform: translate3d(0, 0, 0);
}

.card.player.flipped { /* indicate the card is clickable*/
  cursor: pointer;
}
.card.player.in.flipped:hover {   /* ensure only player,
  flipped and the just in card get this hover event */
  transform: translate3d(0, -10px, 0);
}
.card.selected {
  bottom: 250px;
  left: 300px;
}
```

2. The card elements are the key elements that we are going to query several times during the gameplay. We can cache the querying element instead of asking the DOM to find them every time, as shown in the following code:

```
;(function(){
  // cache node querying
  var allPlayerCardElms =
    document.querySelectorAll('.card.player');
  var allCardElms = document.querySelectorAll('.card');
  // rest of game-scene.js code
```

3. Next, we build the card selection logic after gameScene:

```
gameScene.onShow = function() {
  this.startGame();
}
gameScene.startGame = function() {
  this.restartGame();
}
gameScene.restartGame = function() {
  var animatePlayerCardsIn = function() {
    allPlayerCardElms.forEach(function(elm){
      elm.classList.remove('out');
      elm.classList.add('in');
      elm.classList.add('flipped');
    });
  }
  setTimeout(animatePlayerCardsIn, 800); // delay a while
}
gameScene.setup = function() {
  // each player card
  allPlayerCardElms.forEach(function(elm){
    elm.onclick = function(){
      /* select a card */
      elm.classList.remove('flipped');
      elm.classList.add('selected');

      /* remove non-selected cards */
      document.querySelectorAll('.flipped').forEach(function
  (elm){
        elm.classList.remove('in');
        elm.classList.add('out');
      });
    }
  });
}
```

Objective complete – mini debriefing

We created a CSS transition to flip and move the selected card from the deck to the center of the game screen.

Resetting the card's initial position

In the `restartGame` method, we rest the cards in their initial position. The position and states have been designed in the CSS rule. The logic of resetting the cards is just about removing any added classes and setting the class list to the initialized one.

Selecting the card with a click event

During the setup stage of the game scene, we listen to the click event of all the card elements for the players. Once a card is selected, we remove the `flipped` class and add the `selected` class.

 Note that we put the click event registration in `setup` instead of `onShow` because `setup` is called only once and `onShow` is called every time the scene shows. We just need to register the event listeners once.

Removing the non-selected cards

After any card is selected, we hide the other non-selected cards to let the player focus on the battle animation. This is done by toggling the in/out state on all the flipped cards. Note that we do not cache this querying on the `flipped` class because the result is different in every round after a player selects any card.

Short delay before the card goes into transition

We used `setTimeout` to create a short delay before the player's cards go into transition. This delay provides the illusion of refreshing the cards between two rounds of battle.

Besides the `setTimeout` JavaScript, there is a delay feature available in the CSS property. Normally, we prefer using the CSS delay property to make all the styles and animations defined in CSS consistent. However, we chose to use the JavaScript `timeout` element in this task because this is a new animation that appears in the first round of the game. This means that the previously used battle ending styles may just be added to the element, and having the same element setting for the `out` and `in` class will immediately cause unusual troubles, for example, the out styles are ignored. Having a delay before adding the `in` class makes both the out and in styles and the animation being executed.

Classified intel

There are several ways to place the game elements inside a parent HTML element. In this example, we used the absolute position. It works because our game dimension is fixed by the #game element.

The other approach is to use the translate function instead of the transform function. By using translate3d to define position and positional changes, we get a performance boost from the GPU-accelerated rendering.

In this example, we actually mixed both the approaches.

The third approach is to add the **CSS flexbox** module. The flexbox module allows us to describe how the elements flow within the container. Take the three cards as an example. We can define the three cards to be distributed evenly in the bottom area, according to the width of the container. This approach works better than hardcoding the absolute position when our game requires flexible dimensions, for example, to be installed into different mobile devices with a full-screen playing experience.

The *Learn CSS Layout* website provides an introduction on how we can use different methods to layout DOM elements with CSS at http://learnlayout.com/.

Adding a power value to the cards

In this task, we will add a power value to the cards. We will also create a Card object to get the original value back.

Prepare for lift off

Before going into the core part, we will get the interface prepared.

There is not much to add in HTML. Add the power element inside the front face element, as shown in the following code:

```
<div class="front face">
  <div class="power">100</div>
</div>
```

Also, add some very basic CSS styling to define the power text, which is large and aligned in the center, as shown in the following code:

```
.card .power{
  position: absolute;
  width: 100%;
```

```
    text-align: center;
    bottom: 30px;
    font-size: 2em;
}
```

Engage thrusters

The core part of this task is the JavaScript logic, explained as follows:

1. First, we create a new module to randomize all the power values. Prepend the following code in the `game-scene.js` file. The benefit of separating this logic is to make changing the power formula easy in the future:

```
;(function() {
  var game = this.cardBattleGame = this.cardBattleGame
    || {};

  // Cache elements query
  var allPowerElms = document.querySelectorAll('.power');

  game.randomizePower = function() {
    allPowerElms.forEach(function(elm){
      elm.textContent = Math.round(Math.random() * 60)
        + 40;
    });
  }
})();
```

2. The power value is stored as a text value inside the power elements. We need an easy way to get the value to be used in the battle formula later. Create the following `Card` definition inside the `gameScene` object:

```
var Card = (function(){
  function Card(node) {
    this.node = node;
  }
  Card.prototype.power = function() {
    return 1 *
      this.node.querySelector('.power').textContent
// convert string to integer
  }
  return Card;
})();
```

3. Now, before we restart the game every time, we randomize the power value. It provides different values on every round of card selection:

```
gameScene.restartGame = function() {
  game.randomizePower();
  // rest of the existing code in restartGame.
}
```

4. Now, we mark the selected card as a new Card instance, and then check the power of the card after logging into the game:

```
/* select a card */
selectedCard = new Card(elm);
console.log("Power of selected card: ", selectedCard.power());
// rest of original code for card selection.
```

Objective complete – mini debriefing

We have added a power value to the cards. These values will be used for comparison when we add the battle logic later.

Randomize logic

The game randomizes the power values in all cards for every round when the game begins. It is a separate logic that selects all the power elements and adds a randomized value ranging from 40 to 100 to it. After we get the value, we use the textContent property to set the string value to the card node.

Card definition

Most of the card logic is done on the HTML node directly, such as the toggling classes. But the power is stored in the node as a string type. We want to get the integer type of the power value to make the battle calculations easier. That's why we create a Card object definition.

The Card object contains the original HTML node reference and a power method to get the integer power value from the text content of the HTML node.

The reason why we only instantiate the selected card is because we don't read any power value of the non-selected card.

> The official way to convert a string to an integer is the parseInt method. But the fastest way is to multiply the string by 1. The following URL tests the performance between these two methods:
>
> http://jsperf.com/parseint-vs-x1

Classified intel

When do you define an object definition and when do you declare an object instance directly?

When something is going to be reused many times, declaring the definition allows us to create many instances using the `new` operator. Otherwise, if we just need the object once, an object instance is more than enough.

Creating the opponent's card

It is time to prepare for the battle. In this task, we will create the opponent's card.

Prepare for lift off

As usual, we will prepare the interface before adding logic to the game using the following steps:

1. In the `index.html` file, append the following opponent's card object after our player's cards:

    ```
    <div class="card opponent out">
      <div class="front face">
        <div class="power">100</div>
      </div>
      <div class="back face">back</div>
    </div>
    ```

2. The opponent's card is going in from the left side of the game scene. We define the style of placement and also the out and in classes for the JavaScript to toggle:

    ```
    .card.opponent {
      bottom: 250px;
    }
    .card.opponent.out {
      left: -200px;
    }
    .card.opponent.in {
      transition-delay:.8s;
      left: 40px;
    }
    ```

Engage thrusters

Let's follow these steps to create the opponent's card:

1. During the setup inside the gameScene module, we create a Card instance for that element so that we can get the power of this card later:

```
var opponentCard = new
  Card(document.querySelector('.card.opponent'));
```

2. Next, we define the entry point of the battle animation function. Place the following function code inside the gameScene.setup method. It toggles the opponent state to make it visible in the game scene. Also, note that we are using opponentCard. node because it is a Card instance instead of the raw element node:

```
var beginBattleAnimation = function() {
  opponentCard.node.classList.remove('out');
  opponentCard.node.classList.add('in');
  console.log("Power of opponent card: ",
    opponentCard.power());
}
```

3. Now, when any player's card is selected, we execute the battle animation after all the existing code:

```
allPlayerCardElms.forEach(function(elm){
  elm.onclick = function(){
    /* original code: select a card */

    /* original code: remove non-selected cards */

    /* battle */
    beginBattleAnimation();
  }
});
```

Objective complete – mini debriefing

We created the opponent's card and started the battle by showing the opponent's card in the game scene.

The opponent card's transition

We have defined the transition duration and easing function in the card-flipping task. In this task, we only need to define the in and out position for the opponent's card. Also, we have added a 0.8 second delay to the transition in animation to make the animation look smooth.

The entry point of the battle animation

There is going to be a long animation sequence after the player selects a card. In this task, we get the entry point of the battle prepared. We define the `beginBattleAnimation` method where we move in the opponent's card. In the next task, we will add the entire animation sequence inside this method.

Building the battle animation

This is a major task that defines the entire battle animation. After both the player's card and opponent's card are on stage, the player's card emits a flame blaze towards the opponent and then the opponent emits another blaze towards the player. The following screenshot shows the blaze being emitted from the player's card on right-hand side towards the opponent's card:

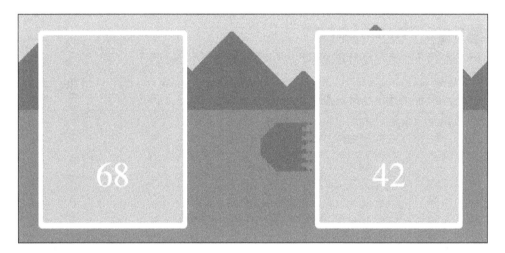

Prepare for lift off

First, we need two more game objects—the blaze towards the left and the blaze towards the right. Add them to the HTML before the end of the game-scene element, as shown in the following code:

```
<div class="blaze toward-left"></div>
<div class="blaze toward-right"></div>
```

We need the following two images for these two newly added game objects:

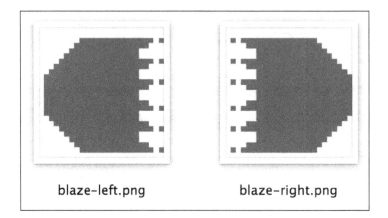

blaze–left.png   blaze–right.png

Engage thrusters

Let's create the battle animation sequence with the following steps:

1. Here, we prepare a CSS animation, **keyframes**, to shake the card. Add the following code before the card styling definition in the game.css file:

```
@keyframes shake {
    0%   { transform: translate3d(0, 0, 0);  }
    20%  { transform: translate3d(-5%, 0, 0);}
    40%  { transform: translate3d(5%, 0, 0); }
    60%  { transform: translate3d(-5%, 0, 0);}
    80%  { transform: translate3d(5%, 0, 0); }
    100% { transform: translate3d(0, 0, 0);  }
}
```

2. Then, we make use of the animation by defining a new shake state for the card elements:

```
.card.shake {animation: shake 300ms ease-out;}
```

3. Next, we have styles for our newly created blaze elements. Append the following styling and animation to the end of the game.css file:

```
.blaze {
  position: absolute;
  bottom: 300px;
  width: 50px;
  height: 50px;
  opacity: 0;
  animation-timing-function: ease-out;
```

```
    animation-duration: 1000ms;
  }
  .blaze.toward-left {background-image:url(images/blaze-
    left.png);}
  .blaze.toward-right {background-image:url(images/blaze-
    right.png);}

  @keyframes blaze-toward-left {
    0%,20%{ opacity: 1; transform: translate3d(300px, 0,
      0);}
    80% { transform: translate3d(100px, 0, 0); }
    100%{ opacity: 0; transform: translate3d(100px, 0, 0);
      }
  }
  @keyframes blaze-toward-right {
    0%,20%{ opacity: 1; transform: translate3d(130px, 0,
      0);}
    80% { transform: translate3d(330px, 0, 0); }
    100%{ opacity: 0; transform: translate3d(330px, 0, 0);
      }
  }
  .blaze.toward-left.attack { animation-name: blaze-toward-
    left; }
  .blaze.toward-right.attack {animation-name: blaze-toward-
    right;}
```

4. Before we have our battle animation sequence, we define two prototype methods to the `Node` element object. They are used to keep track of the transition and animation completion. Add the following code to the `patch.js` file:

```
Node.prototype.onAnimationEnd = function(callback) {
  var listener = function(e){
    e.target.removeEventListener('webkitAnimationEnd',
      listener);
    callback(e);
  }
  this.addEventListener('webkitAnimationEnd', listener);
}
Node.prototype.onTransitionEnd = function(callback) {
  var listener = function(e){
    e.target.removeEventListener('webkitTransitionEnd',
      listener);
    callback(e);
  }
  this.addEventListener('webkitTransitionEnd', listener);
}
```

5. Here, we have the long battle animation sequence. It starts by showing the opponent's card. After the opponent's card is in, it starts the blaze and shake animations one-by-one, accordingly:

```
var beginBattleAnimation = function() {
  opponentCard.node.classList.remove('out');
  opponentCard.node.classList.add('in');
  console.log("Power of opponent card: ",
    opponentCard.power());
  opponentCard.node.onTransitionEnd(function(e) {
    //only execute the attack animation when opponent at
      'in' state.
    if (!e.target.classList.contains('in')) return;

    var blazeLeft =
      document.querySelector('.blaze.toward-left');
    blazeLeft.classList.add('attack');
    blazeLeft.onAnimationEnd(function(e){
      e.target.classList.remove('attack');
      opponentCard.node.classList.add('shake');
      opponentCard.node.onAnimationEnd(function(e){
        opponentCard.node.classList.remove('shake');

        var blazeRight =
          document.querySelector('.blaze.toward-right');
        blazeRight.classList.add('attack');
        blazeRight.onAnimationEnd(function(e){
          e.target.classList.remove('attack');
          selectedCard.node.classList.add('shake');
          selectedCard.node.onAnimationEnd(function(e){
            selectedCard.node.classList.remove('shake');
          }); // player shake end handler
        }); // blaze right end handler
      }); // opponent shake end handler
    }); // blaze left end handler
  }); // opponent transition end handler
} // end beginBattleAnimation
```

Objective complete – mini debriefing

In these steps, we created the battle animation by using CSS and JavaScript elements.

The animation sequence

1. Here is how we can create the animation sequence: We enable the animation state by adding a specific class to the game elements.

2. We listen to the `transitionEnd` or `animationEnd` event.

3. When the event is trigged, we remove the event listener.

4. Inside the event handler, we repeat step 1 for the next game elements.

 Please note that we need to remove the event listener after it is triggered; otherwise, the animation completion event will be triggered several times when the game repeats the battle animation. Multiple `addEventListener` events will trigger the same handlers.

So, we have the following sequence for the battle:

1. Opponent card transits in.

2. Blaze moves from right to left.

3. The opponent card shakes.

4. Blaze moves from left to right.

5. The player card shakes.

 The `transitionEnd` and `animationEnd` elements also come with the vendor prefix until they are stable and officially supported by browsers. That's why we used `webkitTransitionEnd` and `webkitAnimationEnd`.

Using the CSS keyframes animation

Keyframes allows us to define how the styles change within the animation duration. It is a collection of keyframes with two things: the percentage of time and a block of styles. The time must start at 0 percent and end at 100 percent.

The keyframes block often generically describes the movement. So, you will not see information about missing elements and duration. This missing information is for the styles of the selector. That's why we have the duration and easing function defined in the `.card.shake` selector.

The card shaking animation

The shaking animation is done by having the card's x-axis move from -5 percent to 5 percent several times.

The blaze animation

The blaze is an animation that moves from one side to the other along the x-axis. At the same time, it fades out during the last 20 percent of time.

We can create a pause between the animations by setting the same value in two adjacent keyframes. The blaze attacking animation sets a 20 percent pause at the beginning by adding the following code:

```
0%,20%{ opacity: 1; transform: translate3d(300px, 0, 0);}
```

Classified intel

If we want to add a pause at the beginning, we can also use the `animation-delay` property. But the delay is not the same. The delay property adds the delay duration to the total duration using the following formula:

The duration user sees = delay duration + animation duration

Using the keyframes pause makes the total duration follow the `animation-duration` property.

Adding health points to the game

In this task, we are going to add health points to both the player and the opponent. We reduce the health points during the battle if any side gets hurt.

Prepare for lift off

First, we define the user interface of the health points in HTML. Put the following code in the `index.html` file, right after opening the `#game-scene` tag. We also create a battle indicator:

```
<div class="hp-background">
  <div class="hp opponent"></div>
  <div class="hp player"></div>
</div>
```

Engage thrusters

We are now going to put all the health points code in a new file:

1. Let's create a new file named `hp.js` under the `js` folder. Then, we include the newly created JavaScript file in HTML before importing our `game-scene.js` file:

    ```
    <script src='js/hp.js'></script>
    ```

2. Next, as usual, the styling will be for our health points interface. We can append it to the end of the `game.css` file:

    ```css
    .hp-background {
      border-bottom: 1px solid #333;
      background: #ababab;
      height: 30px;
    }
    .hp {
      position: absolute;
      width: 210px;
      height: 30px;
      transition: all .3s ease-out;
    }
    .hp.opponent {
      background: url(images/blue-hp.png) repeat;
      left: 0;
    }
    .hp.player {
      background: url(images/red-hp.png) repeat;
      right: 0;
    }
    ```

3. In the newly created `hp.js` file, we have the following code for the HP module. It is an object managing both the player's and opponent's health points, including the value and displaying the calculation methods:

    ```js
    ;(function(){
      var game = this.cardBattleGame = this.cardBattleGame
        || {};

      var HP = game.HP = {
        playerHP: 100,
        opponentHP: 100,
        playerHPView: document.querySelector('.hp.player'),
    ```

```
    opponentHPView:
      document.querySelector('.hp.opponent'),
    reset: function() {
      this.playerHP = 100;
      this.opponentHP = 100;
      this.playerHPView.style.width = '210px';
      this.opponentHPView.style.width = '210px';
    },
    isSomeoneDead: function() {
      return (this.playerHP <= 0 || this.opponentHP <= 0)
    },
    isPlayerDead: function() {
      if (this.playerHP <= 0) return true;
      return false;
    },
    hurtPlayer: function(attackPower, defensePower) {
      var diff = attackPower - defensePower;
      if (diff > 0) {
        this.playerHP = Math.max(this.playerHP - diff,
          0);
        this.playerHPView.style.width = this.playerHP /
          100 * 210 + 'px';
      }
    },
    hurtOpponent: function(attackPower, defensePower) {
      var diff = attackPower - defensePower;
      if (diff > 0) {
        this.opponentHP = Math.max(this.opponentHP -
          diff, 0);
        this.opponentHPView.style.width = this.opponentHP
          / 100 * 210 + 'px';
      }
    }
  }
};
})();
```

4. Now, we go back to the game-scene.js file. When the game scene is displayed, usually after the menu screen dismisses, we reset the health points:

```
gameScene.onShow = function() {
  game.HP.reset();
  this.startGame();
}
```

5. We need to add the health points calculation in between the battle animation. The first step is to add the hurtOpponent method calling after we start the opponent-shaking animation:

```
opponentCard.node.classList.add('shake');//Existing code.
game.HP.hurtOpponent(selectedCard.power(),
  opponentCard.power());
```

6. The second one is the hurtPlayer method calling after the player-shaking animation starts:

```
selectedCard.node.classList.add('shake');//Existing code.
game.HP.hurtPlayer(opponentCard.power(),
  selectedCard.power());
```

7. Now, we have health points, and they will get to zero. Add the following game-over check after we complete the player's shake animation:

```
selectedCard.node.onAnimationEnd(function(e){
  selectedCard.node.classList.remove('shake');
//Existing code.

  if (game.HP.isSomeoneDead()) {
    game.flow.gameOver();
  } else {
    //gameScene.restartGame();
  }
});
```

Objective complete – mini debriefing

We have calculated the battle damages and visualized it in the health bar at the top of the game screen.

The health point module

The first part of the module defines the health point value for the opponent and player. It also caches the query selector of both the views.

It comes with a resetting method to reset both the health points of the player and opponent to their initial state, that is, 100. The method, isSomeoneDead, is to determine if anyone died with 0 health points. This is useful to determine if the game should end. Then, we have another similar method, isPlayerDead. This is useful to determine who the winner is, the opponent or player.

At last, we get two methods to reduce health points from both the sides. After doing the deduction of the health points, it updates the interface.

The health points are on the scale of 0 to 100. When displaying it in HTML, we control the width of the element in the same proportion. The formula of the width is *hp_width = hp / 100 * full_width*.

The health points reduction formula

During the battle, the first blaze goes from the player's card towards the opponent and then the opponent's card performs the shake animation. At this time, we tell the health point module to calculate the point reduction from the given attacker's power and defender's power.

The same applies to the player when the player's card is being attacked by the blaze.

Ending the game

There are two options after one battle round. If anyone is dead, the game is over; otherwise, the cards should be reset for the next round of battle. We haven't coded the resetting logic yet; that's why the `gameScene.restartGame()` function is commented out.

Classified intel

The point calculation is very simple in this game. It just checks which side has the higher power and reduces the difference to the weaker side. A more complicated calculation can be introduced to create more fun. For example, there can be some point reduction on both sides when both sides have the same or similar power.

Restarting the game for the next round of battle

We now come to the last task—resetting the cards for the next round of battle. At this stage, the battle animation runs once and then the game stalls there. In this task, we reset all the card states so that the player can select another card and trigger another round of battle until either side is dead.

Engage thrusters

Let's continue the battle with the following steps:

1. Inside the `gameScene.restartGame` method, we add the following code to toggle the `out` and `flipped` state for all the cards:

```
/* reset the transition state */
allCardElms.forEach(function(elm){
  elm.classList.remove('in');
  elm.classList.add('out');
});
allPlayerCardElms.forEach(function(elm){
  elm.classList.remove('selected');
  elm.classList.add('flipped');
});
```

2. Remember that we have commented out the `restartGame` method calling in the previous task. Now, we can enable this method calling by removing the comments. The battle round then repeats until the game ends:

```
gameScene.restartGame();
```

3. At last, when the game over scene appears, we determine which side wins and then show the win/loss screen correspondingly:

```
gameOverScene.onShow = function() {
  if (game.HP.isPlayerDead()) {
    this.node.classList.add('loss');
    this.node.classList.remove('won');
  } else {
    this.node.classList.add('won');
    this.node.classList.remove('loss');
  }
}
```

Objective complete – mini debriefing

The onShow method is called whenever the scene.show method is called. So, this is a good time to change the background to show the win or loss background.

Mission accomplished

Throughout the eight tasks, we successfully created a card battle game with lots of CSS transition and animation. The player has to keep fighting until he/she beats the opponent as shown in the following screenshot:

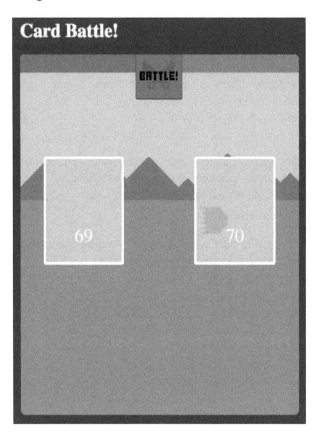

Hotshot challenges

There are different ways we can further improve the game.

> ► **Adding special items**:
>
> There can be special items that can affect the battle result. For example, there can be an item that heals the health points before the battle. Or, there can be an item that adds 10 power values to the card for three rounds.

These cards can be purchased at the in-game store. And this usually involves virtual coins. The coins can be earned by winning the game.

▸ **Multiple players**:

By setting up a socket server and using the HTML5 web socket API, we can make the opponent a real player. On each selection, one side sends the selected power value to the server and a push to the other player. On the other side, the value from the server appears on the opponent's card. In this way, the power value on the opponent's card is not a random number, but a value from the real opponent player. The server then stores the health point calculation and determines the end of the game.

Project 3

Space Runner

In the previous project, we created two game examples that take mouse inputs. In this project, we are going to create another game example with game loop and keyboard inputs. The player controls an avatar that runs from the moon station towards space. The goal is to run as far as possible without hitting any obstacles.

We will learn how to create sprite sheet-based animations with a CSS background and use JavaScript to handle keyboard inputs.

Mission briefing

We will learn how to create a CSS-based sprite sheet animation. We will also learn the concept of parallax scrolling and use JavaScript to handle keyboard inputs. You can visit the URL http://makzan.net/html5-games/space-runner/ to play the example game in order to have a better understanding of what we will build throughout this project.

A screenshot of the game is shown as follows:

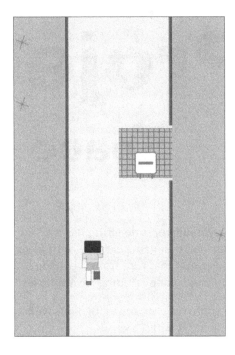

Why is it awesome?

After covering two game examples that used a mouse in the earlier projects, this is the first time we will handle keyboard inputs.

We will use a game loop in this project. The Game loop is an important technique in a game that drives the updates for both the logic and as well as the view rendering. We will further work on the animation by using a sprite sheet that animates frame by frame. **Game loop** and **sprite sheet animation** are two essential concepts of game development. We will even use these techniques in the later project that build games with canvas and game library.

In addition, we will learn how to add depth to the game with parallax scrolling. These are all the essential techniques that are required to create HTML5 games.

Your Hotshot objectives

This project consists of the following tasks:

- ▶ Managing the scenes
- ▶ Defining the floor and tiles in the game
- ▶ Controlling tiles creation in JavaScript

- ▸ Using a game loop
- ▸ Parallax background scrolling
- ▸ Controlling a player with the keyboard
- ▸ Determining a collision between the player and tiles
- ▸ Spritesheet animation

Mission checklist

What do we need to prepare before we start the project? Firstly, we need a project directory for all the game files. Let's create a directory with the folder and file structure, as shown in the following screenshot:

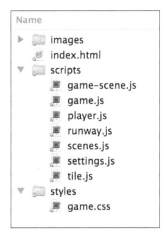

We need some graphics in order to complete this project. You can find the graphics in the sample code bundle. The `images` folder for all the eight tasks is the same in this project. Let's put the `images` folder inside our project directory.

Managing the scenes

In this first task, we will prepare the scenes, which act as a container for all our game objects.

Prepare for lift off

Before creating the scene flow, we prepare the basic scenes definition.

The scene is set up in the same way as the previous project. However, this time we simplified it into two scenes only. Add the following code in the game.js file:

```
;(function(){
  var game = this.spaceRunner || (this.spaceRunner = {});

  // Main Game Flow
  game.flow = {
    startGame: function() {
      game.gameOverScene.hide();
      game.gameScene.startOver();
    },
    gameOver: function() {
      game.gameOverScene.show();
    }
  };

  // Entry Point
  var init = function() {
    console.log("Welcome to Space Runner Game.");
    game.isGameOver = true;
    game.gameScene.setup();
    game.gameOverScene.setup();
  };
  init();
}).call(this);
```

Then, we move to the scene.js file to define a scene object. This scene object has basic abilities such as showing and hiding itself. Moreover, it provides a hook for the scene implementation to add initialization logic in the setup function and the onShow function:

```
;(function(){
  var game = this.spaceRunner = this.spaceRunner || {};

  // Generic Scene object.
  var scene = game.scene = {
    node: document.querySelector('.scene'),
    setup: function(){},
    onShow: function(){},
    show: function() {
      this.node.classList.remove('out');
      this.node.classList.add('in');
      this.onShow();
    },
    hide: function() {
```

```
        this.node.classList.remove('in');
        this.node.classList.add('out');
      }
    };
```

After this, comes the `GameOver` scene, which is a clone instance of the basic scene object. It adds logic to the `setup` function for the restart button:

```
// Gameover Scene
var gameOverScene = game.gameOverScene = Object.create(scene);
gameOverScene.node = document.getElementById('gameover-scene');
gameOverScene.setup = function() {
  document.getElementById('back-to-menu-button').onclick =
    function() {
    game.flow.startGame();
  };
};

}).call(this);
```

Game scene is an object that extends from the generic scene:

```
// game scene module
;(function(){
  var game = this.spaceRunner || (this.spaceRunner = {});

  var gameScene = game.gameScene = Object.create(game.scene);
  gameScene.node = document.getElementById('game-scene');
  gameScene.onShow = function() {};

}).call(this);
```

We need CSS styles for the scenes element and the in/out transition. The CSS for scenes is exactly the same as seen in *Project 2, Card Battle!*. Please refer to the task *Creating the game scenes* in *Project 2, Card Battle!*, for the CSS style.

Engage thrusters

Since it is an HTML-oriented game, we first work on the game's HTML file by performing the following steps:

1. We construct the scenes and game objects in the HTML file:

```
...
<section id="game" class="row">
    <div id="game-scene" class="scene">
    </div>
```

```
        <div id="gameover-scene" class="scene out">
          <p><a href="#" id="back-to-menu-button"
            class="button"></a></p>
        </div>
      </section>

      . . .
```

2. The following CSS (`game.css`) rules are for the game over scene. In the game over screen, we need a background and a restart button:

```
.button {
  position: absolute;
  width: 100%;
  height: 100%;
  top: 0;
  left: 0;
}
#gameover-scene {
  background: rgba(0, 0, 0, .5) url(../images/gameover.png);
}
```

3. Next, we initialize the game with a temporary code that toggles the game into the game over state after a 3 seconds delay:

```
gameScene.setup = function() {

  this.startOver();
};
gameScene.startOver = function() {

  game.isGameOver = false;

  // temporary code to test game over scene
  setTimeout(function(){
    game.flow.gameOver();
  }, 3000);
  // end temporary code
};
```

It's time to check whether the code works. When we open the HTML file in a web browser, the game should start at the game scene. Wait for 3 seconds after starting the game and the game switches to the game over scene. Then, try to click anywhere in the game and it will lead us to the game scene again.

Objective complete – mini debriefing

We completed the task of setting up the scene. We have defined two scenes: the game play scene and the game over scene. We have created a button in the game over scene that starts the game again. We have also added a temporary code to trigger the game over scene after a delay of 3 seconds. After the game logic flow is ready, we will remove the temporary code that triggers the game over state.

Classified intel

Scene management provides a central place to control the game flow so that we can change the game state whenever needed.

There are two scenes in this game: the game scene and the game over scene.

The game autostarts when it is loaded. When the player hits any obstacles, the game ends with an overlay of the game over scene.

The game over scene has a half-transparent background. When the game over scene appears, we want the game scene to stay so the player can know how the game ends.

The following figure shows how the game scene is unchanged and the game over scene moves in from the right-hand side:

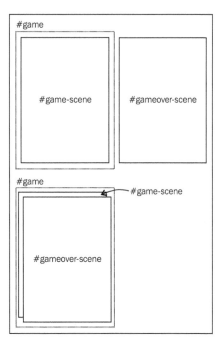

That's why the game flow only controls the visibility of the game over scene.

Defining the floor and tiles in the game

In this task, we would like to define an essential game object—tiles. We use tiles to construct the running floor, and the types of tiles include the runway terrain and obstacles.

Prepare for lift off

We will put our code in several places. Make sure that you have the following files ready before you start:

▸ `setting.js`

▸ `tile.js`

▸ `player.js`

Engage thrusters

First, let's put the game objects inside the game scene in the HTML file. There is an element that represents the floor, an element that represents the player, and a few temporary elements that represent the tiles, these are given in more detail in the following steps:

1. The tile elements come with an inline style for placement on the floor:

```
<div id="game-scene" class="scene">
  <div id="floor" class="floor">
    <div id="player"></div>
    <!-- temporary code to be removed in next task -->
    <div class='tile tile-1'   style=
      'transform: translate3d(100px,      0, 0)'></div>
    <div class='tile tile-2'   style=
      'transform: translate3d(200px,      0, 0)'></div>
    <div class='tile tile-1'   style=
      'transform: translate3d(100px, 100px, 0)'></div>
    <div class='tile tile-100' style=
      'transform: translate3d(200px, 100px, 0)'></div>
    <div class='tile tile-1'   style=
      'transform: translate3d(100px, 200px, 0)'></div>
    <div class='tile tile-2'   style=
      'transform: translate3d(200px, 200px, 0)'></div>
    <!-- end temporary code -->
  </div>
</div>
```

2. It is time for the visual part. Let's move on to the CSS file (`game.css`) and append the following code. The following styling rules define how the running floor and the tiles look visually:

```css
.floor {
  position: relative;
  width: 400px;
  height: 100%;
  margin: auto;
  background: url(../images/space-runner-bg.png) 0 0;
}
.tile {
  position: absolute;
  width: 100px;
  height: 100px;
}
.tile-0 {}
.tile-1 {
  background: url(../images/runway.png);
}
.tile-2 {
  background: url(../images/runway2.png);
}
.tile-100 {
  background: url(../images/block.png);
}
.tile-4 {
  background: url(../images/star.png) center center no-repeat;
}
```

3. We have an HTML element with a `#player` ID to represent the player. Later, we will need to reference that player element in another JavaScript module. To make things clearer, we will create an object dedicated to the player code, which currently only includes the reference to the player element. Put the following player module in the `player.js` file:

```javascript
// Player module
;(function(){
  var game = this.spaceRunner || (this.spaceRunner = {});

  var player = game.player = {};
  player.element = document.getElementById('player');

}).call(this);
```

4. In the `setting.js` file, we set the width and height of each tile for the JavaScript logic:

```
;(function(){
  var game = this.spaceRunner || (this.spaceRunner = {});

  game.TILE_HEIGHT = game.TILE_WIDTH = 100;

}).call(this);
```

Objective complete – mini debriefing

We have accomplished the task by putting the essential game objects in the game scene, and created related CSS visual styles.

The tiles

We use JavaScript to create tiles on the floor dynamically. Before creating the tiles in logic, let's create some dummy tiles to explore how we present the tiles.

The tile pattern

We will use `tile-<id>` to represent a specific tile pattern. The following screenshot shows the tile patterns we have in the game. Here, **tile-0** is an empty tile, **tile-1** and **tile-2** are used for the runway, **tile-10** is for decoration, and **tile-100** is the obstacle.

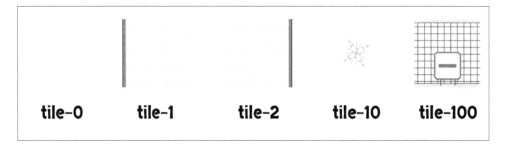

| tile-0 | tile-1 | tile-2 | tile-10 | tile-100 |

We will use the `class` attribute so that it is easy to change the tile graphics in the CSS styling file. In addition, on the logic side, it is easy to use `classList` to switch the tile ID.

For example, if we want to set a tile to the pattern **tile-10** in JavaScript, we can use the following code:

```
tileElement.classList.add('tile-10');
```

The setting.js file

The setting.js file is useful to store constants of the game. For example, it can be used to store the tile dimension that JavaScript needs to know in order to place the tiles programmatically.

Classified intel

We will use class to represent which type of tile an HTML is. Sometimes, we can use the HTML5 data- attribute to embed element-specific data. For example, the following HTML represents a gold coin object having an **amount** value of 50:

```
<div class='gold coin' data-amount='50'></div>
```

The role of HTML, CSS, and JavaScript

Keep in mind that we put a lot of effort to separate logic, data, and view. The following figure shows how different parts are separated; data, view, and the logic controlling these parts. Separating the data and view helps make our code easier to maintain:

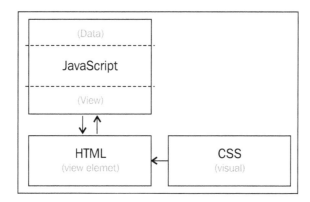

You may notice that we only tell the JavaScript and HTML what ID the tile is, but we never define how they look there. All visual properties are defined in CSS.

As a DOM element-oriented game, HTML is where we define the game objects—scenes, player, tiles, and the user interface.

CSS is the visual part of these elements. It defines the visual look, dimension, and position of the elements.

 JavaScript stores the game data and game states. It also controls and updates the game objects.

Controlling the tiles creation in JavaScript

In the previous task, we placed the tile elements directly in HTML. In this task, we will change the placement of tiles using JavaScript.

Prepare for lift off

At first, we remove the dummy tiles in HTML. We put those tile elements in HTML just to test whether the CSS visual part works. After getting rid of the temporary code for dummy HTML tiles, the `#floor` HTML element reverts to the following state with just the `#player` element:

```
<div id="game-scene" class="scene">
  <div id="floor" class="floor">
    <div id="player"></div>
  </div>
</div>
```

We are going to need the reference of the floor element. Let's put the following code in the `runway.js` file. It creates a new view object and refers to the `#floor` element with an object property:

```
// runway view
;(function(){
  var game = this.spaceRunner || (this.spaceRunner = {});
  game.view = game.view || {};
  game.view.floor = document.getElementById('floor');
}).call(this);
```

Engage thrusters

We wish to have flexibility in terms of how the tiles are placed on the runway. To do that, we will dynamically create the tile's DOM element in JavaScript using the following steps:

1. There are many tile instances in a runway. Let's define the following tile definition in the `tile.js` file:

```
;(function(){
  var game = this.spaceRunner || (this.spaceRunner = {});

  function Tile(element, type, x, y){
    this.x = x || 0;
    this.y = y || 0;
```

```
        this.type = type || 0;
        this.element = element;
        this.updatePosition();
    }
//The behavior we expect from each tile is the ability to update
its own position from the x and y property. It uses the CSS
translate3d function for positioning.
    Tile.prototype.updatePosition = function() {
        if (this.element) {
            this.element.style.webkitTransform = "translate3d(" + this.x
+ "px, " + this.y + "px, 0)";
        }
    }

    game.Tile = Tile;
}).call(this);
```

2. Now, we work on the `view` module that manages the display and rendering of the tiles inside the runway. We put the following code inside the `runway.js` file. It is a runway object that contains tiles' data. It also comes with two methods — `createTile` and `reset`:

```
// runway view
;(function(){
    var game = this.spaceRunner || (this.spaceRunner = {});
    game.view = game.view || {};

    game.view.floor = document.getElementById('floor');

    game.view.runway = {
        tiles: [],
        createTile: function(type, x, y) {
            // Create tiles
            var newTileDiv = document.createElement('div');
            newTileDiv.classList.add('tile');
            newTileDiv.classList.add('tile-' + type);
            this.tiles.push( new game.Tile(newTileDiv, type, x,
                y) );
            game.view.floor.insertBefore(newTileDiv,
                game.player.element);
        },
        reset: function() {
            for (var i=0, len=this.tiles.length; i<len; i++) {
                var tile = this.tiles[i];
```

```
            if (tile.element) {
              game.view.floor.removeChild(tile.element);
            }
          }
        }
        this.tiles.length = 0;
      }
    };
  }).call(this);
```

3. Before moving on, we will test the tile creation code. When the game starts over, we create some dummy tiles:

```
gameScene.startOver = function() {

  game.view.runway.reset();

  game.isGameOver = false;

  // temporary code to test tile creation
  game.view.runway.createTile(0  ,   0,   0);
  game.view.runway.createTile(1  , 100,   0);
  game.view.runway.createTile(2  , 200,   0);
  game.view.runway.createTile(0  , 300,   0);

  game.view.runway.createTile(0  ,   0, 100);
  game.view.runway.createTile(1  , 100, 100);
  game.view.runway.createTile(2  , 200, 100);
  game.view.runway.createTile(0  , 300, 100);

  game.view.runway.createTile(0  ,   0, 200);
  game.view.runway.createTile(1  , 100, 200);
  game.view.runway.createTile(100, 200, 200);
  game.view.runway.createTile(0  , 300, 200);

  game.view.runway.createTile(0  ,   0, 300);
  game.view.runway.createTile(1  , 100, 300);
  game.view.runway.createTile(2  , 200, 300);
  game.view.runway.createTile(0  , 300, 300);
  // end temporary code
};
```

Objective complete – mini debriefing

We have completed the task by moving the tile creation code from HTML to JavaScript.

The Tile definition

We define the `Tile` function, with a capital `T`, as a definition that is used to create instances. In traditional object-oriented programming, this is known as **class definition**. We can define a class definition whenever we have logic that requires many copies. We have a lot of tile elements in the HTML file. The HTML file element is just a part of the view. All the logic belonging to tiles is written in JavaScript. There will be many copies of such tile logic. This `Tile` definition allows us to create an instance for each tile that includes a reference to the HTML element. The `Tile` definition also adds the ability to set the tile position on the game view and more behaviors in later tasks.

The view object for the runway

We used a new object for the manipulation of view of the game objects on the runway.

This is helpful for code separation. Every time we call something using the `game.view` namespace, we know that it should be something related to the view. Otherwise, our code may need refactoring.

The `createTile` method groups the following steps involved in creating a dynamic tile element:

1. Create a tile element.
2. Create a new instance of the tile data object.
3. Store the tile data object in an array.
4. Insert the elements on the floor.

The `reset` method removes all the tile elements on execution. This is useful when we want to reconstruct the game after the game is over.

The temporary code

In this task, we prepared the code that defines the game objects. We need to test it before having all the code ready. That's why we created some temporary code to call our tile creation from JavaScript.

Using translate3d for 2D translation

We have used translate3d for a 2D translation because the translate3d function gains GPU accelerated performance in some devices. HTML5 rocks provides a deeper insight on how and what we can benefit from the hardware accelerated performance. Please refer to `http://www.html5rocks.com/en/tutorials/speed/html5/`, for more information on HTML5 rocks.

Classified intel

The `Tile` function takes four parameters. We want to define only the required element parameter; the rest are optional with a default value of zero:

```
function Tile(element, type, x, y){}
```

In the current version of JavaScript, we cannot set the default value of the missing parameters directly in the function definition.

We need to check whether the parameter is undefined and then assign a default value to the undefined ones. This can be done with the following statement:

```
this.x = x || 0;
```

We have been using the || operator in our code. Now, we take a closer look at it. The || operator is an OR operator. In most of the languages, it returns a `true` or `false` value. JavaScript returns the first non-false and non-undefined value; otherwise, it returns a false value. Some examples on what JavaScript returns are given as follows:

```
return true || "HTML5"; // return true
return "HTML5" || true; // return "HTML5"
return x || 0; // return x if x is not undefined, otherwise it returns
0.
```

Using a game loop

In the previous section, we placed the tiles in HTML directly, and then moved the temporary code for the creation of tiles from HTML to JavaScript.

Although the tiles are created programmatically, it is a one-time creation only. The tiles do not move. No new tiles are created after the initialization.

What we will do in this task is continuously create tiles based on a predefined pattern, and keep moving the existing tiles down.

Prepare for lift off

In this task, we are going to create tiles based on the data provided by the user instead of having the tile patterns hardcoded.

Before we start, let's remove the temporary code that creates testing tiles in JavaScript. The `startOver` function is reverted to the following state:

```
gameScene.startOver = function() {
  game.view.runway.reset();
```

```
  game.isGameOver = false;
};
```

We need to prepare the data for the tiles so that the game can loop and create more tiles.

We have used an integer value in both HTML and CSS to represent different types of tiles. Now, we need the same integer representation in JavaScript.

You can imagine the following runway data as a map represented by an integer value. This is essential because everything first happens in data and then we visualize the data in view. Let's put the following code in the `runway.js` file:

```
// runway data
;(function(){
  var game = this.spaceRunner || (this.spaceRunner = {});
  game.data = game.data || {};
  game.data.runway = [
    [0,   1,   2, 0],
    [0,   1,   2, 0],
    [0,   1,   2, 0],
    [0,   1,   2, 4],
    [0,   1,   2, 0],
    [0,   1,   2, 0],
    [0,   1,   2, 0],
    [0,   1,   2, 0],
    [4,   1,   2, 0],
    [0,   1,   2, 0],
    [0,   1, 100, 0],
    [0,   1,   2, 0],
    [0,   1,   2, 0],
    [0,   1,   2, 0],
    [0,   1,   2, 0],
  ];
}).call(this);
```

Engage thrusters

By performing the following steps, we start working on the Game loop:

1. Game loop is an important topic. Every 800 milliseconds, a new row of tiles is created and existing tiles are moved down. In the `gameScene.js` file, we append the following code to the `startOver` function. It starts two loops: timeout and `requestAnimationFrame`:

```
gameScene.startOver = function() {
...
   /* existing code goes here */
```

```
  this.round = 0;
  setTimeout((this.tick).bind(this), 800);
  requestAnimationFrame((this.onFrame).bind(this));
};
```

2. Before the onFrame function ends, it requests another animation frame to trigger another position update:

```
gameScene.onFrame = function() {
  game.view.runway.updateTilesPosition();
  requestAnimationFrame((this.onFrame).bind(this));
}
```

3. Let's move to the runway.js file and add the updateTilesPosition function to the existing runway view object. What it does is update all the tile placements using the CSS style:

```
game.view.runway = {
  ...
  /* existing runway code here */
  updateTilesPosition: function() {
    for(var i=0, len=this.tiles.length; i<len; i++) {
      var tile = this.tiles[i];
      tile.updatePosition();
    }
  },
```

4. Go back to the gameScene.js file and add the following tick function to the gameScene object:

```
gameScene.tick = function() {
  this.round += 1;

  game.view.runway.tick(this.round);

  if (!game.isGameOver)
  {
    var duration = Math.max(801-this.round, 100);
    setTimeout((this.tick).bind(this), duration);
  }
};
```

5. In the existing runway view object, we add the logic related to the integer map and the Game loop. This view object has reference to all the created tiles:

```
game.view.runway = {
...
  /* existing runway code here */
  runwayIndex: 0,
  tick: function(round) {
    // move existing tiles
    for(var i=0, len=this.tiles.length; i<len; i++) {
      var tile = this.tiles[i];
      tile.moveDown();
    }

    // increase the runway Index
    this.runwayIndex += 1;
    if (this.runwayIndex >= game.data.runway.length) {
      this.runwayIndex = 0;
    }

    // create new tiles
    var row = game.data.runway[this.runwayIndex];
    for(var i=0, len=row.length; i<len;i++){
      this.createTile(row[i], i * game.TILE_HEIGHT, 0);
    }
  }
};
```

6. Inside the `Tile` definition, we define a new method, movedown, to change the tile position:

```
Tile.prototype.moveDown = function() {
  this.y += game.TILE_HEIGHT;

  if (this.element && this.y > game.BOUNDARY) {
    game.view.floor.removeChild(this.element);
    this.element = undefined;
  }
}
```

7. We don't want to move a tile forever after it is out of the viewable screen area. Therefore, we will set a boundary in the `setting.js` file:

```
game.BOUNDARY = 1000;
```

Objective complete – mini debriefing

We have created a loop that continuously creates tiles from the top and the tiles keep moving. The tile types are based on our integers map defined in JavaScript.

Integer map

We use an integer to represent each type of tile. In our code, we used the following integer-type mappings:

```
0: empty
1: left runway
2: right runway
10: star in the space
100: obstacle
```

It is up to the development team to decide which integer values represents each type. Just make sure that no two types of tiles share the same integer. The following figure shows the mapping of our tile and integer values:

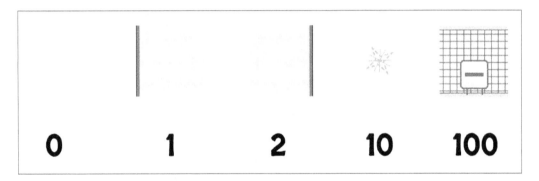

In my experience, I would suggest grouping the integer by types. For example, normal tiles have a single digit; a decoration tile starts from 10 and obstacle tiles start from 100.

There are two benefits of grouping by types:

▶ When you look at your integer map, you can instantly have a sense of what your map looks like. Where are the blocks? Where is the runway edge? Are there any broken tiles? You can answer these questions easily if you have grouped the integer by types. Have a look at the following map; which map in the following figure do you find easier to distinguish?

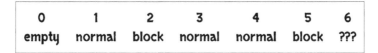

- You may want to extend the types later. For example, now you need ten types of obstacles and five types of runway terrains. Imagine you just increase the tile ID every time you introduce a new tile. This way, you will end up messing up the integers' sequence, as shown in the following figure:

0	1	2	3	4	5	6
empty	normal	block	normal	normal	block	???

We use a single digit for normal tiles and the obstacle starts at 100. It is logical to think that 101, 102, and so on, will be another type for an obstacle. The new map will be similar to the following figure:

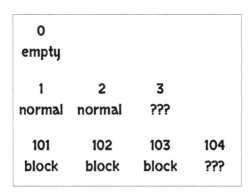

Game loop

The timeout loop is used for data and logic updates, while the animation frame is used to redraw the view.

The `setTimeout` or `setInterval` function is used to keep a time interval that keeps updating things in the game, such as a timer and a game score that is based on time or the movement of game objects.

The `requestAnimationFrame` function, on the other hand, is useful to draw loops. The browser executes the callback when computer usage is relatively low, and the browser will automatically slow down the frequency of the callback when the CPU is under heavy load.

Note that these two loops are created in the `gameScene` object. Then, inside each loop handler, it invokes the child objects for a tick event.

This is because the loop acts like a global clock. We want to place it in the parent object, say the game scene.

The main Game loop

The tick function is the main Game loop controlling the runway movement. It does several things, which are listed as follows:

- Increases the loop count
- Updates the runway movement, which updates the position of the tiles and determines any collision
- Updates the duration to trigger the next tick
- Registers another `setTimeout` function with a duration

Moving the tiles down

We need a way to illustrate a running and moving scenario. In this simple game, we animate the running by moving each tile down one grid at a time.

We update the *y* position in the timeout loop but draw the new position in the request animation frame callback.

The duration

We decrease the timeout duration between each timeout callback. This makes the game run faster gradually, and thus increases the game difficulties from time to time:

```
var duration = Math.max(801-this.round, 100);
```

The duration starts at around `800` milliseconds and it decreases gradually until it reaches `100` milliseconds.

Classified intel

In both the `setTimeout` and `requestAnimationFrame` function calling, we used the following binding syntax:

```
(this.tick).bind(this)
```

It makes sure that `this` inside the tick function refers to the current `this`—gameScene.

It doesn't work without the bind function because there is no context in both the `setTimeout` and `requestAnimationFrame` functions.

For more detail on this context, please refer to the following two articles from the Mozilla documentation that explain the bind method and the usage of the `this` operator:

https://developer.mozilla.org/en-US/docs/Web/JavaScript/Reference/
Global_Objects/Function/bind

https://developer.mozilla.org/en-US/docs/Web/JavaScript/Reference/
Operators/this

Parallax background scrolling

We will create a background movement that moves in a different speed than the runway. This is also known as parallax scrolling, and creates an illusion of depth.

Prepare for lift off

Make sure the following image is ready in the project inside the `images` folder:

Engage thrusters

Let's adjust the movement of the background with the following steps:

1. Inside the `runway.js` file, we append the following code before the end of the `tick` function:

    ```
    game.view.floor.style.backgroundPositionY = round * game.
    BACKGROUND_MOVEMENT_SPEED + 'px';
    ```

2. This moving speed is something that we may fine-tune later. We will put such a variable in the `setting.js` file for easier access:

    ```
    game.BACKGROUND_MOVEMENT_SPEED = 5;
    ```

When we test the game in the browser, the background moves slower than the runway. This creates a perception of depth. The background appears to be far away from us.

Objective complete – mini debriefing

We have completed the task by adding a background that looks like it's far away from the player and runway.

Parallel scrolling background

I guess you have had this experience already. Imagine you are inside a car and you are looking outside. Things nearer to you will pass by the car very fast; things that are far away seem to move slower. Things that are very far away, like the mountain in the background, do not seem to move at all:

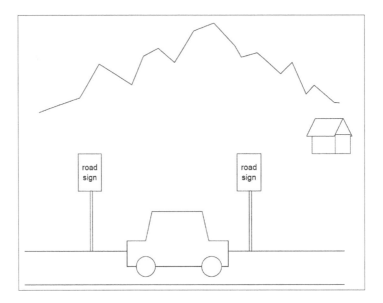

This is because of how we see things in the perspective view. In the digital world, we call this parallax scrolling.

Therefore, when we are moving game objects around, we can make use of the speed differences to create an illusion of depth.

In our game, the background is something far away in space. The movement of the background should move much slower than the player's running speed.

The normal speed is 50. We can set the background movement speed to be 1/10 of the normal speed:

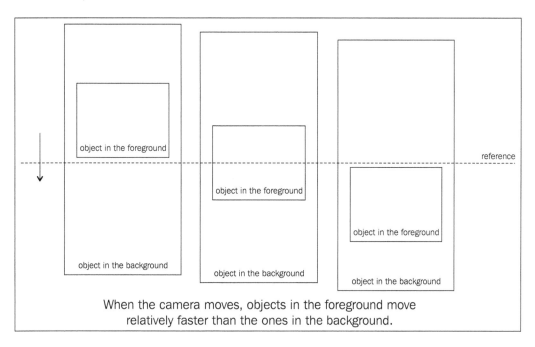

When the camera moves, objects in the foreground move relatively faster than the ones in the background.

Controlling a player with the keyboard

In this task, we will allow the player to control the character to switch between the left and right lanes.

Engage thrusters

The following steps add the keyboard input logic to control the running avatar:

1. We will set the visual and initial placement of the player by using CSS styles. Append the following styles to the `game.css` file:

```
#player {
  position: absolute;
  width: 100px;
  height: 100px;
  background-image: url(../images/running.png);
  bottom: 100px;
}
```

2. Now, we use the translate function to set the lane position of the player:

```
#player.lane1 {-webkit-transform: translate3d(100px, 0, 0); }
#player.lane2 {-webkit-transform: translate3d(200px, 0, 0); }
```

3. Let's move to the logic part. In the `player.js` file, we append the following function that handles lane changing. To change the lane, we toggle the player element between the `lane1` and `lane2` classes:

```
player.changeLane = function(lane) {
  player.currentLane = lane;

  player.element.classList.remove('lane1');
  player.element.classList.remove('lane2');
  player.element.classList.add('lane'+player.currentLane);
};
```

4. When the player clicks on the left or right button, we move the player left or right correspondingly. Therefore, we define the following `moveToLeftLand` and `moveToRightLane` methods to map with the left and right keys:

```
player.moveToLeftLane = function() {
  player.changeLane(1); // special case for 2 lanes.
};
player.moveToRightLane = function() {
  player.changeLane(2); // special case for 2 lanes.
};
```

5. We then set the player to be on lane 1 by default:

```
player.currentLane = 1;
player.changeLane(1);
```

6. Next, we get the keyboard input in the game scene. Put the following code inside the `setup` method in the `game-scene.js` file:

```
window.onkeyup = function(e) {
  if (e.keyCode === 37) { // Left
    game.player.moveToLeftLane();
  } else if (e.keyCode === 39) { // Right
    game.player.moveToRightLane();
  }
  return false;
};
```

Objective complete – mini debriefing

We have added keyboard inputs to control the player.

Each key on the keyboard is assigned one ID. In JavaScript, the keyboard event handler allows us to access the unique ID for each key. This way, we know what key the player has pressed. In our game, we need the game to listen for the left and right keys. To know which key to press, we can print the value of any pressed keys and observe the key code in the console:

```
window.onkeyup = function(e) {
  console.log(e.keyCode);
};
```

The following figure shows the key codes of the common arrow keys:

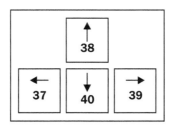

Alternatively, there is reference table on the Internet that allows you to check all the character codes. The following link contains the character codes:

```
http://www.cambiaresearch.com/articles/15/javascript-char-codes-key-
codes
```

Classified intel

This is a special case since we have only two lanes.

It seems redundant to have three functions: `changeLane`, `moveToLeftLane`, and `moveToRightLane`, for this simple task. This makes sense when we have more than two lanes, where the move left and right logic can't be hardcoded anymore.

Determining a collision between the player and tiles

In this task, we will determine the collision between the player and obstacles tiles.

Prepare for lift off

We need an array to store the tile IDs (obstacles). Let's put the following code in the `setting.js` file:

```
game.BLOCKS = [100];
```

Engage thrusters

Let's add collision detection with the following steps:

1. Inside the constructor of the `Tile` definition, we store a Boolean value to determine whether this tile is an obstacle. Since most of the tiles aren't obstacles, we initialize this variable with `false`:

    ```
    this.isBlock = false;
    for (var i = 0, len=game.BLOCKS.length; i < len; i++) {
      if (type === game.BLOCKS[i]) {
        this.isBlock = true;
      }
    };
    ```

2. The following code inside the `moveDown` function of a tile, checks whether the tile collides with the player, when the tile itself is an obstacle:

    ```
    if (this.isBlock) {
      this.checkCollison();
    }
    ```

3. Next, we define the `checkCollision` function inside the `Tile` definition. It uses the position coordinates to determine collision:

```
Tile.prototype.checkCollison = function() {
  if (this.y === 400) {
    if ( (this.x === game.TILE_WIDTH &&
      game.player.currentLane === 1) ||
        (this.x === (game.TILE_WIDTH*2) &&
          game.player.currentLane === 2)) {
      game.isGameOver = true;
      game.flow.gameOver();
    }
  }
}
```

Objective complete

We have successfully made the game over scene when a player hits an obstacle.

Determining collision

There are different approaches that we can use to determine a collision between two game objects.

In this running game example, we use a very basic one that uses only the position in the coordinate system to determine a collision.

The following figure shows the coordinates of the game. The player's *y* position is always at 400 pixels. When the player is in the first lane, he/she has 100 pixels as the *x* position, which is the tile's width. When the player is in the second lane, he/she has 200 pixels as the *x* position. When the obstacle tile has the same coordinates as the player, they collide.

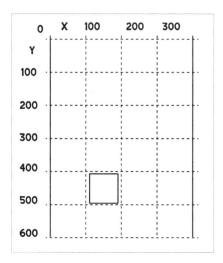

Spritesheet animation

In this task, we will animate the player frame by frame with spritesheet graphics.

Prepare for lift off

Before we start the task, make sure we have the following spritesheet graphics ready in the `images` folder:

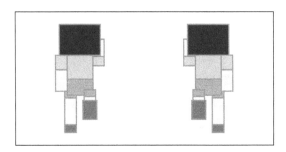

Engage thrusters

In the following steps, we will apply the key frames technique on the player's avatar:

1. The spritesheet animation is done in CSS. We define the key frames, duration between each frame, and steps in between:

```
@-webkit-keyframes running {
    from { background-position:     0px; }
      to { background-position: -200px; }
}
#player {
  animation: running .4s steps(2) infinite;
}
```

2. This animation works without the need of JavaScript. However, we will still use JavaScript to update the animation duration so it runs faster from time to time:

```
// view animation related
player.updateAnimationDuration = function(duration) {
  if (duration % 50 === 0) {
    player.element.style.webkitAnimationDuration = duration +
'ms';
  }
}
```

3. We calculated the duration in the tick function. Therefore, inside the `gameScene.tick` function, we tell the player to update the animation duration:

```
game.player.updateAnimationDuration(duration);
```

Objective complete – mini debriefing

A sprite sheet animation creates an illusion by playing a set of graphics very fast. The spritesheet is a large image file that contains all the frame graphics. In this game, we have two frames for the running animation.

We can set a mask, or frame, to display only one part of the image at a time. Then several milliseconds later, we show another frame. The following figure explains how the large spritesheet with two frames shifts left:

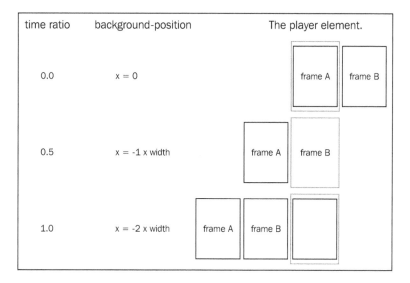

Creating the spritesheet image

The spritesheet graphic contains multiple frames. Certainly, we can put the individual images together using an image editor. There are different tools that will help us generate a sprite sheet image. The following are some examples of sprite sheet generation tools. These are just suggestions and you can actually use any tool on the Web as long as they add all the frames into one image file:

▶ Instant Sprite (`http://instantsprite.com`)

▶ SpritePad (`http://spritepad.wearekiss.com`)

▶ Texture Packer

▶ Flash CS6 along with a spritesheet generator

Take the InstantSprite web tool as an example and perform the following steps:

1. Drag all the frames to the browser.

2. Reorder the frames in the correct order.

3. Adjust the spacing between the frames to 0.

4. Right-click and save the sprite sheet image in the project folder.

The following screenshot shows the add-building button from three separated images into one sprite:

Spritesheet using CSS3 animation

In the CSS keyframe animation, the browser interpolates the value of the property within the specified duration. This section explains how we set the interpolation as a stepping value.

The `steps` function allows the animation to be played in frames. The following figure explains how the interpolated values are evenly divided. After dividing the CSS into steps, we have two modes: `start` and `end`. The difference is whether the beginning or the ending shows. This is shown in the following figure where the x axis is the keyframe's ratio, from 0.0 to 1.0:

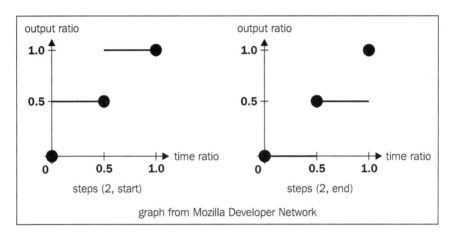

graph from Mozilla Developer Network

Please find the definition in the following Mozilla documentation:

```
https://developer.mozilla.org/en-US/docs/Web/CSS/timing-function#The_
steps()_class_of_timing-functions
```

Changing the animation speed

The running loop gradually gets faster. We want to reflect this in the player's running animation too. Therefore, we decrease the animation duration gradually, and thus make the animation appear faster.

Classified intel

In the console, we can inspect an element's style property to know the property name for a specific style. Some non-stable styles may have the vendor prefix appended such as `webkitAnimationDuration`.

Spritesheet animation versus CSS3 transition

In the previous project, we created an animation with CSS transition. Those animations are good for position, scale, or rotation changes that describe how the value changes in time. The value and time we describe is the key frame. Then, the computer helps generate the frames in between.

On the other hand, in this player animation, the spritesheet approach is good for visual changes. This is the animation where we have to draw all the frames. For example, we need to draw all the frames in order to animate a character that is turning its body.

Mission accomplished

Throughout the eight tasks, we have created a running game where a player needs to avoid the obstacles while running, as shown in the following screenshot:

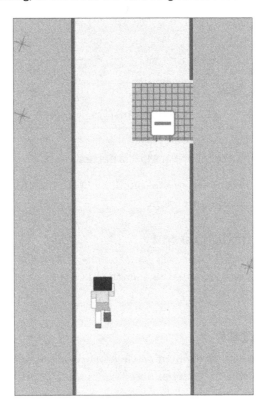

We learned several key concepts in this project, including the Game loop, `requestAnimationFrame`, the concept of parallax scrolling, keyboard input, and spritesheet animation.

Hotshot challenges

There is room to improve the game and make the game more enjoyable:

- We have only two different movement speed levels in this game. If you want more depth in the game, you can add more layers that move at different speed levels.

- Now we have only two lanes; the player is running either on the left or right lane. That makes the game a little boring. How about making the runway wider with four lanes?

- Having a game score encourages the player to repeat the game to achieve a better score. It also adds competition between different players. We can create a game score that increases based on the timer, or how many obstacles the player can pass.

- We have a variable to count how many rounds a user plays in the game. This can also be an indicator of how far away the player runs. How about using this indicator to design a scoring system?

Project 4

Multiply Defense

We built a DOM-based HTML game in the previous project. In this project, we will create a game using the HTML5 canvas. We will also introduce a game library named **CreateJS** to help us manage the game objects.

Mission briefing

We are going to create an education-based game to help students practice multiplication.

In this game, there are numbered boxes that fall from the top of the screen and a numeric pad placed at the bottom. When two numbers are selected from the numeric pad, we get the result of the multiplication.

The goal of this game is to eliminate the numbered boxes before they fall on the bottom. To do this, the player needs to click on the two correct numbers in the numeric pad to match the number value of the falling numbered box.

You may visit `http://makzan.net/html5-games/multiply-defense/` to play an example game in order to have a better understanding of what we will build throughout this project:

Why is it awesome?

Throughout the project, we will learn to manage game objects inside the HTML5 canvas tag. We will draw shapes on the canvas and create a tween animation.

We are going to use a canvas and a game library to create the game. Using a canvas allows us to manipulate the game at the pixel level. The performance is independent of the number of game elements we use.

We start by using a game library that helps us easily create games that are more complex. We will learn how to create a logical hierarchy using inheritance in JavaScript. Inheritance allows us to reuse similar code and still have variation among our game elements. This is an essential technique especially when our game becomes more complex.

The following screenshot shows what we are going to achieve in this project:

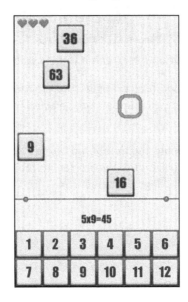

Your Hotshot objectives

We are going to divide our mission into eight objectives, which are as follows:

- Setting up the canvas and EaselJS
- Defining the numbered box

- The game loop and falling boxes
- Inputs and equations
- Removing the boxes
- Ending the game
- Restarting the game
- Replacing the rectangle shape with bitmap graphics

Mission checklist

We need the EaselJS library code. Let's do this before we start the project. We can download it from `http://EaselJS.com`, or we can find it from our code bundle.

 EaselJS is a canvas-drawing library. On the other hand, CreateJS is a suite that contains EaselJS and other libraries, such as the web audio helper and the tweening library. When we are referring to EaselJS in this book, it means that we are referring to the canvas-drawing library.

Setting up the canvas and EaselJS

In this task, we will get the project prepared for the CreateJS canvas game.

We will have the code skeleton ready for different modules, and we will initialize the CreateJS environment with a "Hello" message.

Prepare for lift off

Let's create a new folder for our project. Inside the project folder, we will create the following files/folders structure:

`index.html`

`scripts/game.js`

`styles/game.css`

`vendors/easeljs-0.7.1.min.js`

The `vendors` folder is used for external code. In this task, we put the downloaded `easeljs.0.7.1.min.js` file in this folder.

In the `index.html` file, we will construct a basic HTML structure, which is shown as follows:

```html
<!DOCTYPE html>
<html lang="en">
<head>
  <meta charset="utf-8">
  <title>Multiply Defense</title>
  <link rel="stylesheet" href="styles/game.css">
</head>
<body>
  <header>
    <div class="row">
      <h1>Multiply Defense</h1>
    </div>
  </header>
  <section id="game" class="row">
  </section>
  <section class="how-to-play row">
    <h2>How to Play?</h2>
    <p>Run as far away as possible.</p>
  </section>
  <footer>
    <div class="row">
      <p>Copyright goes here.</p>
    </div>
  </footer>

  <script src="vendors/easeljs-0.7.1.min.js"></script>
  <script src="scripts/game.js"></script>

</body>
</html>
```

Engage thrusters

It's time to define the canvas of the game and the component's skeleton.

1. First, let's put a canvas element into our HTML file:

    ```html
    <section id="game" class="row">
      <canvas id="canvas" width="300" height="480"></canvas>
    </section>
    ```

2. In CSS, we set the dimension of the game's section and basic positioning for both the game and canvas elements:

    ```css
    #game {
      position: relative;
      width: 300px;
    ```

```
    height: 480px;
    border: 1px solid black;
  }
  canvas {
    background: #333;
    position: absolute;
  }
```

3. Let's move to the JavaScript code. At first, we have a setting object that contains variables that configure the values of different game components. These are variables that may change during the development process:

```
;(function(){
  var game = this.game || (this.game={});

  game.setting = {
    gameWidth: 300,
    gameHeight: 480
  };
}).call(this);
```

4. Then, we prepare several object skeletons such as the game view, input, and calculation:

```
// Game View
;(function(){
  var game = this.game || (this.game={});

  game.gameView = {
    init: function() {
      var hello = new createjs.Text('Hello CreateJS', '18px
Impact', 'white');
      game.stage.addChild(hello);
    }
  };
}).call(this);
```

5. We define a placeholder for the input module. In this task, we modularize the logic. In later tasks, we will add code to the module:

```
// Input
;(function(){
  var game = this.game || (this.game={});

  // inputs logic here later

}).call(this);
```

6. We have another module for mathematical calculations. It's a placeholder for now, but we will add logic to the object later:

```
// Calculation
;(function(){
  var game = this.game || (this.game={});

  game.calculation = {};
}).call(this);
```

7. Next, we have the core game logic defined with the most basic setup:

```
// The Game Logic
;(function(){
  var game = this.game || (this.game={});

  game.start = function() {
    var canvas = document.getElementById('canvas');
    // passing the canvas to EaselJS.
    game.stage = new createjs.Stage(canvas);


    game.gameView.init();
    game.stage.update();
  };
}).call(this);
```

8. Finally, we have our entry point to connect the modules:

```
// Entry Point
;(function(){
  if (this.game) {
    this.game.start();
  } else {
    throw "No game logic found.";
  }
}).call(this);
```

After performing these steps, we have the following text painted on the `canvas` tag:

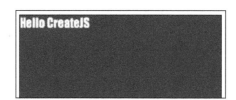

Objective complete – mini debriefing

Game view is responsible for drawing things on a canvas. For this project, we are going to use EaselJS for most of the canvas drawings.

It is recommended that you check their documentation in order to have a big picture of what classes and functionalities it provides. The following is the EaselJS documentation URL:

```
http://createjs.com/Docs/EaselJS/modules/EaselJS.html
```

We used the `Text` class to draw a Hello message on the canvas. It takes three parameters: text value, font style, and text color. All the three parameters are of string type. The format of the font's style and text color is the same as how we define them in CSS. We can use color name, Hex code, or the `rgba` function.

Why use library to draw on a canvas?

Canvas is stateless. It is like a real painting canvas. Once you have drawn something on it, there are just colors.

We need logic to keep track of things and then redraw it every time on a canvas. The libraries, including EaselJS, help us manage objects and draw on a canvas for us.

 Note that all the classes in the CreateJS suite have namespace `createjs`. It prevents conflicts on the other variables. This is why we used `createjs.Text` when referring to the EaselJS's `Text` class.

The addChild method

The simplest way to display anything in the EaselJS-controlled canvas is by adding it to the stage using the `addChild` method. Don't confuse the `addChild` method with the `appendChild` method from JavaScript. We are not adding new DOM elements to the game. We are handling all the game object hierarchies inside the `canvas` tag. We also manage the children hierarchy in JavaScript and draw them on the canvas.

We can think of the canvas area as a stage. Throughout the development, we will keep on adding things to the stage.

We will learn more on adding children to a non-stage object in the next task when creating numbered boxes.

The CreateJS namespace

If you find it too long to call `createjs` every time, it can be aliased to a shortened form. For example, the following code aliases it to a `c` variable:

```
var c = createjs;
```

We can even remove the namespace by assigning it to `window`:

```
createjs = window;
```

Having the JavaScript logic separated into placeholders helps you define the role clearer before we add too much code to it. We have the game view to render things on the canvas, input for taking button-clicking events, and calculation for the multiply mathematics.

Classified intel

The canvas only redraws whenever the `stage.update()` method is called. It is because rendering is a CPU time-consuming task. In EaselJS, we can freely change what we want to display by adding or removing display objects. However, the screen only redraws and updates when we explicitly call the `stage.update()` method. This helps us to improve the performance because we can have a batch update to the game structures and redraw the whole stage in only one call. Otherwise, the CPU will be overloaded with too many drawing requests if we redraw every time we add a new child.

The following table demonstrates the different concepts between drawing every time and drawing only in the `stage.update()` method:

Data	Rendering	Data	Rendering
addchild ()	draw	addchild ()	
addchild ()	draw	addchild ()	
for (.....) {		for (.....) {	
addchild ()	keep drawing	addchild ()	
}		}	
		stage.update()	draw

It's worth noting that we can clear and redraw only part of the canvas if we use the native canvas API. This gives us more control and further helps to improve the performance. We can set `stage.autoClear` to `false` if we need to manually clear the canvas.

Defining the numbered box

In this step, we will define the core game object of the game. We draw a square shape and add a number value to the box. We will learn how to create a prototype inheritance, which is one of the most important concepts when creating a JavaScript game.

Engage thrusters

Let's use the following steps to create a square-shaped numbered box.

1. First, we put the width and height of the box in `game.setting` so that we can easily adjust the box's size in future:

```
game.setting = {
    boxWidth: 50,
    boxHeight: 50,
    // existing settings here
}
```

2. Next, we define the rectangle shape as illustrated in the following code snippet. We are going to use it quite often before we apply graphics:

```
// RectShape
;(function(){
  var game = this.game || (this.game={});

  game.RectShape = (function(){
    function RectShape(width, height, style){
      createjs.Container.call(this); // super init

      // set default shape style for missing ones.
      style = style || {};
      style.strokeWidth = style.strokeWidth || 0;
      style.strokeColor = style.strokeColor || '';
      style.fillColor = style.fillColor || 'rgba(255, 0, 0, 1)';

      // draw the rect with graphics API
      var shape = new createjs.Shape();
      shape.graphics
      .setStrokeStyle(style.strokeWidth)
      .beginStroke(style.strokeColor)
      .beginFill(style.fillColor)
      .drawRect(0, 0, width, height);
      this.addChild(shape);
```

```
      }

     // Prototype inheritance.
     RectShape.prototype = Object.create(createjs.Container.
   prototype);

     return RectShape;
   })();
 }).call(this);
```

3. Then, we create a definition of the box based on `RectShape`. Next, we define a new `Box` class:

```
;(function(){
  var game = this.game || (this.game={});

  game.Box = (function(){
    function Box(){
       game.RectShape.call(this, game.setting.boxWidth, game.
  setting.boxHeight); // super with argument
    }
    Box.prototype = Object.create(game.RectShape.prototype);

    return Box;
  })();
}).call(this);
```

4. The `NumberBox` object is of the shape of a rectangle with a number on top of it. So, it is a container that contains the box and the numbered text. The box is created when it extends the `Box` logic. So we only add `Text` to this logic block:

```
// Number Box
;(function(){
  var game = this.game || (this.game={});
  game.NumberBox = (function(){
    function NumberBox(value){
      game.Box.call(this); // super, it draws rect shape.
      this.value = value;

         // Text on top of the rect shape.
      var text = new createjs.Text(value, '24px Impact', 'white');
      text.textBaseline = 'middle';
      text.textAlign = 'center';
      text.x = game.setting.boxWidth/2;
      text.y = game.setting.boxHeight/2;
```

```
      this.addChild(text);
    }
    NumberBox.prototype = Object.create(game.Box.prototype);

    return NumberBox;
  })();

}).call(this);
```

5. Then, we want to place the numbered box on the stage. We need an array to keep track of all the generated boxes:

```
game.gameView = {
  numberBoxes: [],
  // existing gameView code here
}
```

6. Generating a box means simply creating a box instance and putting it on the stage. However, we make it more fun by adding a random _x_ position:

```
game.gameView = {
  generateNumberBox: function(){
    // helper function that returns a random integer value between
min and max, both included.
    function randomInt(min, max) {
      return Math.floor(Math.random() * (max-min+1) + min);
    }
    var value = randomInt(1, 12) * randomInt(1, 12);

    var box = new game.NumberBox(value);
    box.x = Math.random() * (game.setting.gameWidth - game.
setting.boxWidth);
    box.y = 0;
    game.stage.addChild(box);

    this.numberBoxes.push(box);
  },
  // existing gameView code here
}
```

7. Now, we can start generating the box by calling the `generateNumberBox()` function. During the game view initialization, we generate the box:

```
game.gameView = {
  init: function() {
    this.generateNumberBox();
  },
  // existing gameView code here
}
```

Objective complete – mini debriefing

One core class of the EaselJS library is `DisplayObject`. The `DisplayObject` class is a base that displays graphics on the screen. It has several implementations in EaselJS. The `Shape` class, which defines vector shapes, extends `DisplayObject`. The `Bitmap` class, which displays the bitmap image file, extends `DisplayObject`. The `Container` class is `DisplayObject` that contains other display objects. The three display object classes are shown in the following figure:

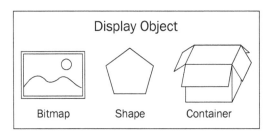

Drawing a shape with the Graphics object

If we draw with the native canvas API, we can draw lines, rectangles, and arc curves. However, we used the EaselJS library to take in charge of the canvas in order to benefit from the game object's management. We need to draw via the EaselJS library. We can use the `Graphics` class to draw shapes and attach them to the `Shape` class.

Here is an example that will show you how to draw a rectangle:

```
var g = new createjs.Graphics();
g.setStrokeStyle(style.strokeWidth)
.beginStroke(style.strokeColor)
.beginFill(style.fillColor)
.drawRect(0, 0, width, height);
```

Note that `Graphics` is not based on `DisplayObject`. It is usually attached to `Shape` to represent the vector drawings:

```
var shape = new createjs.Shape(graphics);
```

If we create a new `Shape` instance without providing our `Graphics` object, the `Shape` instance will create a new empty `Graphics` object for us:

```
var shape = new createjs.Shape();
shape.graphics
.setStrokeStyle(style.strokeWidth)
.beginStroke(style.strokeColor)
.beginFill(style.fillColor)
.drawRect(0, 0, width, height);
```

For more vector drawing options, refer to the graphics documentation at `http://createjs.com/Docs/EaselJS/classes/Graphics.html`.

Class inheritance

In EaselJS, it follows the traditional class-based object-oriented programming approach.

So how does class inheritance work in EaselJS? Take our project as an example.

We need to have a class, `RectShape`, dedicated to draw a rectangular shape. We define it as a kind of `Container` (or we can say we will extend it from `Container`) that will contain a `Shape` object that draws a rectangle, which is shown as follows:

```
RectShape.prototype = Object.create(createjs.Container.prototype);
```

You may wonder why we use `Container` here instead of using `Shape` directly. It is because of the extensibility. We may need to add more things to the rectangular shape later, say a numbered text. Making it `Container` at an early stage ensures that there will be no need to change the code from `Shape` to `Container` later.

Container

The Container class is the most generic class that extends DisplayObject. It contains other display objects too. For example, a solar system can be a container that contains the sun, the earth, and other planets. For earth, it can also be a container that contains the bitmap of the earth and a moon bitmap graphics.

Often, game objects are composited by smaller parts; thus, we have Container. From the solar system example, we know that containers can be put inside another container.

It's worth noting that a stage is actually one special kind of container.

Chaining the prototype and inheritance

JavaScript is a prototype-based language. We extend an object's abilities by chaining the prototype. The following code shows how we chain the `Container` object's prototype to our `RectShape` class:

```
RectShape.prototype = Object.create(createjs.Container.prototype);
```

The code creates a new object with the given parameter as the prototype. We defined the `RectShape` function as a constructor. That makes the `RectShape` prototype a new object along with the `Container` prototype. The following figure shows the prototype relationship when we create a new `RectShape` instance:

```
new RectShape()
    └──► prototype of RectShape
            └──► Object of Container
                    └──► prototype of Container
```

The following *Mozilla Developer Network* article shows an example of class inheritance using `Object.create`:

```
https://developer.mozilla.org/en-US/docs/Web/JavaScript/Reference/
Global_Objects/Object/create
```

There is one more step to make the inheritance work. The `Container` object has its own constructor to initialize its logic. We need to call the parent definition function or "constructor" in an object-oriented programming term inside our custom `RectShape` class as follows:

```
createjs.Container.call(this);
```

We haven't changed the namespace, so we need the `createjs` namespace whenever we refer to the `Container` class. In JavaScript, class is a concept. In reality, `Container` is a function object. So we can invoke the `Container` function to initialize it. This has the same effect of calling `super()` in other class-based, object-oriented programming languages.

The following essay provides an introduction to applying the object-oriented programming technique in JavaScript:

```
https://developer.mozilla.org/en-US/docs/Web/JavaScript/Introduction_
to_Object-Oriented_JavaScript
```

In summary, the following simplified code block shows how we can define a new class that extends an existing one:

```
function RectShape(arguments){
    createjs.Container.call(this); // calling super
```

```
  // logic of RectShape constructor goes here
}

// inherit via prototype
RectShape.prototype = Object.create(createjs.Container.prototype);

RectShape.prototype.newMethod = function(){
  // instance method definition goes here.
}
```

Random position

We drop the newly generated boxes from the top edge in a random *x* position. The default reference point (0, 0) is at the top-left corner of the box. When we generate the box, the *x* position ranges from **0** to the **game width-box width**. Otherwise, a generated box may be out of the visible area and the player will not be able to eliminate it. The following figure shows the relationship between the game width, box width, and the random range:

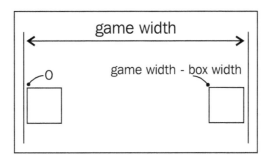

The built-in JavaScript's random function returns a random floating number between 0 and 1. However, what we want is a random integer between two integers. This can be done by using the following formula:

```
// Random number between A (inclusive) and B (exclusive)
X * (B-A+1) + A  where X is the random result
```

Its implementation is as follows:

```
function randomInt(min, max) {
  return Math.floor(Math.random() * (max-min+1) + min);
}
```

Classified intel

Whenever I have questions on how to follow the CreateJS game structure to build a game, I often check their source code at https://github.com/CreateJS/EaselJS. It helps to know how each class inherits from the other and how we can create our custom EaselJS object that integrates well with those built-in classes.

The game loop and falling boxes

In *Project 3*, *Space Runner*, we created the game loop ourselves. In this project, we have help from the CreateJS game library. Here, we will make use of the `Ticker` class to create a game loop that drops the generated boxes.

Prepare for lift off

We need two more settings: falling speed and the duration between each new box for this task. Let's set them before getting into real logic:

```
game.setting = {
  fallingSpeed: 0.8,
  ticksPerNewBox: 80,
  // existing setting code here
};
```

The `ticksPerNewBox` variable controls the duration between the generation of the next box and the current box.

Engage thrusters

Let's code the game loop in the `game.js` file with the following steps:

1. CreateJS comes with a `Ticker` class to handle the game loop. All we need to do is add our custom tick function to the `Ticker` class's event listener. Put the following code in the game's `init` logic:

    ```
    createjs.Ticker.setFPS(40);
    createjs.Ticker.addEventListener('tick', game.tick);
    ```

2. Then, we define our `tick` function in the core game object. It generates a new box and makes the box fall:

    ```
    game.tick = function(e){
      game.stage.update();

      if (!e.paused) {
        game.gameView.moveObjects();
    ```

```
      var ticksCount = createjs.Ticker.getTicks(/*exclude_pause=*/
  true);
      if (ticksCount % game.setting.ticksPerNewBox === 0) {
        // logic for every 80 ticks
        game.gameView.generateNumberBox();
      }
    }
  }
```

3. In the game view, we make each box fall at a short distance:

```
game.gameView = {
  moveObjects: function() {
    for (var i=0, len=this.numberBoxes.length; i<len; i++) {
      var box = this.numberBoxes[i];
      box.y += game.setting.fallingSpeed;
    }
  },
  // existing gameView code here
};
```

Now, the boxes should keep showing up at the top and falling down to the bottom when the game loads.

Objective complete – mini debriefing

The ticker is a centralized clock for the entire game. The clock moves and ticks in every unit. In every tick, we refresh the canvas rendering by calling `stage.update()`.

Besides rendering, we will move down all the existing boxes to make them fall. After a while, we will make a numbered box fall from the top of the screen.

Inside the tick event handler, we can check whether `Ticker` is under the pause state by `e.paused`. It is useful to globally pause a game and still be limited to the logic that runs in every game's loop regardless of the pause state.

The benefit of having a global `Ticker` is that we can control the start and pause of all the game elements at only one place. We can use `Ticker.setPaused(true)` to pause the game.

Inputs and equations

In this task, we will allow the player to input numbers by clicking on the numeric pad interface, and we will show a multiplication equation according to the input.

Prepare for lift off

We need to set up some input buttons to use the game logic. These input buttons are set up in HTML. We will put the following number controls in HTML, inside the #game section and after <canvas>:

```html
<div id="control-box">
  <a class="control" data-value="1" href="#">1</a>
  <a class="control" data-value="2" href="#">2</a>
  ...
  <a class="control" data-value="11" href="#">11</a>
  <a class="control" data-value="12" href="#">12</a>
</div>
```

We will use CSS to place the controls in proper place, as follows:

```css
#control-box {
  width: 100%;
  overflow: auto;
  position: absolute;
  bottom: 0;
}

.control {
  display: block;
  float: left;
  width: 50px;
  height: 50px;
  background: gray;
  text-decoration: none;
  color: white;
  text-align: center; // center align
  line-height: 50px; // vertical align
  font-size: 24px;
  font-family: impact;
}
.control:active {
  background: white;
  color: red;
}
```

Engage thrusters

We have prepared the interface with HTML and CSS. Let's work on the logic by adding appropriate code to our `game.js` file, as mentioned in the following steps:

1. We want to provide feedback to players when they click on the inputs. So we will display an equation, just like any calculator, that reflects the player's inputs:

```
game.gameView = {
  init: function() {
    // text for calculation equation
    this.calculationText = new createjs.Text('1x1=1', '18px
Impact', 'white');
    this.calculationText.textAlign = 'center';
    this.calculationText.x = game.setting.gameWidth / 2;
    this.calculationText.y = game.setting.gameHeight - game.
setting.controlHeight - 30;
    game.stage.addChild(this.calculationText);

    // existing init code goes here.
  },
  // existing gameView code goes here.
}
```

2. The game view should be able to change the equation over time:

```
game.gameView = {
  updateText: function(string) {
    this.calculationText.text = string;
  },
  // existing gameView code goes here.
}
```

3. The equation text is placed just above the input controls. We will store the height of controls under setting for an easier placement of the equation:

```
game.setting = {
  controlHeight: 100,
  // existing settings go here.
}
```

4. Next, we loop through all the number inputs and handle the click action:

```
// Input
;(function(){
  var game = this.game || (this.game={});
```

```
    // 1-12 inputs
var allControls = document.querySelectorAll('.control');
for(var i=0, len=allControls.length; i<len; i++) {
    var control = allControls[i];
    control.onclick = function() {
      var value = this.dataset.value;
      var string = game.calculation.addInput(value);
      game.gameView.updateText(string);
      // check result later
    }
  }
}).call(this);
```

5. Then, we work on the `calculation` object to take the inputs and form the equations. We would like to clear the inputs as well when there are two or more of them:

```
game.calculation = {
  inputs: [],
  result:1,
  addInput: function(value) {
    if (this.inputs.length >= 2) {
      this.clearInputs();
    }

    this.inputs.push(value);
    this.result *= value;

    return this.inputs.join('x') + '=' + this.result;
  },
  clearInputs: function(){
    this.inputs.length = 0;
    this.result = 1;
  }
};
```

Now, when we load the game, we will see 12 number inputs at the bottom of the game. When we press on an input, the calculation responds with the correct equation.

Objective complete – mini debriefing

The following screenshot displays what we have done in this task. We have added inputs and the multiplication equation to the game.

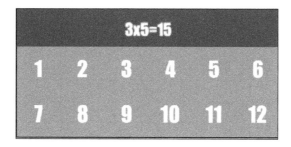

We use HTML for mouse input because this is independent of the game elements. It is easier to handle the hover and active state with CSS. In *Project 5*, *Building an Isometric City Game*, we will explore a canvas-based mouse input on the in-game objects.

We need to come up with a way to represent two numbers in the format, *A x B = Result*.

Here, *A* and *B* are elements in the array. *Result* is calculated every time a new input is entered. The multiplication format can be set by using the `join` method in the build-in array object. For example, consider an array: `[1, 2, 3, 4]`. Joining this array with character `x` will result in the following format:

`1x2x3x4`

Then, we just add the equal to sign and the result to form the equation.

Actually, in this game, we just accept a maximum of two inputs for each multiplication because all the generated numbers are composited by two of the input integers.

Classified intel

We put the equation inside the canvas by using the CreateJS text object. Since this equation text is independent of any other game elements, it is our choice to put the text as a DOM element or inside the canvas. In *Project 5*, *Building an Isometric City Game*, we will discuss more on grouping user interface elements inside the EaselJS object's structure.

In the EaselJS text object, `textAlign` is for horizontal alignment and `textBaseline` is for vertical, which can be found at `http://createjs.com/Docs/EaselJS/classes/Text.html#property_textAlign`.

Removing the boxes

In this task, we remove the boxes that we no longer need by using tweens. A box can be removed either when it passes the boundary at the bottom of the game or when the player matches the calculation's result.

Prepare for lift off

We will need two additional files for this task. First, add the `circle.png` file to the `images` folder. You can find the images from the code bundle.

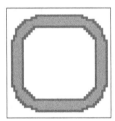

We also need the **TweenJS** library from the CreateJS suite. Download the `TweenJS` file from the CreateJS code repository (`https://github.com/CreateJS/TweenJS/tags`) or locate the file from the code bundle.

Copy the `tweenjs-0.5.1.min.js` file and put it into the `vendors` folder; the same folder where we put the EaselJS file.

Next, we import the TweenJS library in HTML before we import our `game.js` file; refer to the following code:

```
<script src="vendors/tweenjs-0.5.1.min.js"></script>
```

Engage thrusters

Let's add the following code for the box-removing logic:

1. First, we work on the falling boundary because it is easier. Define where the y position of the boundary is in the setting object:

```
game.setting = {
  boundaryY: 320,
  // existing settings go here.
}
```

2. Then, we draw the boundary line when `gameView` initializes:

```
game.gameView = {
  init: function() {
    // boundary line
    var line = new game.RectShape(game.setting.gameWidth, 3,
{fillColor:'#600'});
    line.y = game.setting.lineY;
    game.stage.addChild(line);

    // existing init code goes here.
  },
}
```

3. Once a box falls below the boundary, we will remove it. Add the following function to the game view so that we can remove a specific box:

```
game.gameView = {
  removeNumberBox: function(target) {
    for (var i=0, len=this.numberBoxes.length; i<len; i++) {
      var box = this.numberBoxes[i];
      if (box === target) {
        this.numberBoxes.splice(i, 1);
        game.stage.removeChild(box);
        return;
      }
    }
  },
  // existing gameView code goes here
};
```

4. Now, after the game loop makes the boxes fall, we loop through each object and remove any boxes that are below the boundary line:

```
game.gameView = {
  moveObjects: function() {
    // existing move objects code goes here.

    for (var i=0, len=this.numberBoxes.length; i<len; i++) {
      var box = this.numberBoxes[i];
      // remove the box when it is below deadline
      if (box.y>game.setting.boundaryY) {
        this.removeNumberBox(box);
      }
    }
  },
  // existing gameView code goes here
};
```

5. The other case to remove a box is when the player successfully matches a box with the calculation's result. We need to find a box with the given number. Let's add the following function to the `gameView` object:

```
game.gameView = {
  findNumberBoxWithValue: function(value) {
    for (var i=0, len=this.numberBoxes.length; i<len; i++) {
      var box = this.numberBoxes[i];
      if (box.value === value) {
        return box;
      }
    }
  },
  // existing gameView code goes here
};
```

6. On every player's input, we will tell the game logic to check the matching. Put the following `checkResult` call inside the input click handlers:

```
control.onclick = function() {
  // existing code goes here.
  game.checkResult();
};
```

7. The game logic will ask the game view to find a box with the given value. If this box exists, the game removes the box with a success signal:

```
game.checkResult = function() {
  var box = game.gameView.findNumberBoxWithValue(game.calculation.
result);
  if (box) {
    game.gameView.showCircle(box.x, box.y);
    game.gameView.removeNumberBox(box);
    game.calculation.clearInputs();
  }
};
```

8. When removing tiles, we want to make it clear and obvious. We will show a circle for a few seconds to let players know they did something correctly:

```
game.gameView = {
  showCircle: function(x, y) {
    var circle = new createjs.Bitmap('images/circle.png');
    circle.x = x || 0;
    circle.y = y || 0;
    game.stage.addChild(circle);
    createjs.Tween.get(circle).wait(500).to({alpha:0}, 1000).
call(function(){
      game.stage.removeChild(circle);
    });
```

```
    },
    // existing gameView code goes here
};
```

Objective complete – mini debriefing

The green circle displays and hides for just a short moment. It would be too troublesome to have dedicated logic that keeps track of them. We will use TweenJS to help us here.

TweenJS is similar to the transition in CSS that animates between keyframes, but TweenJS is for a canvas object. We define the target and it animates the properties for us by interpolating the steps in between. It makes it easy to select an EaselJS display object, change its property over time, and execute the logic after the animation is completed.

The following code is an example that selects the circle, sets the *x* position to 0, and uses a second to animate it to 300 px *x* position in the `bounceIn` easing function. The `to` method takes three arguments. They are the properties object, duration, and easing function, shown as follows:

```
createjs.Tween.get(circle).to({x:0}, 0).to({x:300}, 1000, Ease.
bounceIn);
```

The properties object can be any property changes that are made for the selected display object. The duration is how long it takes to transform from the current state to the target properties. When the duration is 0, it changes to the target properties immediately. The easing function is optional and is used to define how the animation spreads within the duration. By default, the easing function is linear.

In our code based on the green circle, we first show the circle, wait for a while, fade out the circle, and then make the circle remove itself once the animation is over:

```
createjs.Tween.get(circle).wait(500).to({alpha:0}, 1000).
call(function(){
  game.stage.removeChild(circle);
});
```

Classified intel

In EaselJS, we can add a stage as one of the Ticker-listener events directly. The default `tick` function inside `stage` will invoke the `stage.update` method for us, as shown in the following code:

```
createjs.Ticker.addEventListener("tick", stage);
```

In some cases where we don't have the custom game-loop logic, we can make use of this technique.

The easing function

The easing function often defines the animation style. We have different choices on how tweening values are calculated. Linear may look boring; however, ease-out ends the interpolation subtly. A bouncing effect may make it look lively. We can set the animation mood with a proper easing function. The following link to the TweenJS documentation lists all the built-in easing functions:

```
http://www.createjs.com/Docs/TweenJS/classes/Ease.html
```

The following link to the TweenJS example provides an interaction chart that demonstrates the difference among the easing functions:

```
http://www.createjs.com/#!/TweenJS/demos/sparkTable
```

Ending the game

In this task, we will add a life system to give the game an ending. For each box that passes through the dead line, we deduce one life. The game continues until a player loses all the life points.

Prepare for lift off

Before we get into the logic, we would like to define how many lives a player gets in each game. We define this value in the setting object, as shown in the following code:

```
game.setting = {
  initialLifes: 3,
  // existing settings go here.
};
```

Engage thrusters

Let's code the game-end logic with the following steps:

1. We have defined three lives per game so we will use three hearts to represent three lives. Before we add bitmap graphics, we use a RectShape function to represent a heart. Furthermore, we will use a container object to store all the hearts so it can be easily placed on the stage. In the final task, we will replace all these RectShapes functions into bitmap graphics of the shape of a heart. Append the following code inside the gameView object:

```
game.gameView = {
  init: function() {
```

```
    // hearts for the lives
    this.hearts = [];

    this.heartsContainer = new createjs.Container();
    this.heartsContainer.x = 5;
    this.heartsContainer.y = 5;
    game.stage.addChild(this.heartsContainer);

    this.resetHearts();

    // existing init code goes here.
  },
};
```

2. When we restart the game later, we will need to recreate the hearts. We use the following code to empty the hearts' container and recreate hearts inside it:

```
game.gameView = {
  resetHearts: function() {
    this.heartsContainer.removeAllChildren();
    this.hearts.length = 0;
    for (vari = 0; i<game.setting.initialLifes; i++) {
      var heart = new game.RectShape(18, 18, {fillColor:'red'})
      heart.x = i * 20;
      this.heartsContainer.addChild(heart);
      this.hearts.push(heart);
    }
  },
  // existing gameView code here
};
```

3. We add a function to the game view to remove a heart whenever this function is called:

```
game.gameView = {
  deduceLife: function(){
    var heart = game.gameView.hearts[game.lifes];
    this.heartsContainer.removeChild(heart);
  },
  // existing gameView code here
};
```

4. The `gameView` event responds to the process of removing a heart from the game view, whereas the logic is in charge of determining when the lives run out and the game is over:

```
game.deduceLife = function() {
  this.lifes -= 1;
  game.gameView.deduceLife();

  if (this.lifes <= 0) {
    this.gameOver();
  }
}
```

5. When the game is over, we pause the ticker using the following code:

```
game.gameOver = function() {
  createjs.Ticker.setPaused(true);
}
```

Now the game will pause and the boxes will stop falling after three boxes are passed through the deadline.

Objective complete – mini debriefing

When the game is over, we pause the ticker by setting the `Ticker.setPaused` function to `true`. Since our game loop depends on the ticker, the game loop is paused; thus, no new box is created and all existing boxes are stopped.

Making the game run again is simply achieved by setting the `setPaused` Boolean to `false`. This is the advantage of having a centralized `Ticker` that controls everything; everything is paused with just one Boolean.

Classified intel

Although we know that we are going to use a heart bitmap to represent a life, we are still using a rectangular shape. The benefit of using a rectangular shape here is that we can focus on implementing the logic without switching to the visual creativity of the brain. Thinking in both logical as well as visual ways is just too difficult. Once we get to the core of the working of the gameplay, we can switch to the artistic work of creating bitmap graphics for the game elements.

Restarting the game

In this task, we provide a game over screen with a button to let the player restart the game.

Prepare for lift off

We will first set up the game-over overlay in HTML. We add the following HTML script inside the `#game` section after the existing elements and just before closing the `</section>`, as shown in the following code:

```
<div id="game-over" class="hide">
  <a href="#" id="replay-btn"></a>
</div>
```

An HTML often comes with its styles. We will add the following style from CSS:

```
// game over scene
#game-over {
  position: absolute;
  width: 100%;
  height: 100%;
  background: rgba(0, 0, 0, 0.3);
}
// visibility controlling
.show {
  display: block;
}
.hide {
  display: none;
}

#replay-btn {
  background: url(../images/replay.png);
  display: block;
  width: 100px;
  height: 60px;
  margin: auto;
  position: relative;
  top: 200px;
}
#replay-btn:hover {
```

```
      background-image: url(../images/replay_hover.png);
    }
    #replay-btn:active {
      background-image: url(../images/replay_active.png);
    }
```

Now the game-over layer is ready and we can get into the JavaScript code.

Engage thrusters

Let's work on the JavaScript code to restart our game after the game is over.

1. In the `gameView` JavaScript object, we define two more methods to show and hide the game-over overlay, which are shown as follows:

    ```
    game.gameView = {
      gameOverOverlay: document.getElementById('game-over'),

      showGameOver: function() {
        this.gameOverOverlay.classList.remove('hide');
        this.gameOverOverlay.classList.add('show');
      },
      hideGameOver: function() {
        this.gameOverOverlay.classList.remove('show');
        this.gameOverOverlay.classList.add('hide');
      },

      // existing gameView code goes here.
    };
    ```

2. We handle the click event of the restart button. Put the following code inside the `input` module:

    ```
    // replay button in game over scene
    var replay = document.getElementById('replay-btn');
    replay.onclick = function(){
      game.resetGame();
    };
    ```

3. We need the `resetGame` method that resets all the game objects to their initial statuses:

    ```
    game.resetGame = function() {
        this.lifes = game.setting.initialLifes;
        game.gameView.removeAllNumberBoxes();
        game.gameView.hideGameOver();
    ```

```
      game.gameView.resetHearts();
      createjs.Ticker.setPaused(false);
   };
```

4. In the last task, we pause the ticker whenever the game is over. We go one step further to show the game overlay in this task:

```
game.gameOver = function() {
   createjs.Ticker.setPaused(true);
   game.gameView.showGameOver();
};
```

Objective complete – mini debriefing

We have created a game-over scene and are now able to restart the game. The game-over scene makes use of the DOM element overlay on top of the canvas game. This allows us to use the CSS hover and active pseudo classes for the button effect. We are not locked into any one library even when we use a canvas to render our game elements. From the Web, we can choose the solution that's most suitable. Overlaying a DOM element is not a bad idea at all before we learn to create buttons using the CreateJS library.

Classified intel

Before the game starts over again, we reset the game to its initial state. Resetting the game means that we remove all the existing boxes and reset the lives. After the reset is complete, we resume the game and the game starts over and runs again.

Pausing the game

If we want to let the player pause the game in the middle, we can overlay a pause screen similar to the game-over screen and also pause the ticker. Then, we may provide a pause button to trigger the pause state.

Replacing the rectangle shape with bitmap graphics

In this task, we will decorate the game with bitmap graphics. We replace the current code-drawing shape with bitmap graphics drawn in the painting software.

Prepare for lift off

We will need several bitmap images in this task. They will be used as images for the background, box, heart, and the deadline. Please find them attached in the code bundle.

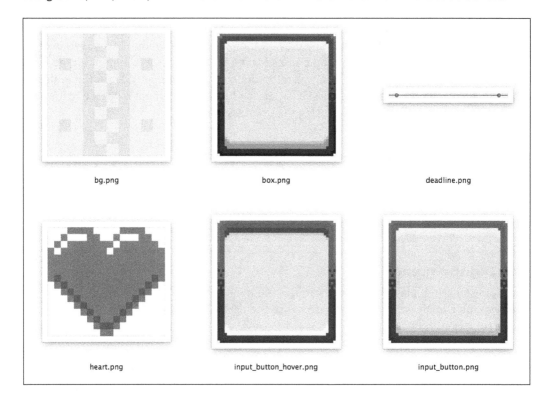

Engage thrusters

Let's start by replacing the canvas's background and input.

1. The following code elements are the HTML elements and we can set the graphics in CSS:

```
canvas {
  background: #333 url(../images/bg.png);
}
.control {
  background: gray url(../images/input_button.png);
}
.control:active {
  background: white url(../images/input_button_hover.png);
}
```

2. Then, we use bitmap to replace the canvas's `RectShape` function. We start with the box:

```
function Box(){
  createjs.Container.call(this);

  var bitmap = new createjs.Bitmap('images/box.png');
  this.addChild(bitmap);
}
```

3. Then, we replace the `deadline` shape with the bitmap:

```
var deadline = new createjs.Bitmap('images/deadline.png');
```

4. Finally, we replace the red square shape into a heart shape image to represent the remaining lives:

```
var heart = new createjs.Bitmap('images/heart.png');
```

Objective complete – mini debriefing

What we have done is change the rectangular shape to a bitmap graphic. Because we have put the numbered box as a container, we are free to change what's inside the container without the need to change any of the logical part. It is independent of whether we use a shape or a bitmap to display it.

Specifically, we use pixel art because it looks better in a smaller dimension.

Classified intel

The `RectShape` function is a useful class that helps to build the game's prototype. We can rapidly represent game elements with colored shapes. Once we get the game logic implemented, we can replace the shape into gorgeous graphics.

From the first task until just now, we have used `RectShape` to represent boxes, lives, and the falling deadline. Now, its job is done and we can get rid of it until we need a new game element in future.

Mission accomplished

With the eight tasks, we have successfully created an educational canvas-based game. The game makes use of a simple-to-use game loop ticker. A well-structured game library helps us manage the game elements' hierarchy. And finally, we make the game ready to be published with some pixel art-style graphics.

The following screenshot shows what we have accomplished in this project:

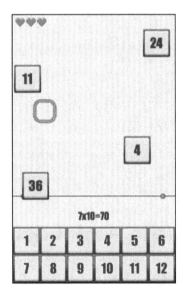

A Hotshot challenge

We can make the game more challenging by gradually increasing the boxes' falling speed. Let's say we set the initial falling speed to 0.3 and gradually increase the falling speed to 1.0 over a time span of 5 minutes. The boxes fall faster when the player plays longer. This can make the game more fun by challenging the player's limit.

Project 5

Building an Isometric City Game

We created a canvas-based game in the last project. We will continue working on canvas and CreateJS library in this project. We are going to create a game where players build their own city. We give the city depth by using an isometric projection, the so-called *2.5D world*. We also will learn more essential CreateJS techniques that help us build canvas-based games.

Mission briefing

At the beginning of the game, we will show the player a new city. The player will act as its mayor, create buildings in his/her way, and earn coins.

We'll build a tiny economy system, which is made up of coins, diamonds, a power supply, and populations. Coins are the major currency, diamonds are the luxury resource, each building increases the population of the city, and the power supply building generates power to support the population. The power capacity of the supplies must be larger than the required population in order to create new buildings.

We introduced three types of buildings that affect the economy. They are the coins generator, power supply, and merchant. The player's goal is to create a beautiful city and collect as many coins and diamonds as possible.

You can visit `http://makzan.net/html5-games/isometric-city/` to play the example game in order to have a better understand of what we will build throughout this project:

The following is a screenshot of the game that is created after we complete all the objectives in this project:

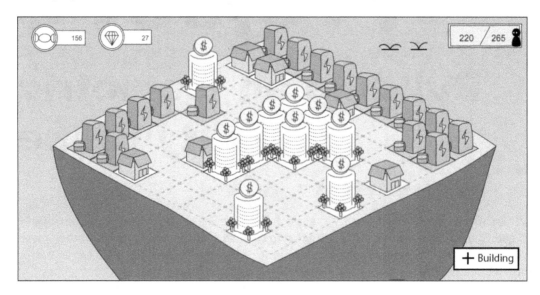

Why is it awesome?

We will learn how to place the building on a map and visualize the map in a 2.5D isometric projection.

The skill to place buildings is useful in different ways. We will use some common techniques to place buildings in *Project 6*, *Space Defenders*.

The isometric projection creates depth in the game. This technique can be used in a wide range of games, such as RPG games, building games, or strategy games such as tower defense.

By changing the graphics and game parameters, we can easily modify this project into games of different themes. It may become a zoo park game or any business simulation game such as a hospital, restaurant, museum, or logistics company.

Your Hotshot objectives

This project consists of the following tasks:

- ▸ Designing the game's user interface
- ▸ Placing the tiles and grid in the city layer
- ▸ Choosing which building to build
- ▸ Placing buildings on the floor
- ▸ Growing buildings
- ▸ Generating coins and diamonds
- ▸ Collecting pop-up diamonds
- ▸ Saving and loading game progress

Mission checklist

We need the EaselJS and TweenJS library code. Before we start the project, we have to download these library code from `http://CreateJS.com`, or from the code bundle.

Designing the game's user interface

In this task, we will set up the project and create the essential interface elements.

Prepare for lift off

The first thing we will do is create our project directory with the following file structure:

```
index.html
styles/game.css
scripts/game.js
vendors/easeljs-0.7.1.min.js
vendors/tweenjs-0.5.1.min.js
images/
```

In this task, we need the following image files. You can get them from the code bundle.

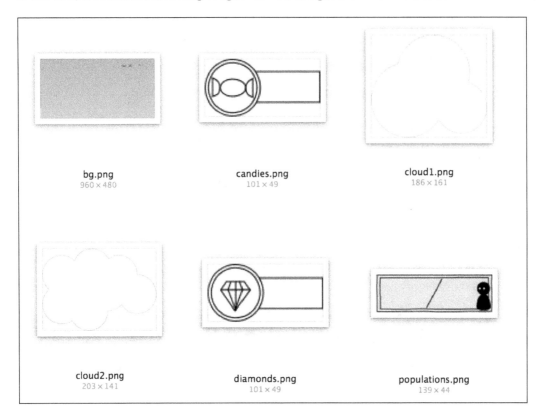

bg.png 960 × 480	candies.png 101 × 49	cloud1.png 186 × 161
cloud2.png 203 × 141	diamonds.png 101 × 49	populations.png 139 × 44

The `index.html` file is very similar to the previous examples. We'll only show the most relevant HTML code here. We have defined the following game section:

```html
...
<section id="game" class="row">
  <canvas id="canvas" width="960" height="480"></canvas>
</section>
...
```

Just before closing the `body` tag, we include the libraries and the `game.js` JavaScript files:

```html
...
<script src="vendors/easeljs-0.7.1.min.js"></script>
<script src="vendors/tweenjs-0.5.1.min.js"></script>
<script src="scripts/game.js"></script>
...
```

Inside the `game.js` file, we prepare the following game settings object at the start of the file:

```
var game = this.game || (this.game={});
var createjs = createjs || {};

// Settings
;(function(game){
  game.canvas = document.getElementById('canvas');
  game.setting = {
    gameWidth: game.canvas.width,
    gameHeight: game.canvas.height,
  };
}).call(this, game);
```

In this game, we set up three layers. All the game elements will be put in any one of the layers. The following figure shows the planning of layers. These layers are the background layer, city layer, and user interface layer. For example, city graphics and buildings are placed in the city layer. Buttons and interface indicators are placed in the UI layer. The background and clouds will be placed in the background layer.

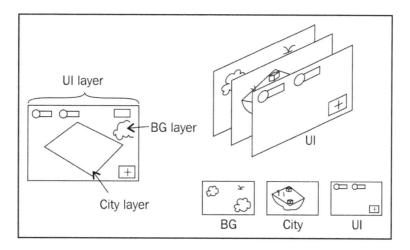

Engage thrusters

In the following steps, we will code the planned layer structure:

1. The layer's block of code defines the three layers. We wrap all the layers' code into a self-invoked function:

```
;(function(game, cjs){
  // all following layers' code goes here.
}.call(this, game, createjs);
```

2. Then, we define a generic layer definition. A layer will contain other game elements so it extends the EaselJS `Container`. This definition is used only within this code block; that's why we define it as a local variable:

```
var Layer = (function(){
  function Layer() {
    cjs.Container.call(this); // super
  }
  Layer.prototype = Object.create(cjs.Container.prototype);
  return Layer;
})();
```

3. Then, we create a new definition for `CityLayer`, which extends `Layer`. The city layer doesn't contain any real logic yet. We are going to work on it in later tasks:

```
// City Layer
game.CityLayer = (function(){
  function CityLayer() {
    Layer.call(this);
  }
  CityLayer.prototype = Object.create(Layer.prototype);
  return CityLayer;
})();
```

4. Next, we have the background layer definition. It also extends `Layer`. We put two cloud animations in it that move from right to left in order to make it less boring:

```
game.BGLayer = (function(){
  function BGLayer(){
    Layer.call(this); // super

    // background image
    var bitmap = new cjs.Bitmap('images/bg.png');
    this.addChild(bitmap);

    // Cloud 1 Bitmap
    var cloud1 = new cjs.Bitmap('images/cloud1.png');
    cloud1.y = 30;
    cloud1.alpha = 0.4;
    this.addChild(cloud1);

    // Cloud 1 Tween Animation
    cjs.Tween.get(cloud1, {loop:true})
    .to({x:game.setting.gameWidth + 300}, 0)
    .wait(15500)
    .to({x:-300}, 50*1000);
```

```
    // Cloud 2 Bitmap
    var cloud2 = new cjs.Bitmap('images/cloud2.png');
    cloud2.y = 300;
    cloud2.alpha = 0.4;
    this.addChild(cloud2);

    // Cloud 2 Tween Animation
    cjs.Tween.get(cloud2, {loop:true})
    .to({x:game.setting.gameWidth + 50}, 0)
    .wait(500)
    .to({x:-300}, 50*1000);
  }
  BGLayer.prototype = Object.create(Layer.prototype);
  return BGLayer;
})();
```

5. The user interface layer contains indicators and buttons. We will add the buttons in later tasks. In this task, we set up the heads-up display using a separated setupHUD method:

```
// User Interface
game.UILayer = (function(){
  function UILayer() {
    Layer.call(this);
    this.setupHUD();
  }
  UILayer.prototype = Object.create(Layer.prototype);
  // prototype functions to be placed here.
  return UILayer;
})();
```

6. Setting up a user interface programmatically may require long and redundant code. Thus, we create the following two methods to reuse bitmap and text creation:

```
UILayer.prototype.placeBitmap = function(path, x, y) {
  var bitmap = new cjs.Bitmap(path);
  bitmap.x = x;
  bitmap.y = y;
  this.addChild(bitmap);
};
UILayer.prototype.placeText =
  function(text, size, x, y, align) {
  var text = new cjs.Text(text, size +
    'px Arial', '#222');
  text.x = x;
```

```
      text.y = y;
      text.textAlign = align;
      this.addChild(text);
      return text; // text content needs to be changed later.
   }
```

7. We can then use the helper methods we just defined to set up the heads-up display. This includes several indicators for the game parameters, such as the coins and diamonds collected:

```
UILayer.prototype.setupHUD = function() {
   this.placeBitmap('images/candies.png', 28, 16);
   this.placeBitmap('images/diamonds.png', 154, 14);
   this.placeBitmap('images/populations.png', 810, 14);

   this.coinsIndicator = this.placeText('12345', 12, 123,
      34, 'right');
   this.diamondsIndicator = this.placeText('0', 12, 250,
      34, 'right');
   this.powerSupplyIndicator = this.placeText('100', 16,
      905, 32, 'center');
   this.populationIndicator = this.placeText('100', 16,
      845, 32, 'center');
};
```

8. That's all for the layers. Next, we move to the main game logic. Append the following code to the end of the game.js file. It initializes the canvas stage, adds the layers, and sets up the game ticks:

```
// The Game Logic
;(function(game, cjs){
   game.start = function() {
      game.stage = new cjs.Stage(game.canvas);

      game.backgroundLayer = new game.BGLayer();
      game.cityLayer = new game.CityLayer();
      game.uiLayer = new game.UILayer();

      // in correct order: from background to foreground
      game.stage.addChild(game.backgroundLayer);
      game.stage.addChild(game.cityLayer);
      game.stage.addChild(game.uiLayer);

      cjs.Ticker.setFPS(40);
      cjs.Ticker.addEventListener('tick', game.stage);
```

```
   // add game.stage to ticker make the stage.update call
automatically.
   };
}).call(this, game, createjs);
```

9. Finally, we define the entry point to invoke the game logic:

```
;(function(game){
  if (game) {
    game.start();
  } else {
    throw "No game logic found.";
  }
}).call(this, game);
```

At this point, we will have the result that's shown in the following screenshot. We can see that the interfaces are in front of the background elements. Please note that we have not added any objects in the city layer yet, so we can't see the city layer in the screenshot:

If you get a security error in your browser about accessing the
images or the canvas due to cross-domain issues, you may want
to run your code from a server. The following are some software
that you can use to set up a local development server:

▶ **Mac**: Anvil/Pow.cx

▶ **Windows**: XAMPP

▶ **Linux**: Apache/Nginx

Objective complete – mini debriefing

The benefit of having layers is that we don't need to worry about having background stuff
coming in front of the essential game elements. We divide the game elements into layers.
This is a way to organize and structure the game. They are nothing special but containers.
This helps to create a clear hierarchy for display objects. We add the layers arranged in the
order from background to foreground. The default *z* index follows the order of `addChild`.
The child added later is in front of the child added earlier.

We can ensure that things added to the background will always be at the back. Objects
we add in the city layer will never be on top of the user interface. The user interface layer
is always the top layer. The following figure illustrates how three layers separate the display
objects clearly:

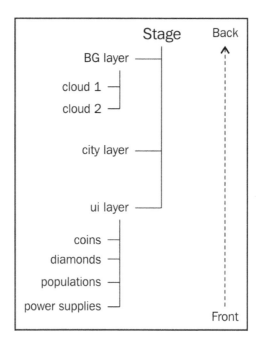

Tween-based cloud animation

We have made the background less boring by including the cloud animations. We used the TweenJS library for this tween-based animation.

We move the cloud from right to left in a slow pace. The distance and tween duration of the two clouds are intentionally different so they do not appear the same. This has been highlighted in the following figure:

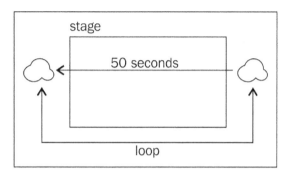

We used the TweenJS library in the previous project, *Project 4*, *Multiply Defense*. This time, we will add a second argument to the `Tween.get` method by setting the loop option to `true`. This allows the tween animation to keep running in loops. In addition, we set a delay to both the cloud animations by using the `wait` method, shown as follows:

```
Tween.get(cloud1, {loop:true});
```

Classified intel

Additionally, we can do more activities in the background. For example, we can change the darkness of the background based on the current time. The game may show sunlight during the day and gradually turn dark from evening to night. This can be done using two background images, light and dark, and tuning the opacity on them based on the time using JavaScript.

Placing the tiles and grid in the city layer

We created the layers' foundation in the last task. The city layer was empty. In this task, we focus on the city layer where we put tiles and buildings.

Prepare for lift off

First, we will draw some graphics for the isometric city. Any graphic editor should work. To draw a floor tile, we use the steps shown in the following figure:

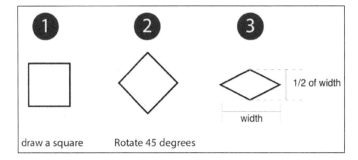

1. Draw a square shape.
2. Rotate it by 45 degrees to form a diamond shape.
3. Set the current vertical diagonal of the resulting rhombus to 50 percent of the width.

The resulting graphic is our base floor and we can start drawing buildings on top of it. Besides the tile graphic, we also put the `city-bg.png` file in the `images` folder, as shown in the following screenshot:

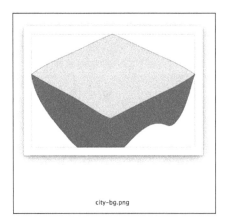

city-bg.png

We will need two more JS files for this task. Create the following two JS files inside the `scripts` folder:

```
scripts/view-sprites.js
scripts/helpers.js
```

For newly created files, we need to include them inside our `index.html` file before loading the `game.js` file:

```
<script src="scripts/view-sprites.js"></script>
<script src="scripts/helpers.js"></script>
```

The `view-sprites.js` file defines individual game sprites, such as `Tile` and `Buildings`.

The `helper.js` file provides useful utilities. In this task, we need to create a 2D array and add the following `create2DArray` function to help.

Insert the following code inside the `helper.js` file:

```
var game = this.game || (this.game={});
var createjs = createjs || {};

;(function(game, cjs){
  game.helper = game.helper || {};

  game.helper.create2DArray = function(rows, cols, initialValue) {
    var array = [];
    for(var i=0; i<rows; i++) {
      array[i] = [];
      for (var j=0; j<cols; j++) {
        array[i][j] = initialValue;
      }
    }
    return array;
  };
}).call(this, game, createjs);
```

Engage thrusters

In the following steps, we will lay the tiles on the city floor in a 9 x 9 tile grid:

1. In the `view-sprites.js` file, we define the `Tile` class. Every tile on the map has its own coordinates in the isometric array. The function argument is the bitmap path. By default, we use our `tile.png` file:

```
var game = this.game || (this.game={});
var createjs = createjs || {};
```

```
   // Tile View
   ;(function(game, cjs){
     function Tile(imagePath) {
        imagePath = imagePath || 'images/tile.png';
        cjs.Bitmap.call(this, imagePath);
        this.regX = 0;
        this.regY = 21;
     }
     Tile.prototype = Object.create(cjs.Bitmap.prototype);
     Tile.width = 86;
     Tile.height = 43;
     game.Tile = Tile;
   }).call(this, game, createjs);
```

2.   In the previous task, we coded the bare city layer without adding any object.
     Now, we work on the `CityLayer` object. Add the following code to the
     `CityLayer` constructor function:

```
function CityLayer() {
  Layer.call(this);

  // city background.
  var bg = new cjs.Bitmap('images/city-bg.png');
  bg.regX = 370; // adjust to fit the 9x9 tiles.
  bg.regY = 30;
  this.addChild(bg);

  this.cols = this.rows = 9; // 9x9 map.

  // tiles container to contains all Tile instance.
  this.tiles = new cjs.Container();
  this.addChild(this.tiles);

  // 2D array that holds the ref. of building sprites
  this.viewMap = game.helper.create2DArray
    (this.rows, this.cols);

  // center align the city layer to the stage.
  this.x = game.setting.gameWidth /2 -
    game.Tile.width / 2;
  this.y = game.setting.gameHeight /2 -
    (this.rows-1) * game.Tile.height / 2;

  this.redraw(); // create the visual of the city
}
```

3. Then, we define the `redraw` method that visualizes the data:

```
CityLayer.prototype.redraw = function() {
  // loop the 2D array for visualization
  for (var i=0; i<this.rows; i++) {
    for (var j=0; j<this.cols; j++) {
      var tile = new game.Tile();

      // layout tiles in rombo shape.
      tile.x = (j-i) * game.Tile.width / 2;
      tile.y = (j+i) * game.Tile.height / 2;
      this.tiles.addChild(tile);

      this.viewMap[i][j] = tile;
    }
  }
};
```

After performing these steps, the result will be as shown in the following screenshot:

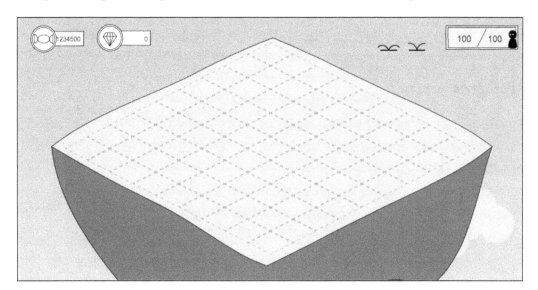

Objective complete – mini debriefing

We have placed 9 x 9 isometric tiles on the floor.

Registration point

The registration point is the reference point of the display object in its container. The key to correctly laying out the tile is the registration point. For any shape of a building, we set the registration point to the left corner of the floor tile. The following draft drawings show how the registration point is already set to the left corner of the tile regardless of the building's shape. This allows us to sort the depth of the buildings with their *y* position by setting a registration point on the left (or right) corner. We'll work on the sorting of buildings in later tasks when we place buildings on the floor.

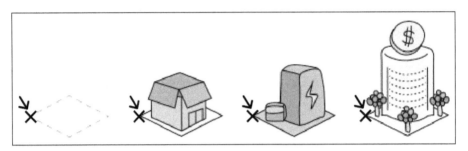

Isometric formula

In isometry, we think of a rhombus shape as shown in the following figure. Each tile is laid out in a diagonal shape. Let's call these tiles isometric coordinates:

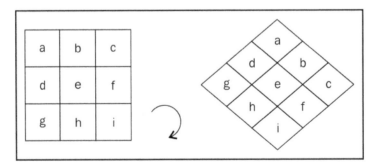

No matter how we transform and place the tiles, we need to place them in screen coordinates that are normal to each other eventually. The following figure illustrates the translation between isometric *x* / *y* into the screen coordinates:

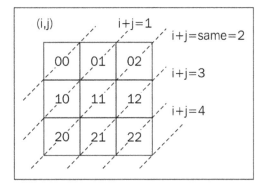

We use the following formula to position the tiles in the isometric perspective on the floor:

```
X :(col-row) x tile_width /2
Y :(col+row) x tile_height /2
```

Choosing which building to build

In this task, we let the player choose three types of buildings to create. These buildings are the power supply, coins generator, and merchant building. We create a building panel interface for this purpose.

Prepare for lift off

This is going to be a long task. The following screenshot previews what we are going to archive in this task so that we have a better understanding when reading the code:

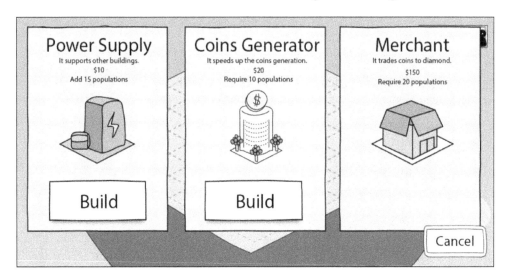

The button image follows a common practice in web design. We put the normal, hover, and active states into one image. Let's prepare the image files. Insert the following images files inside the project folder. We will take a look at how to create the following multistate images later:

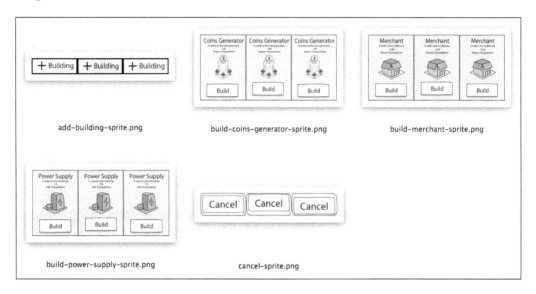

We will have three types of buildings in this game. They are **Power Supply**, **Coins Generator**, and **Merchant**. We'll create the following new file to store some building data:

```
scripts/data.js
```

We will include its code inside the index.html file and place it before the code of the game.js file, shown as follows:

```
<script src="scripts/data.js"></script>
```

When we introduce a building, we need to include the economy parameters too. It is because the availability of the buildings depends on the resources we have. We will initialize the following game parameters in the game.start function:

```
game.coins = 100;
game.diamonds = 0;
game.powerSupplies = 100;
game.populations = 0;
```

Now, we display these parameters in the user interface. Put the following `tick` function inside the `UILayer` definition prototype. The `tick` function displays the economy parameters in the text-based indicators:

```
UILayer.prototype.tick = function(){
   this.coinsIndicator.text = game.coins + ""; // force converting to
string with ""
   this.diamondsIndicator.text = game.diamonds + "";
   this.populationIndicator.text = game.populations + "";
   this.powerSupplyIndicator.text = game.powerSupplies + "";
};
```

We will keep refreshing the `tick` function by adding it to the CreateJS ticker in the following code. We put it inside the `game.start` function. Note that it also binds the `game.uiLayer` object as the context of the tick function:

```
cjs.Ticker.addEventListener('tick'
   , game.uiLayer.tick.bind(game.uiLayer));
```

Engage thrusters

In the following steps, we will create a building panel:

1. The data file defines the buildings and their parameters. Insert the following code inside the `data.js` file:

```
;(function(game){
  game.BuildingsData = {};
  game.BuildingsData['CoinsGenerator'] = {
    className: 'CoinsGenerator',
    needCoins: 20,
    needPopulations: 10,
    power: 0
  };
  game.BuildingsData['PowerSupply'] = {
    className: 'PowerSupply',
    needCoins: 10,
    needPopulations: 0,
    power: 15
  };
  game.BuildingsData['Merchant'] = {
    className: 'Merchant',
    needCoins: 150,
    needPopulations: 20,
    power: 0
  };
}).call(this, game);
```

2. We are going to create several buttons. EaselJS provides a `ButtonHelper` function that makes use of the `SpriteSheet` class. Inside our `helper.js` file, we add the following `createButton` function. Having the common code placed at one place and reusing it would be better than writing it again and again inside the main logic:

```
game.helper.createButton =
  function(spriteImage, width, height) {
  var data = {
    images: [spriteImage],
    frames: {width:width, height:height},
  };
  var spritesheet = new cjs.SpriteSheet(data);
  var button = new cjs.Sprite(spritesheet, 1);
  var helper = new cjs.ButtonHelper(button, 0, 1, 2);

  return button;
};
```

3. Let's move to the `game.js` file. To make use of the button's mouse hover effect, we need to enable mouse over. This is disabled by default because not every CreateJS project needs the mouse hover event and this event could be computationally expensive to generate:

```
game.stage.enableMouseOver();
```

4. The building-choosing panel is part of the user interface. We will set up the panel inside `UILayer`:

```
function UILayer() {
...
  // existing code goes here.
  // we need a flag to know whether we are creating new building.
By default it is false;
  game.isCreatingNewBuilding = false;
  this.setupBuildingPanel();
}
```

5. Now we come to the major logic of this task. We define the following function to set up the building panel user interface. We will split this long function into steps. The skeleton of this function is given in the following code snippet:

```
UILayer.prototype.setupBuildingPanel = function() {
  // Building Panels

  // building buttons data

  // three building buttons
```

```
    // set up 1 building button based on the index and data

    // loop the 3 buttons

    // *Cancel button while choosing place to build

    // *Button for cancel and hide the building panel

    // *Button for showing building panel

};
```

6. We put logic into the `setupBuildingPanel` function one by one:

```
UILayer.prototype.setupBuildingPanel = function() {
  // Building Panels
  this.buildingPanel = new cjs.Container();
  this.buildingPanel.visible = false; // hide it at initialize.
  this.addChild(this.buildingPanel);

  var _this = this;
```

7. We define three sets of the building data. We will loop this data to set up the buttons. Insert the following code into the `setupBuildingPanel` function following the preceding step:

```
// building buttons data
var buildings = [ // 3 buttons data into array.
  {
    name:'PowerSupply', // class name
    image: 'power-supply', // image name
    x: 20  // x-position of this button
  },
  {
    name:'CoinsGenerator',
    image: 'coins-generator',
    x: 338
  },
  {
    name:'Merchant',
    image: 'merchant',
    x: 650
  }
];
```

8. We make use of the data from the preceding step and create a button. A button contains the EaseIJS button and a disabled image. We also register a clickable button:

```
// set up 1 building button based on the index and data
function setupBuildingButton(i) {
  var b = buildings[i];
  var button = _this['build'+b.name] =
    game.helper.createButton('images/build-'
    + b.image + '-sprite.png', 286, 396);
  button.x = b.x;
  button.y = 16;
  _this.buildingPanel.addChild(button);

  button.on('click', function(){
    game.buildingTypeToBePlaced = b.name;
    _this.readyToPlaceBuilding();
  });

  // disabled image
  var buttonDisabled = _this
    ['build' + b.name + 'Disabled'] = new cjs.Bitmap
    ('images/build-' + b.image + '-disabled.png');
  buttonDisabled.x = button.x;
  buttonDisabled.y = button.y;
  buttonDisabled.visible = false;
  _this.buildingPanel.addChild(buttonDisabled);
}

// loop the 3 buttons
for (var i=0; i<3; i++) {
  setupBuildingButton(i);
}
```

9. After this, we add the two cancel buttons and the button that shows the building panel:

```
//Cancel Button while choosing place to build
var cancelBuildBtn = this.cancelBuildBtn =
  game.helper.createButton
  ('images/cancel-sprite.png', 128, 62);
cancelBuildBtn.x = 820;
cancelBuildBtn.y = 400;
this.addChild(cancelBuildBtn);
cancelBuildBtn.visible = false;
```

```
cancelBuildBtn.on('click', function() {
  game.isCreatingNewBuilding = false;
  cancelBuildBtn.visible = false;
  _this.newBuildingBtn.visible = true;
});

// Cancel button inside building panel
var cancelButton = game.helper.createButton
  ('images/cancel-sprite.png', 128, 62);
cancelButton.x = 820;
cancelButton.y = 400;
this.buildingPanel.addChild(cancelButton);

cancelButton.on('click', function() {
  _this.hideBuildingPanel();
});

// New Building button on stage
this.newBuildingBtn = game.helper.createButton
  ('images/add-building-sprite.png', 124, 42);
this.newBuildingBtn.x = 820
;
this.newBuildingBtn.y = 420;
this.addChild(this.newBuildingBtn);

this.newBuildingBtn.on('click', function() {
  _this.showBuildingPanel();
});
};
```

10. We extract the visible panel to show or hide the logic and create a function for easier invoking. When displaying the panel, we check the condition of each building:

```
UILayer.prototype.showBuildingPanel = function() {
  this.newBuildingBtn.visible = false;
  this.buildingPanel.visible = true;

  var buildings =
    ['Merchant', 'PowerSupply', 'CoinsGenerator'];
  for (var i=0, len=buildings.length; i<len; i++) {
    var name = buildings[i];

    // The Boolean determines that the player has enough power
  supplies to build that building. It returns true if the building
  doesn't need any population requirement.
```

```
        var hasEnoughPowerSupplies =
          (game.BuildingsData[name].needPopulations ===
          0 || (game.powerSupplies-game.populations)   >=
          game.BuildingsData[name].needPopulations);

        // The Boolean determines that the player has enough coins to
    build that building.
        var hasEnoughCoins =
          (game.coins >= game.BuildingsData[name].needCoins);

    if (hasEnoughPowerSupplies && hasEnoughCoins) {
        // show the button and hide the disabled image
        this['build' + name + 'Disabled'].visible = false;
        this['build' + name].y = this['build' + name +
    'Disabled'].y;
      } else {
        // show the disabled image and hide the button
        this['build' + name + 'Disabled'].visible = true;
        this['build' + name].y = 999;
      }
    }
  }
};
```

11. Then, we need a way to quickly hide the building panel:

```
UILayer.prototype.hideBuildingPanel = function() {
  this.newBuildingBtn.visible = true;
  this.buildingPanel.visible = false;
};
```

12. After the player chooses a building to be built, we ready the game to place the building:

```
UILayer.prototype.readyToPlaceBuilding = function() {
  this.buildingPanel.visible = false;
  this.cancelBuildBtn.visible = true;
  game.isCreatingNewBuilding = true;
  // we are going to really place the building in the next task.
};
```

At the end of the task, we will have created the building panel with the building selectable by the mouse. We don't have any building placing logic yet. We are going to work on this in the next task.

Objective complete – mini debriefing

We have a data file to define the basic data of buildings. The class name is used in order to refer to the sprite view. Every building has a minimum number of required coins and population to be created. The power supply building generates power to increase the population capacity.

The following figure shows the user interface flow of the building panel:

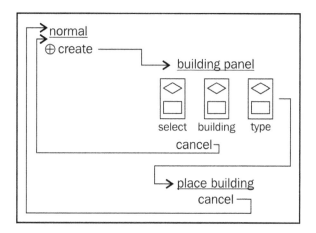

Button helper

There is no Button class in the CreateJS library. The button is actually a combination of a three-frame sprite image and the mouseover and mousedown events. The button is an EaselJS SpriteSheet class that takes the image path and the frame dimension as parameters. The button helper then converts a three-frame spritesheet into a button with mouse interactivity. It automatically adds the rollover and mousedown events to the created sprite. The following code is a recap of the code we added to the logic:

```
var data = {
  images: [spriteImage],
  frames: {width:width, height:height},
};
var spritesheet = new cjs.SpriteSheet(data);
var button = new cjs.Sprite(spritesheet, 1);
var helper = new cjs.ButtonHelper(button, 0, 1, 2);
```

The following screenshot shows the logic behind the button helper:

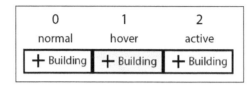

For more details on the button helper, please refer to the official EaselJS documentation at `http://createjs.com/Docs/EaselJS/classes/ButtonHelper.html`.

Classified intel

We have added mouse interaction to the display object. You can take alook at the events section in the Stage documentation for more mouse events:

`http://createjs.com/Docs/EaselJS/classes/Stage.html #event_click`

You can also refer to the following tutorial showcasing several mouse interaction examples:

`http://www.createjs.com/tutorials/Mouse%20Interaction/`

Placing buildings on the floor

We are in the process of creating a building. We let the player choose the type of building in the previous task. In this task, we allow the players to choose where to place the selected building on the floor. There is a half-transparent building image following the cursor when selecting a tile to place the building. If the place is unavailable, we put a red overlay on top of the ghost building.

Prepare for lift off

We need the three building image files to be placed on the floor. Include the following three image files in the `images` folder of our project. The red overlay is added programmatically.

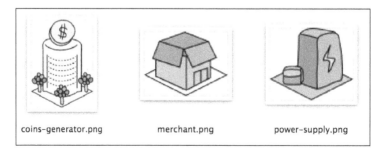

coins-generator.png   merchant.png   power-supply.png

Planning the placing flow

This task involves both the UI layer and the city layer. We will use event dispatching for communication between these two components. There will be two custom events: `newBuildingToBePlaced` and `placedBuilding`. The following figure illustrates the event communication between both the layers in order to place the selected building on the floor:

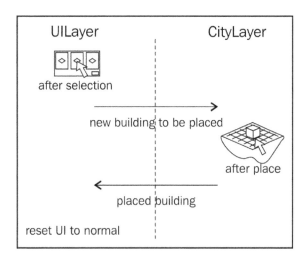

Before we start following the steps for completing this task, we want to have two more helper functions. These functions convert coordinates between the screen and isometric system. Let's insert the following code inside the `helper.js` file:

```
// ISO <-> Screen conversion.
;(function(game, cjs){
  game.isoMaths = {
    screenToIsoCoord: function(screenX, screenY) {
      var ix = Math.floor( (screenY * game.Tile.width +
        screenX * game.Tile.height) / (game.Tile.width *
        game.Tile.height) );
      var iy = Math.floor( (screenY * game.Tile.width
        - screenX * game.Tile.height) /
        (game.Tile.width * game.Tile.height) ) + 1;
      return {x: ix, y: iy};
    },
    isoToScreenCoord: function(isoX, isoY) {
      var sx = (isoX - isoY) * game.Tile.width / 2;
      var sy = (isoX + isoY) * game.Tile.height / 2;
      return new cjs.Point(sx, sy);
    }
  };
}).call(this, game, createjs);
```

Engage thrusters

Let's complete this task with the following steps:

1. We have three more images to place in the city layer now. Define them in the `view-sprites.js` file using the following code:

```
// Buildings View
;(function(game, cjs){
  (game.CoinsGenerator = function() {
    game.Tile.call(this, 'images/coins-generator.png');
    this.regX = 0;
    this.regY = 94;
  }).prototype = Object.create(game.Tile.prototype);

  (game.Merchant = function() {
    game.Tile.call(this, 'images/merchant.png');
    this.regX = 0;
    this.regY = 43;
  }).prototype = Object.create(game.Tile.prototype);

  (game.PowerSupply = function() {
    game.Tile.call(this, 'images/power-supply.png');
    this.regX = 0;
    this.regY = 51;
  }).prototype = Object.create(game.Tile.prototype);
}).call(this, game, createjs);
```

2. Let's move on to the `game.js` file. In the `CityLayer` constructor function, we add the following code that initializes the data of the map. We need `this` to compare when drawing the buildings:

```
// 2D array that holds the type of building in string
this.data = game.helper.create2DArray
  (this.rows, this.cols);
```

3. Next, we define a new code block for the `Building` definition. We also create an empty array that will store the building instances:

```
;(function(game, cjs){
  game.Building = function(isoX, isoY, viewClassName) {
    this.name = viewClassName;
    this.x = isoX;
    this.y = isoY;
  };
  game.buildingsList = [];
}).call(this, game, createjs);
```

4. The `setupMouseInteraction` function is quite a long function. We set up a ghost building to temporarily illustrate where the building is going to be placed. We also define three event-handling callbacks. The skeleton of the temporary building is as follows:

```
CityLayer.prototype.setupMouseInteraction = function() {
  // a ghost building
  var ghostBuilding = new game.CoinsGenerator();
  ghostBuilding.alpha = 0.5;
  ghostBuilding.visible = false;
  this.addChild(ghostBuilding);

  // change ghost building visual based on the building choice.
  var _this = this;
  game.on('newBuildingToBePlaced', function(){
    // initial logic for every new building placement
  });

  // mouse move on city layer
  game.stage.on('stagemousemove', function(e) {
    // mouse over logic
  });

  this.on('click', function(e){
    // click logic
  });
};
```

5. We defined three functions in the previous step without content. In the following three steps, we will define their logic accordingly. The following is the code to handle the `newBuildingToBePlaced` event inside the city layer:

```
game.on('newBuildingToBePlaced', function(){
  _this.removeChild(ghostBuilding);

  ghostBuilding = new game
    [game.buildingTypeToBePlaced]();
  ghostBuilding.alpha = 0.5;
  ghostBuilding.visible = false;
  _this.addChild(ghostBuilding);
});
```

6. Next, we will work on the following code of the mouseover event in the city layer. It shows the ghost building on the tile where the cursor is pointed. We also overlay a red filter on the ghost building when the pointing tile is unavailable:

```
function showGhostBuilding(x, y) {
  ghostBuilding.visible = true;
  // from screen cursor to city layer local x/y.
  var localPt = _this.globalToLocal(e.stageX, e.stageY);
  // from screen's x/y of city layer to isometric x/y.
  var isoCoord = game.isoMaths.screenToIsoCoord
    (localPt.x, localPt.y);
  // back from iso x/y to screen x/y (get tile x/y).
  // in order to get the screen x/y at tile reg point.
  var tileScreenCoord = game.isoMaths.isoToScreenCoord
    (isoCoord.x, isoCoord.y);
  ghostBuilding.x = tileScreenCoord.x;
  ghostBuilding.y = tileScreenCoord.y;
  ghostBuilding.filters = [];
  var isTileAvailable =
    (this.data[isoCoord.y] && this.data[isoCoord.y]
    [isoCoord.x] === 'Tile');
  if (!isTileAvailable) {
    // overlay a red color by using filter
    ghostBuilding.filters = [
      new cjs.ColorFilter(1, 0, 0, 1), // red
    ];
  }
  ghostBuilding.cache(0, 0, 100, 100); // we need to cache the
Display Object as bitmap for the red filter.
}
game.stage.on('stagemousemove', function(e) {
  // mousemove happens all the time, and if we are not creating
new building, we don't need any logic here. And make sure the
ghost building is invisible.
  if (!game.isCreatingNewBuilding) {
    ghostBuilding.visible = false;
    return;
  }

});
```

7. Then, we craft the on-click event handling. The coordinate conversion is similar to the mousemove event:

```
this.on('click', function(e){
  var localPt = this.globalToLocal(e.stageX, e.stageY);
```

```
      var isoCoord = game.isoMaths.screenToIsoCoord
        (localPt.x, localPt.y);
      var isTileAvailable = (this.data[isoCoord.y] &&
        this.data[isoCoord.y][isoCoord.x] === 'Tile');
      if (game.isCreatingNewBuilding && isTileAvailable) {
        var needCoins = game.BuildingsData
          [game.buildingTypeToBePlaced].needCoins;
        // deduce money
        game.coins -= needCoins;

        var event = new cjs.Event('placedBuilding');
        event.buildingType = game.buildingTypeToBePlaced;
        game.dispatchEvent(event); // trigger the event
        game.isCreatingNewBuilding = false;
        ghostBuilding.visible = false;

        var newBuildingData = new game.Building
          (isoCoord.x, isoCoord.y, event.buildingType);

        game.buildingsList.push(newBuildingData);

        // redraw the city tiles and buildings after changes.
        this.redraw();
      }
    });
```

8. Now, we initialize the interaction setup we just created inside the `CityLayer` constructor function:

```
this.setupMouseInteraction();
```

9. We need to refine the `redraw` function to take the building data into the logic of the code:

```
CityLayer.prototype.redraw = function() {
  var newDataMap = game.helper.create2DArray
    (this.rows, this.cols, 'Tile');

  // construct the 2D map data with building list.
  for (var i=0, len=game.buildingsList.length;
    i<len; i++) {
    var b = game.buildingsList[i];
    var className = b.name;

    newDataMap[b.y][b.x] = className;
  }
```

```
                // loop the 2D array for visualization
                for (var i=0; i<this.rows; i++) {
                  for (var j=0; j<this.cols; j++) {
                    if (this.data[i][j] !== newDataMap[i][j]) {
                      this.tiles.removeChild(this.viewMap[i][j]);

                      var className = newDataMap[i][j];

                      // sprite based on the selected building type
                      var tile = new game[className]();

                      tile.x = (j-i) * game.Tile.width / 2;
                      tile.y = (j+i) * game.Tile.height / 2;
                      this.tiles.addChild(tile);

                      this.viewMap[i][j] = tile;
                    }
                  }
                }

                this.data = newDataMap;

                // Reorder the building based on Y
                this.tiles.sortChildren(function(b1, b2) {
                  if (b1.y > b2.y) { return 1; }
                  if (b1.y < b2.y) { return -1; }
                  return 0;
                });
            };
```

10. Inside the `UILayer` constructor function add the following lines of code:

```
    var _this = this; // for event handler to refer 'this'

    game.on('placedBuilding', function(){
      _this.cancelBuildBtn.visible = false;
      _this.newBuildingBtn.visible = true;
    });
```

11. After the player chooses a building from the building creation panel, the `readyToPlaceBuilding` function is invoked. We dispatch the event to let the city layer know that we have a new building to be placed:

```
    UILayer.prototype.readyToPlaceBuilding = function () {
    ...
      // existing code goes here.
      game.dispatchEvent('newBuildingToBePlaced');
    };
```

12. To make the custom event dispatch and listening work, we need to initialize the game object to have the `EventDispatcher` capabilities. We initialize it inside the `game.start` function:

```
cjs.EventDispatcher.initialize(game);
```

Objective complete – mini debriefing

The `BuildingsList` is a list containing all the buildings and their current state. The state includes the building type and the isometric coordinates. Later, we will add more variables to the building data, including the construction statistics.

Conversion from screen coordinates to isometric coordinates

When the mouse moves over to the floor, we have the coordinates of a 2D screen. We need a conversion between the screen and isometric coordinates for the cursor movement and clicks. By calculating the *isoX* and *isoY* coordinates that the cursor is pointing to, we can get the selected tile in the isometric world. We defined each building's registration point on the isometric grid. From the registration point of the selected tile, we know where the ghost building or the new building should be placed. Let's recap the code to archive this conversion:

```
var localPt = _this.globalToLocal(e.stageX, e.stageY);
var isoCoord = game.isoMaths.screenToIsoCoord
  (localPt.x, localPt.y);
var tileScreenCoord = game.isoMaths.isoToScreenCoord
  (isoCoord.x, isoCoord.y);
```

The following figure illustrates the steps to convert a stage's *x* and *y* coordinates into the city layer's isometric world and the final registration point in the screen coordinates:

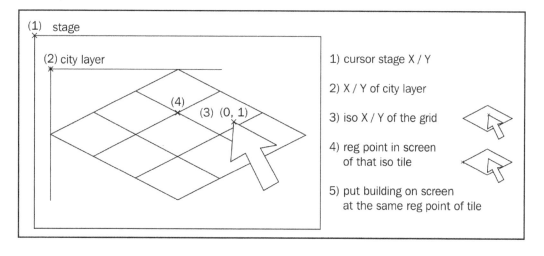

Drawing the building

We have two data maps for comparison: the old one from the last frame and the current one. We only redraw the building that has just changed between the last frame and current frame. For any building changes, we remove the old building sprite on that tile and draw a new instance there.

By avoiding redrawing the entire map every time, we avoid making too many deletions and creations of the display objects in a short period of time. This helps improve the performance. It also helps to avoid a blank screen when all the tiles are being removed from every frame.

Building view classes

We define the building sprite in the `sprite-view.js` file for each type of building that needs to be visualized on the city layer. The following is the merchant sprite definition:

```
(game.Merchant = function() {
  game.Tile.call(this, 'images/merchant.png');
  this.regX = 0;
  this.regY = 43;
}).prototype = Object.create(game.Tile.prototype);
```

Because of the variation in the dimensions of the building drawn, each building view has its own image path and registration point. By encapsulating this information into a class, we can simply create a building instance by name without worrying about misplacing it on the wrong registration point.

Applying color filter

When choosing an invalid place, we show a red overlay on the ghost building image to indicate the invalid place to a player. This overlay is done by the filter:

```
ghostBuilding.filters = [
  new cjs.ColorFilter(1, 0, 0, 1),
];
```

Every display object has a list of filters. There are filters on color adjustment, hue, blur, and so on. In the following link, you will find a demonstration on how to apply multiple filters to an image:

`http://www.createjs.com/#!/EaselJS/demos/filters`

In order to make the filter work, we must cache the display object. It is like prerendering the display objects and effects into one bitmap.

For reference, please refer to the following documentation for more effects that we can apply to a display object:

```
http://www.createjs.com/Docs/EaselJS/classes/Filter.html
```

Classified intel

Let's take a deeper look at the mouse event and screen coordinates translation.

The different mouseover events

We used the `stagemousemove` event to track the movements of the mouse. There are several events related to the mouse move event in EaselJS. They are `mouseover`, `rollover`, and `stagemousemove`. There are a few differences among the following events:

- ▶ `stagemousemove`: This is any mouse move event that takes place on the canvas element. This event is fired whenever the mouse is inside the canvas area and moving. When we want to track smooth mouse moving, we need this event. For example, you need this event in order to draw a linein drawing game.

- ▶ `mouseover`: This event occurs when the cursor enters the target display object. If the target is a container and the cursor moves among its children objects, the `mouseover` event is fired.

- ▶ `rollover`: This event is similar to the `mouseover` event except that it takes the target as one object and doesn't count the movement between its children. The event will fire once when the cursor enters the target.

The EaselJS documentation has an example explaining the difference between various types of events: `http://createjs.com/Docs/EaselJS/classes/DisplayObject.html#event_rollover`. The the following video also demonstrates how mouseover detects each part inside the container and how rollover only detects the container as a whole object:

```
https://www.youtube.com/watch?v=ZU59cO1cmsE
```

Translating coordinates between global and local

We heavily use a container to group the display objects in EaselJS. Each container has its own coordinate reference point. The coordinates (0, 0) are set at the registration point of the container and all the children objects follow it. These are the local coordinates.

For global coordinates, it means the coordinates on stage. The (0, 0) point is located at the top-left corner of the stage. When we handle coordinates inside a specific display object, we need an isolated coordinate system that is independent of the stage. EaselJS provides the `localToGlobal`, `globalToLocal`, and `localToLocal` methods. That's where we need to translate the coordinates from a global stage to the local stage, and vice versa. Sometimes we even need to translate it between two display objects using the `localToLocal` method.

Creating depth illustrations by ordering the buildings

We need to create the depth illustration by placing the buildings in the correct order. When we redraw, we may add a new child in front of the screen, which should be behind a certain building. We can reorder all the tiles' z index after every redraw. EaselJS Container provides a `sortChildren` method to let us define the reorder criteria. We use the y position to determine the z order.

Advancing the construction progress over time

We have placed some building constructions on the floor in the previous task. In this task, we advance the construction progress over time.

Prepare for lift off

We have the following two images to represent two steps of the building construction. Let's add them to the project's `images` folder.

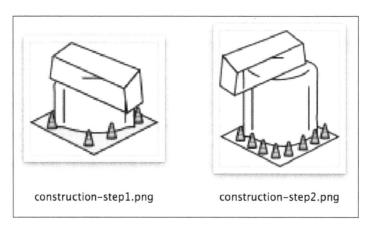

construction-step1.png   construction-step2.png

We defined `BuildingsData` in the previous task. Now, we add one more parameter to each building's data. The new parameter is the duration in seconds that each construction step takes:

```
game.BuildingsData['CoinsGenerator'] = {
...
  // existing building data goes here.
  stepsSeconds: [10, 20]
};
game.BuildingsData['PowerSupply'] = {
...
  // existing building data goes here.
  stepsSeconds: [5, 10]
};
game.BuildingsData['Merchant'] = {
  // existing building data goes here.
  stepsSeconds: [20, 40]
};
```

We added two images and now we insert the following code inside the `sprite-view.js` file to make it available for the city drawing code to use:

```
(game.ConstructionStep1 = function() {
  game.Tile.call(this, 'images/construction-step1.png');
  this.regX = 0;
  this.regY = 51;
}).prototype = Object.create(game.Tile.prototype);

(game.ConstructionStep2 = function() {
  game.Tile.call(this, 'images/construction-step2.png');
  this.regX = 0;
  this.regY = 74;
}).prototype = Object.create(game.Tile.prototype);
```

Engage thrusters

In the following steps, we will add the construction logic to the building:

1. We add several properties to count the growing statuses inside the `Building` function constructor:

```
game.Building = function(isoX, isoY, viewClassName) {
...
  // existing Building code goes here.
  this.isConstructionDone = false;
```

```
      this.currentStep = 1;
      this.stepsSeconds = game.BuildingsData
        [viewClassName].stepsSeconds;
      this.buildTime = (new Date()).getTime();
  };
```

2. Then, we define the following tick method that helps the buildings grow. We may put it next to the `Building` definition:

```
var cityGrowing = game.cityGrowing = {};
cityGrowing.tick = function() {
  for (var i=0, len=game.buildingsList.length;
    i < len; i++) {
    var building = game.buildingsList[i];

    // is consturction in the next stage?
    var secondsDiff = Math.floor(((new Date()).getTime()
      - building.buildTime) / 1000); // seconds
    for (var j=0, length=building.stepsSeconds.length;
      j < length; j++) { // loop the steps
      if (secondsDiff >= building.stepsSeconds[j]) {
        building.currentStep = j+2;
        if (building.currentStep > length) {
          building.isConstructionDone = true;
        }
      }
    }
  }
};
```

3. When we draw the tiles and buildings in the city layer's `redraw` method, we draw the construction building graphics too:

```
// construct the 2D map data with building list.
for (var i=0, len=game.buildingsList.length; i<len; i++) {
  var b = game.buildingsList[i];
  var className = b.name;
  if (!b.isConstructionDone) {
    className = "ConstructionStep" + b.currentStep;
  }

  newDataMap[b.y][b.x] = game.BuildingIDs[className];
}
```

4. Inside the `game.start` function, we add the redraw method of the city layer and building growing tick method to the ticker:

```
cjs.Ticker.addEventListener
  ('tick', game.cityLayer.redraw.bind(game.cityLayer));
cjs.Ticker.addEventListener
  ('tick', game.cityGrowing.tick.bind(game.cityGrowing));
```

The resultant output after completing this task is shown in the following screenshot. Notice that now it takes time to build a building. We should see the construction graphics that indicate the work-in-progress buildings:

Objective complete – mini debriefing

We have added the construction progress display to the building. Newly created buildings now take a while to complete. We assign a time for construction to every kind of building. It is an array of seconds in ascending order. The building step is determined by how many seconds elapsed since it was built:

```
stepsSeconds: [10, 20]
```

The construction is based on world time. We store the starting time of each building. At any given moment, we know the progress of the construction by calculating the time difference between the current time and build time, in seconds:

```
var secondsDiff = Math.floor(((new Date()).getTime() -
  building.buildTime) / 1000); // seconds
```

We determine the current step by looping the `stepsSeconds` array and checking whether the difference reaches the target number of seconds. When it reaches the last step, we mark the construction of the building as done.

The construction states are put onto the data map. When the map redraws on every tick, it will handle the visual changes and draw different stages of the building on the floor.

Generating coins and diamonds

In this task, we create the economy of the game by generating the coins and diamonds.

Prepare for lift off

Before getting into the code, let's summarize how the buildings affect the coins and diamonds:

- The generation of coins and diamonds depends on the number of buildings
- By default, each coin is generated within a fixed duration
- More coin generators speed up the coin generation process
- The merchant building trades 200 coins for a diamond once in a while, unless there are not enough coins
- These buildings are where the population resides
- We count the number of power supplies to know the maximum population capacity

Engage thrusters

To generate coins and diamonds, perform the following steps:

1. First, we define the `tickCountForMerchantDiamond` and `coinsNeededForDiamond` variables in the game settings:

```
game.setting = {
    ...
    // existing game setting
    tickCountForMerchantDiamond: 800,
    coinsNeededForDiamond: 200
};
```

2. Let's create a function to increase the diamond count. We add it to the UI layer because eventually a diamond sprite will pop up for the player to click on. However, in this task, we will simply increase the count to make things simpler:

```
UILayer.prototype.popDiamond = function(building) {
    game.diamonds += 1;
};
```

3. When initializing the game, we add two more variables. The first one is the countdown until we get the next coin. The second one is the count so far:

```
game.coinGenerationCountdown = 90;
game.coinGenerationCount = 0;
```

4. The number of coin generators will affect the countdown to generate a new coin. We define the following function in the game scope that calculates and applies the building's effects:

```
game.calculateBuildingsEffects = function(){
  // refresh population and power supplies based on the building
list.
  game.powerSupplies = 10;
  game.populations = 0;
  game.coinGenerationCountdown = 90; // default value, will be
affected by coins generators

  for (var i=0, len=game.buildingsList.length;
     i<len; i++) {
    var b = game.buildingsList[i];
    var data = game.BuildingsData[b.name];

    evaluatePopulation(data.needPopulations);

    if (b.isConstructionDone) {
      // only count power after it is built.
      evaluatePowerSupply(data.power);

      if (b.name === 'CoinsGenerator') {
        evaluateCoinsGeneration();
      }

      if (b.name === 'Merchant') {
        evaluateMerchant(b);
      }
    }
  }
};
```

5. We called four functions in the previous task. These are evaluatePopulation, evaluatePowerSupply, evaluateCoinsGeneration, and evaluateMerchant. Let's add them one by one after our calculateBuildingsEffects method:

```
function evaluatePopulation(value){
  game.populations += value;
}
```

```
function evaluatePowerSupply(value) {
  game.powerSupplies += value;
}


function evaluateCoinsGeneration() {
  // each coin generator speed up the count down by 3 units.
  game.coinGenerationCountdown -= 3;
}


function evaluateMerchant(building) {
  var b = building
  if (!b.diamondTick) {
    b.diamondTick = 0;
  }
  b.diamondTick += 1;
  if (b.diamondTick >= game.setting.tickCountForMerchantDiamond) {
    // trade coins to diamonds
    if (game.coins >= game.setting.coinsNeedForDiamond) {
      game.coins -= game.setting.coinsNeedForDiamond;
      game.uiLayer.popDiamond(b);
      b.diamondTick = 0;
    }
  }
}
```

6. We have the following tick function to really count the generation of coins and invoke our methods:

```
game.tick = function() {
  game.coinGenerationCount += 1;
  if (game.coinGenerationCount >=
    game.coinGenerationCountdown) {
    game.coins += 1;
    game.coinGenerationCount = 0;
  }
  game.calculateBuildingsEffects();
};
```

7. Finally, we add the tick function to `Ticker` in order to execute it on every frame:

```
cjs.Ticker.addEventListener('tick', game.tick);
```

Objective complete – mini debriefing

We have made a live economy with the generation and consumption of resources.

We looped all the buildings in the list. For each building, we calculated the power and population. For each coins generator, we decreased the duration of new coins generation. For each merchant, we try to trade coins for diamonds.

Instead of increasing the diamond count directly, we invoke the UI layer so that a diamond pops up. It is up to the UI layer to define how a diamond should be collected. In this task, we simply increase the count. In the next task, we will edit this function so that a diamond sprite pops up on the screen for the player to click on and collect.

Classified intel

It is quite common to have two currencies in this type of game. Coins, which are used in this game, are used in most cases to buy new buildings, pay for upgrades, or expand the city. The rare currency in this game, diamond, is used for premium features. For example, we may charge a diamond to finish the building instantly without the construction time. The rare resources should not be easy to obtain. In addition, we may even charge the player real money for the rare resources. That's how a freemium model works in app stores.

Collecting pop-up diamonds

In this task, we make the diamonds pop up from merchant buildings to let the player click on the diamonds and collect them in order to increase the diamond count.

Prepare for lift off

Before getting started with the steps of this task, we want to ensure that we have the following diamond sprite graphic files prepared and placed in the `images` folder:

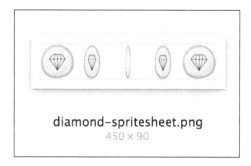

diamond-spritesheet.png
450 × 90

Engage thrusters

In the following steps, we add the diamond animation to the stage and let the players click on it:

1. We have a new display object so we will add the diamond sprite to the `view-sprites.js` file:

    ```
    (game.Diamond = function() {
    cjs.Container.call(this); // super
    var data = {
      framerate: 16,
      images: ['images/diamond-spritesheet.png'],
      frames: {width:90, height:90},
    };
    var spritesheet = new cjs.SpriteSheet(data);
    var diamondSprite = new cjs.Sprite(spritesheet);
    diamondSprite.gotoAndPlay(0);
    diamondSprite.scaleX = diamondSprite.scaleY = 0.5;
    this.addChild(diamondSprite);

    this.on('click', function(){
      game.dispatchEvent('clickedDiamond');
      this.parent.removeChild(this);
    });

    }).prototype = Object.create(cjs.Container.prototype);
    ```

2. We want the player to collect the diamond. We redefine the `popDiamond` function:

    ```
    UILayer.prototype.popDiamond = function(building) {
      var diamond = new game.Diamond();

      var screenCoord = game.isoMaths.isoToScreenCoord
        (building.x, building.y);
      // transform the screen coordinate of city layer to UI layer.
      var globalScreenCoord = game.cityLayer.localToLocal
        (screenCoord.x, screenCoord.y, this);
      diamond.x = globalScreenCoord.x;
      diamond.y = globalScreenCoord.y;
      this.addChild(diamond);
    };
    ```

3. Whenever the diamond is clicked on, we increase the diamond count. We can put the following code inside the `game.start` function:

    ```
    game.on('clickedDiamond', function(){
      game.diamonds += 1;
    });
    ```

Objective complete – mini debriefing

The clicking of diamond and increment of variable happens in different components. The diamond is added to the UI layer and the value of the diamond variable increases.

Diamond sprite animation

The diamond sprite animation uses the same sprite sheet approach for the button. The difference is that button has three frames for the mouseup, mouseover, and mousedown events. The diamond is an animation with the most frames. We can tell EaselJS to play the animation by calling `gotoAndplay(0)`. The frame number starts with 0. By default, the animation is reset to frame 0 and loops after it reaches the last frame of the sprite.

In *Project 6*, *Space Defenders*, we will explore how to export vector animations to CreateJS directly from Adobe Flash.

Classified intel

Besides the diamonds that pop up, we may also allow coins to pop up randomly in the game. This increases the possibility that a player has something to do in the game. This can be a good incentive to make the player stay in the game. They will get bonus coins and diamonds while the buildings are under construction. Moreover, the coins can be of random value too. Some pop-up coins may increase 10 coins and some may increase 100 coins.

Saving and loading the game progress

In the task, we store the game progress locally. When a player loads the game, we use the world time to calculate the building construction.

Engage thrusters

We will use the following steps to store game parameters and load them at the initial stage:

1. Create the `saving` function with the following code:

```
game.autoSave = function() {
  if (cjs.Ticker.getTicks() % 100 === 0) {
    localStorage['city.coins'] = game.coins;
    localStorage['city.diamonds'] = game.diamonds;
    localStorage['city.buildinglist'] = JSON.stringify(game.
buildingsList);
  }
};
```

2. Add the `saving` function to the ticker so that it can autosave:

```
cjs.Ticker.addEventListener('tick', game.autoSave);
```

3. Now, we can load the saved game using the following code:

```
if (localStorage['city.buildinglist']) {
  game.buildingsList = JSON.parse(localStorage['city.
buildinglist']);
} else {
  game.buildingsList = [];
}
```

4. When we initialize coins and diamonds, we load the values from the local storage:

```
game.coins = localStorage['city.coins']*1 || 10; // *1 to force
converting string to number
game.diamonds = localStorage['city.diamonds']*1 || 0;
```

Now, try to play the game in a browser with the latest code loaded. Place some buildings in the city and close the browser. Reopening the game will load the buildings. The game continues from where it stopped the last time. Try to create another building and leave the game once it starts the first step of construction. Then come back to the game 30 seconds later and you will see that your building construction is now complete.

Objective complete – mini debriefing

We have saved and loaded our game. When we saved the building list locally, we saved the starting time of the construction as well. After the game has been closed for a while and the player reopens the game, we load the building list and the city `redraw` method will calculate to see whether the building was 100 percent constructed during the time the game was offline.

Using local storage

Local storage allows a website to store data persistently in the browser. It utilizes very simple key-value access. `LocalStorage` uses only string type for both keys and values. The following is the syntax to save, load, and remove the stored items.

```
// save a string.
localStorage.setItem(key, value);
// load a string.
localStorage.getItem(key);
// remove an item.
localStorage.removeItem(key);
```

Alternatively, local storage provides an array syntax to access the data:

```
localStorage['key here'] = "value goes here"; // set the value
localStorage['key here']; // get the value
```

Since the stored value is in the string format, we should postprocess the loaded data to the format we need. For example, if we saved the coins, we need to type cast the string back to the number:

```
localStorage['coins']= 123; // stored as "123"
var savedCoins = localStorage['coins'] * 1; // x1 to make it a number
```

We have the following things to save in the local storage:

- ▸ The amount of coins
- ▸ The amount of diamonds
- ▸ The list of buildings

What about the list of buildings, which is an array of objects with values?

We can still save an object by converting the object into a string. Technically, we can use any kind of string serialization but JSON is a good choice here. We can use the built-in JSON object. It provides two methods to convert an object into a string and vice versa. They are JSON.stringify and JSON.parse. When we convert an object into a string, we use the stringify method. After we load the serialized string back from the storage, we parse it into a JavaScript object:

```
JSON.stringify(obj) serializes the given object into string.
JSON.parse(string) parses the string into object.
```

We can't assume that the value exists in the local storage. It may be the first time a player opens the game. It can also be that the player deleted the local data manually. Either way, it will lead to an undefined value when we try to retrieve the value from the local storage. It is a good practice to have a default value in case the local storage returns an undefined result. The following code is how we add the default value:

```
game.coins = localStorage['city.coins']*1 || 10; // default 10 coins
```

For a more detailed discussion on the local storage, you can refer to the guide on Mozilla (https://developer.mozilla.org/en-US/docs/Web/Guide/API/DOM/Storage) or the online book *Dive into HTML5*, by *Mark Pilgrim*, published by *O'Reilly Media* at http://diveintohtml5.info/storage.html.

For security reasons, LocalStorage API only allows access to the data that was saved on the same domain.

Classified intel

The `Ticker` ticks the registered function in every frame. We are going to automatically save the game but saving it on every frame would result in frequent I/O operations. Hence, we use the `getTicks` method and invoke the saving after every 100 ticks.

Having more than one saving slot

Both the key and value are stored in string format on the local storage. We learned how to serialize data into values. We can apply a similar approach to the key. For example, if we want to provide three saving slots, we can define the key as `game.<slot_number>.buildingList`. Assuming that at this moment we load the second saving slot, we use the following code:

```
var savingSlot = 2;
var loadData = localStorage
   ['game.' + savingSlot + '.buildingsList'];
```

Since the storage happens on the client side, the player can use a browser as a developer tool to alter any value in the local storage. If your game needs a more secure storage, you may store the values on the server and cache them with local storage. After this, validate the data sent from the client side.

Mission accomplished

We have created a city-building game. The game has a 2.5D depth with an isometric view. This isometric projection requires some mathematics on both the display and mouse interaction. We have also introduced a time delay to let a player wait for the building construction to be completed. Finally, we save everything so that the players can quit and resume the game at any time. The following is a screenshot of my city stacking up coins:

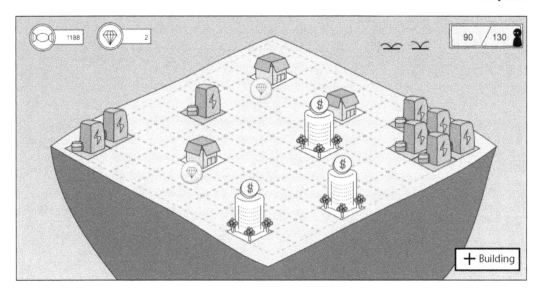

Hotshot challenges

There is room to improve this game.

Eliminating waiting time by paying

The city-building game involves creating different kinds of buildings on the map to balance the city resources. The creation often takes some time to complete. Players may need to wait for seconds or even hours. Some building games offer the option to eliminate waiting time during construction by letting the player pay a small amount of money. This is one approach to sell the premium feature on a free game.

Upgrading buildings

We can add upgrades to our buildings. For example, we can introduce a solar power supply, which charges more but provides more power. The existing power supply may be upgradable to higher levels. We may even have some premium buildings that are only available to paid players. The premium model may use an in-app purchase mechanism while the game is distributed to app stores.

Providing mini quests

Another approach is to introduce some mini quests and mini games that players can play and earn bonus resources. The reward may be a random amount of coins or a diamond. These kinds of random events can engage the player to stay in the game for a longer period of time while not building the city. They will wait for the event when they can earn extra rare resources.

Project 6

Space Defenders

We built a city-building game in the last project. We will build a tower defense game in this project, where players build economy and attack units to protect the earth from enemy invasion. It makes use of similar building techniques that we learned in the last project.

Mission briefing

In this tower defense game, enemies come from the top of the screen. They move down to invade the earth, which is at the bottom of the screen. The player needs to protect the earth by building defense buildings in the space.

The space is divided into grids. The buildings block the enemy movement and some even fire bullets to kill enemies. These enemies also attack the things that block their way. So, the player needs to survive and kill all units within the time limit before the enemy reaches the earth.

You may visit `http://makzan.net/html5-games/space-defenders/` to play the example game in order to have a better understanding of what we will build throughout this project.

The following figure shows the planning of the game:

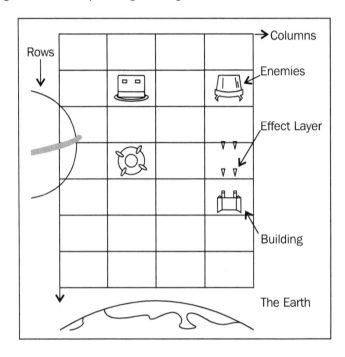

Why is it awesome?

This is a successor of *Project 5, Building an Isometric City Game*. We will be using a similar building placement and grid map. The only difference is that we will use a 2D tile in this game.

This project uses the techniques that we have learned previously and applies them in a well-designed game. By carefully designing the gameplay and fine-tuning the difficulty, this game will be the most fun game to play in this book.

Your Hotshot objectives

This project is divided into eight tasks, which are mentioned as follows:

- ▶ Setting up the user interface
- ▶ Placing the defense buildings
- ▶ Summoning the enemies
- ▶ Generating energy
- ▶ Enemies attacking the buildings
- ▶ Firing bullets and attacking the enemies
- ▶ Controlling enemy waves
- ▶ Loading the bitmap graphics into the game

Mission checklist

Similar to the previous projects, we will create a new project directory and have the CreateJS libraries ready for this project too.

Specifically, we need to have the **EaselJS**, **TweenJS**, **MovieClip**, and **PreloadJS** files downloaded from the CreateJS website: `http://createjs.com`.

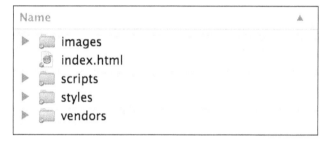

Setting up the user interface

In this task, we will get started with the project by setting up the structure and the user interface.

Prepare for lift off

In this project, we will try a different method of using the graphical assets. We will include the assets.js file, which you can find in the code bundle. This is the file generated by the CreateJS toolkit from **Adobe Flash**. The following screenshot shows that we lay out the graphical symbols on the stage inside the Flash IDE. The assets.js file includes background, buildings, enemies, and the wave-cleared message. They all come with a name that we can reference and instantiate in our game.

Engage thrusters

The following steps build the foundation of our project:

1. First, we only show the core part of the `index.html` file in the following code. When we deploy the code, we always want to have the entire HTML structure:

```
...
<section id="game" class="row">
  <canvas id="canvas" width="640" height="1000"></canvas>
  <div id="hud">
    <div>Lives: <span id="lives"></span></div>
    <div>E: <span id="energies"></span></div>
    <div>Waves: <span id="waves"></span></div>
  </div>
  <div class="add-buttons">
    <a class="add-button" title="Space Junk" data-
type="SpaceJunk">J</a>
    <a class="add-button" title="Satellite" data-
type="Satellite">S</a>
    <a class="add-button" title="Satellite+" data-
type="Satellite2">S+</a>
    <a class="add-button" title="Castle" data-type="Castle">C</a>
    <a class="add-button" title="Castle+" data-type="Castle2">C+</
a>
  </div>
</section>
...
```

2. We will separate our game code into different files in this project for each script file, and we will need to include them in the HTML file:

```
...
<script src="vendors/easeljs-0.7.1.min.js"></script>
<script src="vendors/tweenjs-0.5.1.min.js"></script>
<script src="vendors/movieclip-0.7.1.min.js"></script>
<script src="scripts/assets.js"></script>
<script src="scripts/hud.js"></script>
<script src="scripts/board.js"></script>
<script src="scripts/game.js"></script>

...
```

3. Then, we define the styles that lay out the user interface of the game. Let's put them in the `game.css` file:

```css
#game {
  position: relative;
  width: 640px;
  height: 1000px;
}

#canvas {
  position: absolute;
  background-color: #ddd;
}

#hud {
  position: absolute;
  width: 100%;
  height: 60px;
  background: rgba(0, 0, 0, 0.5);
  color: white;
}

.add-buttons {
  position: absolute;
  width: 100%;
  height: 60px;
  bottom: 0;
  background: rgba(0, 0, 0, 0.5);
}

.add-button {
  display: inline-block;
  width: 50px;
  height: 50px;
  background-color: rgba(255, 255, 255, 0.3);
  color: white;
  text-decoration: none;
  text-align: center;
  line-height: 50px;
  cursor: pointer;
}
.add-button:hover {
  background-color: rgba(255, 255, 255, 0.6);
}
```

4. Next, we work on the game.js file. It acts as a major manager between the components:

```
var game = this.game || (this.game={});
var createjs = createjs || {};

;(function(game, cjs){

  game.start = function() {
    cjs.EventDispatcher.initialize(game); // allow the game object
to listen and dispatch custom events.

    game.canvas = document.getElementById('canvas');

    game.stage = new cjs.Stage(game.canvas);

    // game parameters
    game.lives = 20;
    game.energies = 120; // used to create building

    // layers
    var bgLayer = game.bgLayer = new cjs.Container();
    bgLayer.addChild(new lib.Background);
    game.stage.addChild(bgLayer);

    var boardLayer = game.boardLayer = new game.Board();
    game.stage.addChild(boardLayer);

    var effectLayer = game.effectLayer = new cjs.Container();
    game.stage.addChild(effectLayer);

    cjs.Ticker.setFPS(40);
    cjs.Ticker.addEventListener('tick', game.stage); // add game.
stage to ticker make the stage.update call automatically.
    cjs.Ticker.addEventListener('tick', game.tick); // gameloop
  };

  game.tick = function(){
    if (cjs.Ticker.getPaused()) { return; } // run when not paused
  };

  game.start();

}).call(this, game, createjs);
```

5. Then, we work on the most important file of this project, the `board.js` file. It provides logic about the grid on the board:

```
var game = this.game || (this.game={});
var createjs = createjs || {};
var lib = lib || {};

;(function(game, cjs, lib){
  function Board(){
    cjs.Container.call(this); // super

    this.x = 10;
    this.y = 60;

    // grid parameters
    this.rows = 10;
    this.cols = 7;
    this.tileWidth = 87;
    this.tileHeight = 83;

    // bg graphics
    var sprite = new lib.Board();
    this.addChild(sprite);
    sprite.y = this.tileHeight;

  }
  Board.prototype = Object.create(cjs.Container.prototype);

  game.Board = Board;

}).call(this, game, createjs, lib);
```

6. Next, we work on the `hud.js` file that refreshes the head-up display with the latest game parameters:

```
var game = this.game || (this.game={});
var createjs = createjs || {};

;(function(game, cjs){

  var addButtons = document.querySelectorAll('.add-button');
```

```
    // indicatiors
    var lives = document.getElementById('lives');
    var energies = document.getElementById('energies');
    var waves = document.getElementById('waves');

    for(var i=0, len=addButtons.length; i<len; i++) {
      var button = addButtons[i];
      button.onmousedown = function(e) {
        if (cjs.Ticker.getPaused()) { return; }
        var buildingType = this.dataset.type;

        // have enough energy
        var cost = game[buildingType].cost;
        if (cost && game.energies >= cost) {
          game.energies -= cost;
          var event = new cjs.Event('readyToPlaceBuilding');
          event.buildingType = buildingType;
          game.dispatchEvent(event);
        }
      }
    }

    function tick() {
      lives.textContent = game.lives;
      energies.textContent = game.energies;
      waves.textContent = 1;
    }

    cjs.Ticker.addEventListener('tick', tick);

}).call(this, game, createjs);
```

Objective complete – mini debriefing

We use the following three layers for our display objects:

- bgLayer
- boardLayer
- effectLayer

The background layer only contains the background image. Later, when we extend the game with different scenarios, we can work on this layer to show the different graphical themes or even play the animation inside this layer.

The effect layer is used for the display objects that we need to ensure are on top of any board objects. For example, we will show bullets and clickable energy bubbles in this layer. As we don't want the clickable objects to hide behind other objects, we put them on this top layer.

The major layer we focus on is the board layer. All the enemy movement and the player-building logic happen inside this board layer.

The head-up display

We show three game parameters in the **head-up display** (**HUD**), which are listed as follows:

- Energy (equivalent to coins)
- Lives
- Current waves (level)

A hud.js file is dedicated to the logic of displaying the game parameters to the players. On every tick, it refreshes the data and updates the HTML content.

Classified intel

We added the game stage to Ticker. For every child (and their children) on the stage, Ticker will call the tick method of the child display object if the tick method exists. This is handy as we don't need to add the tick listener to Ticker every time. The HUD object, however, is a literal JavaScript object. This is why we need to add the HUD object as a Ticker listener to get the tick.

The role of Adobe Flash when creating assets

Adobe Flash has shifted to parts of the graphics creation workflow. By making use of the benefits of the animation tool, we can easily create a game animation in Flash. With the latest exporting tool, we can even export the animation into JavaScript assets that we can use in the HTML5 canvas.

Every symbol in the Adobe Flash library is exported to the JavaScript file. When we reference them in JavaScript, we use the symbol name. The name is either the linkage **ActionScript** class name or the library name defined in the Adobe Flash environment. The following screenshot shows the graphics created as Flash symbols inside the library panel, with the symbol name properly created:

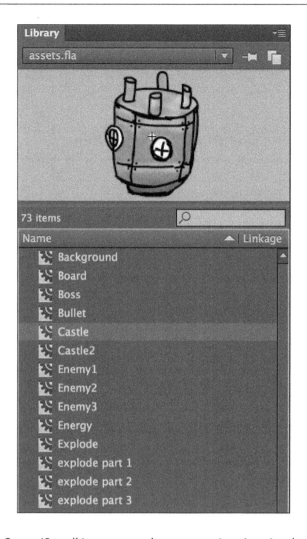

We used the latest CreateJS toolkit to export the vector animation. An alternative exporting option in Flash would be the generation of a spritesheet that was introduced by Flash CS6.

The CreateJS toolkit was introduced in Flash CS6. In the early CC Version, it was one of the commands. In the latest 2013 December update, this toolkit was integrated into the publish workflow. So, you may find it at different places according to the versions. However, they are the same tools that export the animation into a CreateJS-friendly format. Check Adobe's article on using the CreateJS toolkit at `http://www.adobe.com/devnet/createjs/articles/using-flash-pro-toolkit-createjs.html`.

If Adobe Flash is not a part of your workflow, the spritesheet animation or the tween-based animation, which we have discussed in earlier projects, still apply.

For generated graphics, you can get the `assets.js` file and the graphics from the code bundle.

Separating the JavaScript files into modules

At the time of development, the code is more maintainable when separated into files. Each file takes one role. That's why, in this project, we will separate the JavaScript files. The logic is a lot simpler when the code is separated this way.

In production, loading one file is much faster than loading several separated JavaScript files. So, in production, we usually concatenate all the script files back into one JavaScript file.

 To know the reason behind this, please check the Yahoo! Developer Network for the *Minimize HTTP Requests* section at `http://developer.yahoo.com/performance/rules.html`.

There are several approaches through which we can merge the files into one production JavaScript file; some of these are mentioned in the following bullet list:

- We can use the terminal cat approach. In Linux or Mac, we can write a shell script that concatenates all the files inside the project's `scripts` folder.

- We can use a shell-based tool that processes the project's assets. **Grunt** and **Gulp** are some of the shell-based tools that you can use. You can specify how the assets' processes work. For example, we can concatenate all the JavaScripts into one file and compass it.

- We can use GUI assets' processor applications such as **Codekit** or **LiveReload**. With GUI, it is easy to manage how files are merged using simple drags and clicks. The following screenshot shows the configuration of how the `game.js` file prepends all the other files during processing:

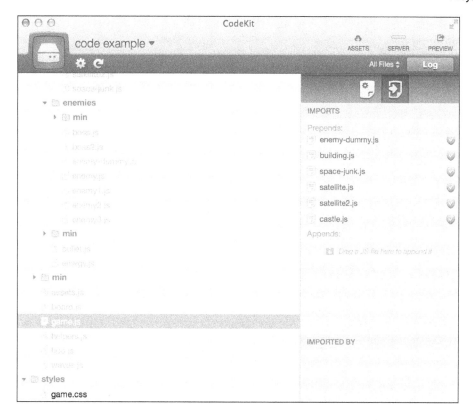

Placing the defense buildings

In this task, we work on the board and allow the player to add buildings.

Prepare for lift off

We are going to need some new files, the helpers and buildings. Specifically, they are `helpers.js`, `building.js`, `space-junk.js`, `satellite.js`, `satellite2.js`, `castle.js`, and `castle2.js`. Create these files and include them into the HTML file. Also, note that the buildings are placed inside the `scripts/board-objects/buildings/` folder:

```
<script src="scripts/helpers.js"></script>
<script src="scripts/board-objects/buildings/building.js"></script>
<script src="scripts/board-objects/buildings/space-junk.js"></script>
<script src="scripts/board-objects/buildings/satellite.js"></script>
<script src="scripts/board-objects/buildings/satellite2.js"></script>
<script src="scripts/board-objects/buildings/castle.js"></script>
<script src="scripts/board-objects/buildings/castle2.js"></script>
```

The first helper that we will add is exactly the same as `create2DArray` that we coded in the previous project:

```
game.helper = game.helper || {};
game.helper.create2DArray = function(rows, cols, initialValue) {
  var array = [];
  for(var i=0; i<rows; i++) {
    array[i] = [];
    for (var j=0; j<cols; j++) {
      array[i][j] = initialValue;
    }
  }
  return array;
};
```

Engage thrusters

In the following steps, we will allow the player to place a building on the board grid:

1. First, let's create a base for the building definition in the `building.js` file. Every type of building is built on top of this logic:

```
var game = this.game || (this.game={});
var createjs = createjs || {};
var lib = lib || {};

// The base of Building definition.
;(function(game, cjs, lib){
  function Building(){
    cjs.Container.call(this);


  }
  Building.prototype = Object.create(cjs.Container.prototype);

  Building.cost = 10; // energy cost
  game.Building = Building;
}).call(this, game, createjs, lib);
```

2. Take the `satellite.js` file as an example. It extends the building base with its own graphics and health points. **Health point (HP)** is useful when buildings take damage from the enemy's attack. Also, each type of building has a different cost:

```
var game = this.game || (this.game={});
var createjs = createjs || {};
var lib = lib || {};
```

```
// Satellite generates energy bubble
;(function(game, cjs, lib){

   function Satellite(){
     game.Building.call(this);

     // graphics
     this.addChild(new lib.Satellite());
     this.cache(-50, -50, 100, 100);

     // override
     this.hp = 150;

   }
   Satellite.prototype = Object.create(game.Building.prototype);

   Satellite.cost = 30;
   game.Satellite = Satellite;

}).call(this, game, createjs, lib);
```

We have five types of buildings: satellite, satellite level 2, castle, castle level 2, and space-junk. We show only the `satellite.js` implementation here.

In the later tasks, we will assign a special logic to the satellites and castles, but for now, these building implementations are almost the same. The differences are mainly in the build cost and the graphics assets.

3. In the `board.js` file, we add the logic for buildings. There is a selection graphic and a 2D map that stores the reference of the building. It also handles the events to add the building:

```
function Board(){
  // existing code
  ...
  // Selection graphic
  this.selection = new lib.Selection();
  this.addChild(this.selection);
  this.selection.visible = false;

  // by default, we are not adding building
  this.isAddingBuilding = false;
```

```
  // list of buildings
  this.buildingMap = game.helper.create2DArray(this.cols, this.
rows);

  // event handling
  game.on('readyToPlaceBuilding', this.readyToPlaceBuilding.
bind(this));

  // mouse interaction
  game.stage.on('stagemousemove', this.onMouseMove.bind(this));
  game.stage.on('stagemouseup', this.onClick.bind(this));
}
```

4. The following two utility methods help in translating the screen coordinate into the board-grid coordinate:

```
// utilities
Board.prototype.screenToRowCol = function(x, y) {
  var col = Math.floor(x / this.tileWidth);
  var row = Math.floor(y / this.tileHeight);
  return {col:col, row:row};
};
Board.prototype.rowColToScreen = function(row, col) {
  var x = this.tileWidth * (col + 0.5); // +0.5 for tile center
  var y = this.tileHeight * (row + 0.5);
  return {x:x, y:y};
};
```

5. We have the following function to add a specific type of building on a given grid coordinate:

```
// Summon new piece on board
  Board.prototype.addBuildingAtTile = function(buildingClass, col,
row) {
  var sprite = new game[buildingClass]();
  this.addChild(sprite);

  var pos = this.rowColToScreen(row, col);
  sprite.x = pos.x;
  sprite.y = pos.y;

  // store row/col for easy access later
  sprite.row = row;
  sprite.col = col;

  this.buildingMap[col][row] = sprite;
};
```

6. The flow related to choosing the building starts from HUD. The selection of a building triggers the `readyToPlaceBuilding` event. The `Board` object captures this event and toggles the `isAddingBuilding` state:

```
// Event Handlings
Board.prototype.readyToPlaceBuilding = function(e) {
  this.upcomingBuildingType = e.buildingType;
  this.isAddingBuilding = true;
};
```

7. When the mouse moves on the board during the state of adding a building, we show the selector on the tile where the cursor is pointing to:

```
Board.prototype.onMouseMove = function(e) {
  if (!this.isAddingBuilding){ return; }

  var pos = this.globalToLocal(e.stageX, e.stageY);
  // convert to tile row and col
  var rowCol = this.screenToRowCol(pos.x, pos.y);
  var pos = this.rowColToScreen(rowCol.row, rowCol.col);

  this.selection.visible = true;

  // finally set the position
  this.selection.x = pos.x;
  this.selection.y = pos.y;
};
```

8. When we perform a mouse click on the board, we determine which tile it is and place a building on that tile:

```
Board.prototype.onClick = function(e) {
  if (!this.isAddingBuilding){ return; }

  //coordinate conversion
  var pos = this.globalToLocal(e.stageX, e.stageY);
  var rowCol = this.screenToRowCol(pos.x, pos.y);
  var row = rowCol.row;
  var col = rowCol.col;

  // check out of bound
  if (row < 0 || row >= this.rows || col < 0 || col >= this.cols)
{ return; }

  if (this.buildingMap[col][row] === undefined) {
    this.addBuildingAtTile(this.upcomingBuildingType, col, row);
```

```
        this.isAddingBuilding = false;
        this.selection.visible = false;
    }
}
```

9. To test the building function, we will temporarily adjust the default energies to a higher value. Change the following code in the game.js file:

```
game.energies = 99999;
```

Objective complete – mini debriefing

There are two coordinate systems in the game: the original screen coordinate and the grid coordinate on the board.

By having a 2D array that stores the building reference, we can easily access the building by rows and columns. We can also easily determine whether a given row and col is empty or not.

There are several types of buildings available, as mentioned:

▶ Space junk has no special features. It's only use will be to block the enemies from moving.

▶ The satellite is very important because it generates energy bubbles that the player needs to collect. Players can create more buildings only by collecting these bubbles.

▶ The castle shoots bullets to attack the enemies. That's our key attacking unit.

You will find that we have a nice balance of building types. We have the space junk, which is the defense unit. We also have the economy unit and the attacking unit.

During the game, players need to plan their strategies on setting the order of the buildings in order to win the game. They also need to decide how many units they need to build for each type of building to maintain the balance between the economy and attack mechanisms. There aren't enough resources to build whatever they want because the enemies will reach very soon.

Classified intel

The mouse's interaction is similar to the techniques we used in the last project. The difference is that in the last project, we converted the screen coordinates into 2.5D isometric coordinates. In this project, the target conversion is still a 2D grid coordinate system.

Summoning the enemies

In this task, we spawn enemies on the board.

Prepare for lift off

We create one file for each type of enemy. They are enemy.js, enemy-dummy.js, enemy1.js, enemy2.js, enemy3.js, and boss.js. Let's create these files and put them inside the scripts/board-objects/enemies/ folder. Then, we include them in the game's HTML. The base enemy.js file comes first because all the other enemy types are based on enemy.js and need its reference:

```html
<script src="scripts/board-objects/enemies/enemy.js"></script>
<script src="scripts/board-objects/enemies/enemy-dummy.js"></script>
<script src="scripts/board-objects/enemies/enemy1.js"></script>
<script src="scripts/board-objects/enemies/enemy2.js"></script>
<script src="scripts/board-objects/enemies/enemy3.js"></script>
<script src="scripts/board-objects/enemies/boss.js"></script>
```

We need one more helper function. The removeItem function finds the given target in the given array and removes it:

```javascript
// remove an item from an array.
game.helper.removeItem = function(array, target) {
  for(var i=0, len=array.length; i<len; i++) {
    if (array[i] === target) {
      array.splice(i, 1); // remove that target
      return true;
    }
  }
  return false;
};
```

 If you are looking for more functions to manipulate arrays, Lo-dash is a good choice to check out (http://lodash.com).

Engage thrusters

With the following steps, we create enemies, make them live on the board, and slowly move them down to the earth:

1. First, we define the base of the `Enemy` class. Put the following code in the `enemy.js` file. A base enemy moves down at a regular speed:

```
// Enemy moves down and attacks buildings
;(function(game, cjs, lib){
  function Enemy(){
    cjs.Container.call(this);

    // these are default values. They can be overriden by
instances.
    this.originalSpeed = 0.5; // speed may change over time. This
one remains constant.
    this.deceleration = 0.004;
    this.hp = 10;
    this.damageDeal = 10;
    this.attackSpeed = 100; // smaller means faster

    // properties
    this.speed = this.originalSpeed;

    this.on('tick', this.tick);
  }
  Enemy.prototype = Object.create(cjs.Container.prototype);
  Enemy.prototype.tick = function() {
    if (cjs.Ticker.getPaused()) { return; }

    // check if speed <0. Min allowed is 0.
    if (this.speed < 0) { this.speed = 0;}
    this.y += this.speed;
  };
  game.Enemy = Enemy;
}).call(this, game, createjs, lib);
```

2. Based on the `Enemy` class, we can define a new type of enemy. For example, it is very easy to kill the following new enemy. It moves slower and has very low health points:

```
// An easy-to-kill enemy
;(function(game, cjs, lib){
  function EnemyDummy(){
```

```
      game.Enemy.call(this);
      this.addChild(new lib.Enemy1);

      this.originalSpeed = 0.3;
      this.deceleration = 0.002;
      this.hp = 1;

      this.speed = this.originalSpeed;
    }
    EnemyDummy.prototype = Object.create(game.Enemy.prototype);

    game.EnemyDummy = EnemyDummy;

}).call(this, game, createjs, lib);
```

3. In contrast, the following `Boss` enemy is a tougher enemy that attacks faster than usual and comes with more HPs. Alternatively, we can design many types of enemies, but we will show only two examples here:

```
;(function(game, cjs, lib){
    function Boss(){
      game.Enemy.call(this);

      this.addChild(new lib.Boss);

      this.originalSpeed = 0.2;
      this.deceleration = 0.002;
      this.hp = 300;
      this.attackSpeed = 50;

      this.speed = this.originalSpeed;
    }
    Boss.prototype = Object.create(game.Enemy.prototype);

    game.Boss = Boss;

}).call(this, game, createjs, lib);
```

4. Let's move to the `board.js` file. We define a 2D array and a list in the `Board` constructor function and use these to keep track of the reference of the summoned enemies:

```
this.enemyMap = game.helper.create2DArray(this.cols, this.rows);
this.enemyList = [];
```

5. We need to give the board an interval loop. Put the following `tick` event listener before the end of the `Board` constructor function:

```
this.on('tick', this.tick);
```

6. We need a `tick` method in the `board` object to keep updating the logic. The first thing we loop will assign the grid coordinate (row and column) to each sprite and also update the 2D array to map the enemy:

```
// Tick Loop
Board.prototype.tick = function() {
  if (cjs.Ticker.getPaused()) { return; }

  // update the row/col for each enemy on the board
  this.enemyMap = game.helper.create2DArray(this.cols, this.rows);
  for (var i=0, len=this.enemyList.length; i<len; i++) {
    var enemy = this.enemyList[i];
    var rowCol = this.screenToRowCol(enemy.x, enemy.y);

    // update both map and enemy's row/col
    this.enemyMap[rowCol.col][rowCol.row] = enemy;
    enemy.col = rowCol.col;
    enemy.row = rowCol.row;
  }

  // check succeed enemies
  // succeed enemies means it goes through the bottom area.
  for(var i=0, len=this.enemyMap.length; i<len; i++) {
    if (this.enemyMap[i][this.rows] !== undefined) { // found
enemy at the last row
      var enemy = this.enemyMap[i][this.rows];
      game.lives -= 1;
      game.helper.removeItem(this.enemyList, enemy);
      enemy.parent.removeChild(enemy);
    }
  }
};
```

7. The `Board` class manages the enemies. We add the following method to allow other objects to add a new enemy through the `board` object:

```
Board.prototype.addEnemy = function(enemyClass) {
  var sprite = new game[enemyClass]();
  this.addChild(sprite);

  var col = Math.floor(Math.random()*this.cols);// random col
```

```
    var pos = this.rowColToScreen(0, col);
    sprite.x = pos.x;
    sprite.y = pos.y;

    // store row/col for easy access later
    sprite.row = 0;
    sprite.col = col;

    this.enemyList.push(sprite);
};
```

8. In order to test the enemies, we manually call the `addEnemy` function in the `game.
   js` file. In a later task, we will use a level controller to control the summoning of
   the enemy:

```
// temporary code
game.boardLayer.addEnemy('EnemyDummy');
game.boardLayer.addEnemy('Boss');
// end temporary code
```

9. In order to end the game for debugging, we temporarily decrease the default lives
   to be less than or equal to the enemies that we have added temporarily:

```
game.lives = 2;
```

Now, we should get the enemy moving down the board.

Objective complete – mini debriefing

We defined a base enemy class. Then, we extended this base to create a wide range of
enemies with different graphics and characteristics. By having a base definition, we can
easily create a new type of enemy with different properties without copying and pasting
all the common logic everywhere.

For example, in the sample game, we created four levels of enemies and two bosses.
Their different movement speeds and HPs create a large combination of difficulties.

Enemies that reach the earth

Each game starts with 20 lives. We reduce the lives for each enemy that passes the bottom line
and reaches the earth. We know that the enemy succeeds when it moves beyond the last row.

Classified intel

The board references the enemies in two places. We have an array to store all the enemies, and we have a 2D array to store where we have enemies on the grid.

We will use the list to check the collision between enemies and buildings. On the other hand, we use the 2D map to detect the collision between bullets and the enemies.

We maintain a 2D map so that we can quickly know how the game objects are distributed on the map without looping all the enemies. This is particularly handy when we are working on a grid-based logic. For example, we may want to know whether the tile selection for a new building hits any enemy. Alternatively, we may alert the player when any enemy is reaching the earth.

We are going to discuss this more after we work on attacking mechanisms and bullets in later tasks.

Generating energy

We need energy to build the buildings. In this task, we generate energy for each satellite built on the board.

Prepare for lift off

Before we start this task, we need to revert the game parameters that we temporarily changed in the previous section. In the game.js file, we set the initial lives to 20 and the energies to 120:

```
game.lives = 20;
game.energies = 120;
```

We have the new display object, an energy bubble, which can be collected when it is generated by satellites. Add the energy.js file to the board-objects folder and include it into the HTML:

```
<script src="scripts/board-objects/energy.js"></script>
```

Project 6

Engage thrusters

Let's work on energy generation:

1. The graphics are defined in the `assets.js` file, but we will add more logic to the sprite with the `energy.js` file:

```
;(function(game, cjs, lib){
  function Energy(x, y) {
    cjs.Container.call(this); //super
    this.addChild(new lib.Energy());

    this.cache(-25, -25, 50, 50); // cache the bitmap to improve
performance.

    this.x = x || 0;
    this.y = y || 0;
    this.baseX = this.x; // store the original X

    // Tween animation
    cjs.Tween.get(this, {loop: true}).to({scaleX:1.2, scaleY:1.2},
600).to({scaleX:1.0, scaleY:1.0}, 600);

    // tick the movement
    this.on('tick', this.tick);
    this.on('mousedown', this.onclick);
  }
  Energy.prototype = Object.create(cjs.Container.prototype);
  Energy.prototype.tick = function(){
    if (cjs.Ticker.getPaused()) { return; }

    var offsetX = Math.sin(cjs.Ticker.getTicks()/10) * 20;
    this.x = this.baseX + offsetX;
    this.y -= .5;
  };
  Energy.prototype.onclick = function(e){
    game.energies += 100;
    this.parent.removeChild(this);
  };

  game.Energy = Energy;
}).call(this, game, createjs, lib);
```

227

2. The energy entity is ready. We use it in the `satellite.js` file. We add the following frequent controls and a `tick` interval to the `Satellite` constructor:

```
function Satellite(){

  ...
  // existing code

  this.energyFrequency = 500;
  this.ticks = 0;
  this.on('tick', this.tick);
}
```

3. On each `tick` of `Satellite`, we check whether it is a good time to generate new energy based on the frequency:

```
Satellite.prototype.tick = function() {
  if (cjs.Ticker.getPaused()) { return; }

  this.ticks += 1;
  // summon energy
  if (this.ticks % this.energyFrequency === 0) {
    this.summonEnergy();
  }
};
```

4. Then, we create the `summonEnergy` method to actually visualize the energy bubble into the stage:

```
Satellite.prototype.summonEnergy = function() {
  var pos = this.localToLocal(0, 0, game.effectLayer);
  var energy = new game.Energy(pos.x, pos.y);
  game.effectLayer.addChild(energy);
};
```

5. To illustrate how we can create more levels of the same type of building, we create a second level of satellite based on the first level. It generates energy at a higher frequency. Also, make sure we charge more energy for premium buildings:

```
this.energyFrequency = 100;
```

Try building a satellite on the board. After a while, it generates an energy bubble that is clickable, as shown the following screenshot:

Objective complete – mini debriefing

We created an energy bubble and generated it from the satellite building. Each energy bubble adds 100 energy points to the player when it is clicked. Energy acts as the currency in the game. Players use energy to buy new buildings.

The mouse-clicking mechanism forces players to pay attention to the bubbles and economy instead of putting all the focus on building the attacking units. This helps us make the game more balanced when we build the level later.

The frequency of the generation of energy is based on a variable inside the `satellite` definition. The first level generates the bubble slower, and the higher level generates the bubble much faster.

Classified intel

Instead of simply moving the bubble up in a straight line, we move it more like a bubble by swinging it to the left and right. This can be done with a base *x* position plus an offset via the sine function.

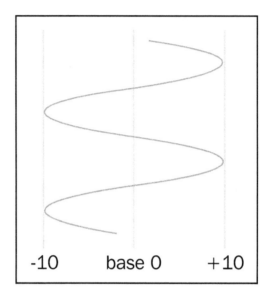

-10   base 0   +10

We further make the bubble not so boring by having it scale up and down continually. This is a looping tween animation:

```
cjs.Tween.get(this, {loop: true})
.to({scaleX:1.2, scaleY:1.2}, 600)
.to({scaleX:1.0, scaleY:1.0}, 600);
```

By having these two animations added to the bubble, we not only make it less boring, but also make it harder to click. This adds fun to the game especially when there are massive enemies coming and the player is running out of energy.

Enemies attacking the buildings

In this task, we allow the enemy to stop and attack the buildings that block their way.

Prepare for lift off

The explode animation is made up of three graphics. We may use the bundled `assets.js` file for this, or we may use the following spritesheet image if we do not have access to Adobe Flash's assets features:

Engage thrusters

Let's code the interactions between the enemies and buildings:

1. We add the following damage logic to the building's base file:

```
// The base of Building definition.
;(function(game, cjs, lib){
  function Building(){
    cjs.Container.call(this);
```

```
      // properties that need to be overridden
      this.hp = 100;
      this.shield = 0;
      this.damageDeal = 0;
      this.attackSpeed = 9999; // smaller means faster
   }
   Building.prototype = Object.create(cjs.Container.prototype);
   Building.prototype.damage = function(damage) {
      var realDamage = Math.max(damage - this.shield, 0); // min 0.
      this.hp -= realDamage;
      if (this.hp <= 0 && this.parent) { // a building may have been
destroyed by more than one enemies and result in no parent.
         this.parent.removeBuilding(this);
      }
   };

   Building.cost = 10; // consume energies
   game.Building = Building;
}).call(this, game, createjs, lib);
```

2. Once the enemy attacks a building, we should be able to remove the building from the board:

```
Board.prototype.removeBuilding = function(building) {
   this.buildingMap[building.col][building.row] = undefined;
   this.removeChild(building);
};
```

3. Inside the `tick` function, we add logic for the duration in which the enemy is in contact with the buildings:

```
// check enemy contacts buildings
for (var i=this.enemyList.length-1; i>=0; i--) {
  var enemy = this.enemyList[i];
  var row = enemy.row;
  var col = enemy.col;

  //contact building
  var target = undefined;
  if (this.buildingMap[col][row] !== undefined) { // current tile
    target = this.buildingMap[col][row];
  }else if (this.buildingMap[col][row+1] !== undefined) { // next
tile
    target = this.buildingMap[col][row+1];
  }
  // has target
```

```
    if (target !== undefined) {
      enemy.speed -= enemy.deceleration;
      enemy.startAttack(target);
    } else {
      enemy.stopAttack();
    }
  }
}
```

4. In the construction function of the `Enemy` class, we add the following properties about the attack:

```
// attack
this.isAttacking = false;
this.attackingTarget = undefined;

this.attackingSmoke = new lib.Explode();
this.attackingSmoke.y = 50;
```

5. We also add the `tick` function that controls the attack on the target:

```
Enemy.prototype.tick = function() {

  ...

  // existing code

  // attack the building every once a while
  if (cjs.Ticker.getTicks() % this.attackSpeed === 0) {
    if (this.isAttacking && this.attackingTarget) {
      this.attackingTarget.damage(this.damageDeal);
    }
  }
};
```

6. We define the following `startAttack` method to attack the building that's in front of the enemy. Whenever we launch an attack, we reassign the target building to make sure it is the correct one:

```
// Attack and damage
Enemy.prototype.startAttack = function(targetBuilding) {
  if (!this.isAttacking) {
    this.isAttacking = true;
    this.addChild(this.attackingSmoke);
  }
  this.attackingTarget = targetBuilding; //reassign target
};
```

7. After the target building is destroyed, the enemy stops the attack. Add the following `stopAttack` method that removes the smoke animation and resets the variables:

```
Enemy.prototype.stopAttack = function() {
  if (this.isAttacking) {
    this.removeChild(this.attackingSmoke);
  }
  this.isAttacking = false;
  this.attackingTarget = undefined;
  this.speed = this.originalSpeed;
};
```

8. The enemy will take damage when we create bullets later. We can define a damage method that takes the damage:

```
Enemy.prototype.damage = function(damage) {
  this.hp -= damage;
};
```

The following screenshot shows that the enemy is attacking the satellite; it shows the attacking smoke as well:

Objective complete – mini debriefing

Each enemy has a child sprite named `attackingSmoke`. We show it when the enemy is attacking, and we hide it when it's not.

Designing the movement of the enemy

We take benefit from storing the building data inside a 2D array. While looping through all the enemies for movement, we can easily know whether there is any building that blocks the way.

When the enemy meets the building, it slows down and stops in front of it.

When the enemy moves very fast, there is chance that the enemy goes through the building before slowing down fully. This lets the enemy look more realistic.

Enemies stop in front of the buildings. When there exists a building in their current tile or the next tile, we stop the movement of the enemy. This happens to all the enemies, so we loop the enemy list and check against the building's 2D map for the collision.

Classified intel

The smoke animation is a tween-based animation done in Flash, as shown in the following screenshot:

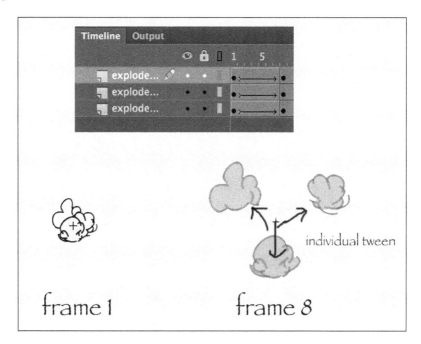

By exporting the graphics using the CreateJS canvas toolkit, we can easily use it in our game with a simple new call, which is shown as follows:

```
var animation = new lib.Explode();
```

When we take a deeper look at the generated code, we find that Adobe Flash has a variety of exporting options. If it is a classic tween animation, Flash exports it to the TweenJS code. If the program fails to transform the animation into TweenJS, Flash generates the animation into a spritesheet and uses the `Sprite` and `MovieClip` timeline code in CreateJS.

Caching graphics inside the assets file

If the exported animation makes use of TweenJS, we can cache the individual graphics inside the animation.

Note that we need to cache individual components because caching the entire animation will stop it from playing. Cached graphics are prerendered as bitmaps inside the EaselJS library. This means that cached graphics act like a bitmap that cannot be changed or animated. That's why we cannot cache the entire `Explode` sprite. It contains three tween animations on each smoke graphic. What we need to do is cache the individual smoke graphics as bitmaps. It works because the cached bitmaps are added to the tween animation. The order is important. We cache the graphics and then animate them with TweenJS, not the reverse of this order, which is shown as follows:

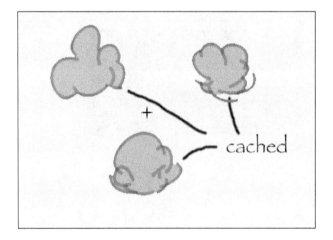

Firing bullets and attacking the enemies

A castle can fire bullets to kill enemies. In this task, we add bullets to the game with enemy-contacting detection.

Prepare for lift off

As usual, we put new things into a dedicated file. We should have an empty `bullet.js` file ready in the project directory:

```
<script src="scripts/board-objects/bullet.js"></script>
```

Engage thrusters

Let's follow the given steps to be able to fire bullets and attack the enemies:

1. Define the `Bullet` class in the `bullet.js` file. It contains the bullet graphics and a default `damageDeal` property with a set value. However, the `Castle` implementation can override this value. It also moves up at a constant speed:

```
// Bullet
;(function(game, cjs, lib){
  function Bullet(damageDeal) {
    cjs.Container.call(this); //super
    this.addChild(new lib.Bullet());

    this.cache(-25, -25, 50, 50);

    this.damageDeal = damageDeal || 1; // default 1

    // tick the movement
    this.on('tick', this.tick);
  }
  Bullet.prototype = Object.create(cjs.Container.prototype);
  Bullet.prototype.tick = function(){
    if (cjs.Ticker.getPaused()) { return; }

    // movement
    this.y -= 1.5;
  };

  game.Bullet = Bullet;
}).call(this, game, createjs, lib);
```

2. In the `Castle` constructor, we add the `tick` listener:

```
this.ticks = 0;
this.on('tick', this.tick);
```

3. The `tick` listener is used to summon the bullets. When the value of the `tick` listener matches the attacking frequency, `Castle` fires the bullet:

```
Castle.prototype.tick = function() {
  if (cjs.Ticker.getPaused()) { return; }

  this.ticks += 1;
  // summon bullet every once in a while
  if (this.ticks % this.attackSpeed === 0) {
    this.summonBullet();
  }
};
```

4. We simply need to put the bullet on the board:

```
Castle.prototype.summonBullet = function() {
  var bullet = new game.Bullet(this.damageDeal);
  bullet.x = this.x + Math.random()*20 - 10;
  bullet.y = this.y;
  this.parent.addBullet(bullet);
};
```

5. The `Castle` class triggers the bullet creation logic, but we manage it with the board object. This makes sense because board is the container of all the game objects. Let's move to the `board.js` file. We maintain a list of all the bullets with `bulletList`. Add the following declaration to the `Board` class constructor:

```
// bullet list for centralized collision detection
this.bulletList = [];
```

6. Then, we need a method for the castle to pass the bullet reference to the board. With this reference, we add the bullet into `effectLayer` and the array:

```
Board.prototype.addBullet = function(bullet){
  game.effectLayer.addChild(bullet);
  this.bulletList.push(bullet);
};
```

7. In the board's tick, we check whether the bullets hit the enemy. The hit is based on the grid coordinate:

```
// check bullet collision
// loop from top because we remove item inside loop
```

```
for (var i=this.enemyList.length-1; i>=0; i--) {
  // loop all bullets
  for (var j=this.bulletList.length-1; j>=0; j--) {
    var bullet = this.bulletList[j];
    var pos = bullet.localToLocal(0, 0, this);
    var rowCol = this.screenToRowCol(pos.x, pos.y);
    if (this.enemyMap[rowCol.col][rowCol.row] !== undefined) {
      var enemy = this.enemyMap[rowCol.col][rowCol.row];

      // damage enemy
      enemy.damage(bullet.damageDeal);
      if (enemy.hp <= 0) {
        this.enemyMap[enemy.col][enemy.row] = undefined;
        game.helper.removeItem(this.enemyList, enemy);
        enemy.parent.removeChild(enemy);
      }

      // remove bullet
      game.helper.removeItem(this.bulletList, bullet);
      bullet.parent.removeChild(bullet);
    }
  }
}
```

The following screenshot shows a bullet that was fired from a castle towards an enemy unit on the board. A few seconds after this screen, the bullet will meet the enemy and deal damage to the enemy. Then, the bullet is removed from the game.

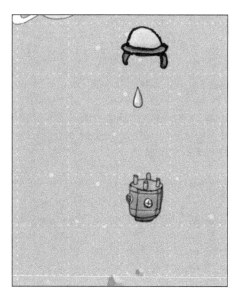

Objective complete – mini debriefing

There is a 2D array to store the enemy reference so that we can perform a grid-based logic on the enemies. We check the bullet and enemy collision based on the grid.

In this game design, we allow enemies to stack together into one tile. Because of the stacking, the 2D array may not contain all the enemy references.

The following screenshot shows two enemy units that are at the same tile. This happened because we used some buildings to delay the first enemy but didn't kill it. Then, the next enemy comes and they are stacked together. Although we allow stacking enemies into the same tile, we do not allow more than one building on each tile.

Each bullet eventually hits only one enemy. At any time, the enemy's 2D map references one and only one enemy for each tile. That's a perfect match. So, we loop the bullet list and check it against the enemy's 2D array.

Classified intel

Note that this process of checking a bullet is true until we later design a kind of bullet that explodes and deals with the area under attack. In such cases, the area under attack should deal with the damage to all the enemies within that bullet's tile. Thus, we will need some other logic for such an "area-damage" deal.

Controlling enemy waves

In this task, we add a leveling system to the game. We will use a dedicated object to manage different combinations of enemies and their spawning frequency.

Prepare for lift off

In this task, we will create a new file for controlling the enemy waves. Let's call it `waves.js` and include it in the HTML:

```
<script src="scripts/waves.js"></script>
```

Engage thrusters

Let's work on leveling:

 Note that we will show only three waves here. The three waves in the book are presented for demonstration purposes. In reality, we have much more waves that are declared. They are just different combinations with different amounts. So, we don't want to paste the whole waves' data here with duplicated content. Please check the code example for the full waves' data code.

1. First, we will work on the `waves.js` file. The `waves` object is simply a literal object because we only want one instance to manage all of the leveling:

```
// controlling waves
;(function(game, cjs){

  game.waves = {};
  game.waves.nextWave = 0;
  game.waves.isActive = false;
  game.waves.enemySummonOrders = ['EnemyDummy', 'Enemy1',
'Enemy2', 'Enemy3', 'Boss', 'Boss2'];
  game.waves.data = [
    { // wave 1
      'EnemyDummy': 1, // summon 1 EnemyDummy during wave
      frequency: 10
    },
    { // wave 2
      'EnemyDummy': 8, // summon 8 EnemyDummy, one by one
      'Enemy1'  : 5, // summon 5 Enemy1 after EnemyDummy
      'Enemy2'  : 5,
      'Boss'    : 2,
```

```
        frequency: 150 // how frequent enemy appears
      },
      { // wave 3
        'EnemyDummy' : 1,
        'Enemy1' : 1,
        'Enemy2' : 1,
        'Enemy3' : 1,
        'Boss'   : 1,
        'Boss2'  : 30,
        frequency: 50
      }
    ];
```

2. We define a `startWave` method as the wave entry point for the game object to call. It resets the game parameters:

```
game.waves.startWave = function () {
  // reset energies
  game.energies = 120;
  this.currentWave = this.data[this.nextWave];
  this.isActive = true;

  this.enemiesSummoned = 0;
};
```

3. When the wave is cleared, we start with the next wave:

```
game.waves.waveCleared = function () {
  this.nextWave += 1;

  if (this.nextWave >= this.data.length) { // bound to max waves
data
    this.nextWave = this.data.length -1;
  }
  this.startWave();
};
```

4. On each `tick`, we check the frequency to see whether it's time to spawn the next enemy:

```
game.waves.tick = function () {
  if (!this.isActive) { return; } // wait until wave started

  // time to summon new enemy
  if (cjs.Ticker.getTicks() % this.currentWave.frequency === 0)
{
```

```
        // determine next enemy type from the enemy summon order.
        var accumunateTargetCount = 0;
        for (var i=0, len=this.enemySummonOrders.length; i<len; i++)
    {
            var enemyType = this.enemySummonOrders[i];
            var targetCount = this.currentWave[enemyType] || 0; //
    default 0 if the wave did not set that enemy type.
            accumunateTargetCount += targetCount;
            if(this.enemiesSummoned < accumunateTargetCount){
              break;
            }
        }

        if(this.enemiesSummoned >= accumunateTargetCount) {
          this.isActive = false;
        } else {
          // summon the enemy
          game.boardLayer.addEnemy(enemyType);
          this.enemiesSummoned += 1;
        }
      }
    };
}).call(this, game, createjs);
```

5. That's all the code we have for the `waves.js` file. Let's go to the `game.js` file. We set up some graphics to celebrate that the current wave is cleared, and we celebrate with the player. By default, we hide this sprite with a large *x* offset:

```
// game waves
game.nextWaveSprite = new lib.WaveCleared();
game.stage.addChild(game.nextWaveSprite);
game.nextWaveSprite.x = 999;
```

6. Then, we start the next wave when the game starts:

```
game.waves.startWave();
```

7. The `game` object is in charge of spawning the enemies through the `waves` object. In the `game.tick` object, we check whether the current wave is cleared and then reset the board for the next wave:

```
game.tick = function(){
  ...
  // existing code goes here.
```

```
    // tick waves
    game.waves.tick();

    // the wave is cleared when:
    // waves not generating new enemies and all existing enemies are
killed.
    if (!game.waves.isActive &&
        game.boardLayer.areEnemiesCleared()) {

      game.boardLayer.isAddingBuilding = false;
      game.boardLayer.removeAllBuildings();
      game.boardLayer.removeAllBullets();
      game.waves.waveCleared();

      // 'Wave Cleared' graphics animation.
      cjs.Tween.get(game.nextWaveSprite)
      .to({x: game.canvas.width/2, y: game.canvas.height/2, alpha:
0}, 0)
      .to({alpha: 1.0}, 300)
      .wait(1000)
      .to({alpha: 0}, 300)
      .to({x: 999});
    }
};
```

8. Next, we need some clearing and resetting logic. In the `board.js` file, we add a method to remove all the buildings:

```
Board.prototype.removeAllBuildings = function(){
  for (var i=0; i<this.cols; i++) {
    for(var j=0; j<this.rows; j++) {
      if (this.buildingMap[i][j]) {
        this.removeBuilding(this.buildingMap[i][j]);
      }
    }
  }
};
```

9. We need to know whether all the enemies are removed to know whether the wave is cleared. We define the following method in the `Board` object:

```
// Have all existing enemies been killed?
Board.prototype.areEnemiesCleared = function(){
  return (this.enemyList.length === 0);
};
```

10. When resetting the game, we need to remove all the bullets from the effect layer. Since the `Board` object manages the bullet list, we remove the bullets from the `Board` object:

```
Board.prototype.removeAllBullets = function(){
  this.bulletList.length = 0;
  game.effectLayer.removeAllChildren();
};
```

11. Finally, we update the `HUD` object and display the next wave number in the `hud.js` file:

```
waves.textContent = game.waves.nextWave + 1; // logic
  starts at 0, our display starts at 1
```

Objective complete – mini debriefing

We have created a leveling system. We separated the game into waves. In each wave, we define how many enemies appear along with their spawning frequency.

We know that each wave is cleared after all the enemies are spawned and removed from the board. The enemies may be killed by the castle bullets, or they may pass the bottom line and get removed.

When no lives remain during the waves, the game is over.

The enemy spawn logic

At each level, we define the amount of each type of enemies that should be spawned. Then, we use a simple counting method to spawn the types in order. The order follows the `enemySummonOrders` variable. The logic compares the sum of spawned enemies and the amount of definition to know the next type of enemy to spawn. The following figure explains how we can compare the total enemies spawned using the waves' data:

Wave data	Total enemies spawned	Spawn type
10 Enemy 1	<10	Enemy 1
15 Enemy 2	<25	Enemy 2
1 Boss	<26	Boss
Stop spawning when >= 26		

Controlling the difficulty of the game

We spawn a new enemy from time to time using the `ticker` loop. We can control the difficulty by controlling the spawning frequency. The faster the enemies come, the less time the player gets to prepare, thus making the game more difficult.

The enemy types also affect the difficulty level of the game. A fast-moving enemy is usually difficult to handle because the player gets much less time to prepare for the defense. Enemies with higher HPs are difficult to handle too. When the enemy takes more time to be killed, it wastes more bullets. This means that fewer bullets reach other enemies and those enemies get more time to advance without getting hurt.

Classified intel

Let's further discuss on how our game design influences the playing strategy.

The tower defense strategy

This game is a kind of tower defense game where a player builds buildings to defend the base and defeat the enemy waves. By introducing waves, we've designed the required strategy to clear the game.

Since the time before the enemies reach the earth is limited, a player needs to find the optimal build order for his/her survival. We will use the unit **E** to represent energy in the following strategy analysis. This makes the calculation easier to read.

Each wave starts at 120E. At the beginning, a player has the following options:

- Build one satellite (30E) and one castle (80E) with the remaining 10E energy. Wait for 300 ms for the first energy and then build another satellite and castle.

- Build two satellites (60E) with the remaining 60E energy. Then, we get two energy bubbles after 300 ms, resulting in a total of 260E energy. Once this is done, we can build three castles within a second.

- Build three satellites (90E) with the remaining 30E energy. Then, we get three energy bubbles almost at once. Now, we have 330E after 300 ms. Once this is done, we can build four castles (320E).

- Build four satellites (120E) and wait for the 400E energy for half a second. Then, we can build five castles.

The ultimate goal is to kill all the enemies. Therefore, the strategy should favor the ability to build many castles in a very short duration.

Building few satellites at the beginning means way too little energy is generated every 300ms. This will result in a weak economy. The enemies don't wait and so there will not be enough energy to build castles when the massive enemies attack. In contrast, building too many satellites results in the generation of too much energy. This is a waste because the cost of building one more satellite means we delay the building of the next castle, thus dealing less damage to the enemies.

The choice of building combinations affects whether the game starts smoothly or not. The strategy even varies more in the middle of the game. Should the player build more satellites to support the economy? Should the player build just enough satellites and build as many castles as possible? Moreover, the amount of "just enough" changes from wave to wave. That's the fun part where players need to find the optimal solution for each wave.

In the previous calculation, we did not take the space junk into account. Space junk costs only five energies and is perfect to delay the enemies' movement. Having multiple satellites at the beginning provides a strong foundation for the economy, but the trade-off is having the castles come alive too late. Fast enemies may already reach the earth before we have enough castles. Therefore, making good use of space junk gives us more time to build the buildings before enemies reach the bottom line.

What's more, when the difficulty increases, the player may consider building the second level of the satellite and castle to survive the wave. The second level of the satellite costs 600E but generates energy bubbles three times faster. The second level of the castle costs 300E and deals more damage with each bullet it fires. The player needs to figure out a good time to add these premium buildings to the army. That's a tough choice because saving 600E for the satellite would mean losing the opportunity of building other buildings during that time.

This is the art of balance that we, as game designers, need to design a game carefully, and the player needs to carefully plan the playing strategy.

Loading the bitmap graphics into the game

In this task, we show the bitmap graphics by loading them into the game.

Prepare for lift off

In this task, we add the colored bitmaps and load them onto the game. These bitmaps are colored and exported from Adobe Flash.

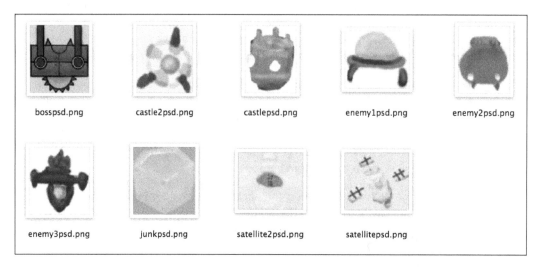

bosspsd.png	castle2psd.png	castlepsd.png	enemy1psd.png	enemy2psd.png
enemy3psd.png	junkpsd.png	satellite2psd.png	satellitepsd.png	

So, make sure we have the `PreloadJS` file ready in the `vendors` folder and in the `index.html` file:

```
<script src="vendors/preloadjs-0.4.1.min.js"></script>
```

Engage thrusters

Let's follow the given steps to load the graphics into the game:

1. In the `game.js` file, we define the `load` method:

```
game.load = function() {
  // load bitmap assets before starting the game
  var loader = new createjs.LoadQueue(false);
  loader.addEventListener("fileload", function(e){
    if (e.item.type === "image") { images[e.item.id] = e.result; }
// assign to images object for assets.js to use
  });
```

```
        loader.addEventListener("complete", game.start);
        loader.loadManifest(lib.properties.manifest);
    }
```

2. We originally have the `game.start()` function calling in the `game.js` file.
   We replace it with the following loading code:

   ```
   game.Load();
   ```

Objective complete – mini debriefing

The artwork outlined in this game is drawn in Flash in the vector format. These vector
graphics can be transformed into an EaselJS-drawing API without issues. Besides vector
outlines, coloring is done in the bitmap format too. Bitmaps cannot be converted into
graphics-drawing instructions. Instead, Flash outputs the bitmaps into JPEGs and loads
them into the sprite using EaselJS's `bitmap` class.

We added a loader to load these bitmap graphics into the game. For each loaded graphic,
we added the bitmap content to a global `images` object. This `images` object is used within
the `assets.js` file to reference the bitmap data.

Let's take a look at the `assets.js` file that is generated by the Flash CreateJS toolkit.
For this, we need to find a manifest array. Most likely, it is at the top of the file and within
a `lib.properties` object:

```
// library properties:
lib.properties = {
    width: 640,
    height: 1000,
    fps: 24,
    color: "#FFFFFF",
    manifest: [
        {src:"images/bosspsd.png", id:"bosspsd"},
        {src:"images/castlepsd.png", id:"castlepsd"},
        {src:"images/castle2psd.png", id:"castle2psd"},
        {src:"images/enemy1psd.png", id:"enemy1psd"},
        {src:"images/enemy2psd.png", id:"enemy2psd"},
        {src:"images/enemy3psd.png", id:"enemy3psd"},
        {src:"images/junkpsd.png", id:"junkpsd"},
        {src:"images/satellitepsd.png", id:"satellitepsd"},
        {src:"images/satellite2psd.png", id:"satellite2psd"}
    ]
};
```

The `LoadQueue` method from the PreloadJS library initializes a loader. The `loadManifest`
method from this loader then takes the files inside the manifest and loads the file source
one by one. The IDs are used internally within the `assets.js` file.

Instead of calling the `game.start` method at the beginning, we load bitmaps and call the `game.start` method only after all the graphics finish loading.

Classified intel

In *Project 8, Creating a Sushi Shop Game with Device Scaling*, we will explore more on using **PreloadJS** by creating a loading progress screen.

Mission accomplished

We have created a fun-to-play tower defense game. The game makes use of what we have learned in the previous projects. In this project, we learned a new way to export the graphics assets with Adobe Flash.

We discussed how the game is well designed to ensure the difficulties are balanced, which will make it fun to play.

Here is a screenshot of what we have created:

Hotshot challenges

We have completed the project. The game is fun to play, but it is just the beginning. Here are some suggestions that we can use to further improve the game.

Providing more statistics

In this kind of game that needs a strategy to play, players may be interested in game statistics. It would be nice to let a player know how much damage is done in each wave or how much energy is collected. The player would be able to explore different strategies by comparing the statistics among their gameplays.

Managing scenes

We skipped the scene management in this project to focus more on making the gameplay complete. Now it's time to add scene management. We can show a starting scene where players can start from wave one or start from the last cleared wave. In the game over scene, we may display the statistics that we discussed in the previous section, for example, how many enemies have been killed.

Adding a pause button

We are using a ticker to provide a global timer. When we pause the timer, all the tickers are paused. We can make use of this characteristic to allow game pausing and resuming. How about designing a pause scene and resume button?

Adding a keyboard shortcut

We may allow the use of keyboard shortcuts to create new buildings. Now, the player needs to keep moving the cursor up and down between the creation buttons and the grid.

We may use the keyup event to add a shortcut to create buildings, for example, using the number keys *1*, *2*, *3*, *4*, and *5* to represent the creation of junk, satellites, and castles.

Introducing an alternate currency

What if we introduce a rare currency, for example, diamonds? Players can obtain diamonds by completing waves or purchasing them with real money. The diamonds can be used to buy special bombs that cause an area attack to the enemies. This should not affect the balance of the game much because a skilled player can clean the waves without powerful bombs and the not-so-skilled players pass the wave by paying an extra cost.

Project 7

A Ball-shooting Machine with Physics Engine

In the previous project, we built a space defender game and also learned how to use vector graphics. In this project, we will still work on the canvas and CreateJS library. We will use an engine called **Box2D** to create a simulated physics world. In this world, we will create a ball-shooting game with some obstacles in the playing court. We will vector graphics from Adobe Flash and attach the graphics to the physical objects from the last project.

Mission briefing

In this project, we focus on the physics engine. We will build a basketball court where the player needs to shoot the ball in to the hoop. A player shoots the ball by keeping the mouse button pressed and releasing it. The direction is visualized by an arrow and the power is proportional to the duration of the mouse press and hold event.

There are obstacles present between the ball and the hoop. The player either avoids the obstacles or makes use of them to put the ball into the hoop. Finally, we use CreateJS to visualize the physics world into the canvas.

You may visit `http://makzan.net/html5-games/ball-shooting-machine/` to play a dummy game in order to have a better understanding of what we will be building throughout this project.

The following screenshot shows a player shooting the ball towards the hoop, with a power indicator:

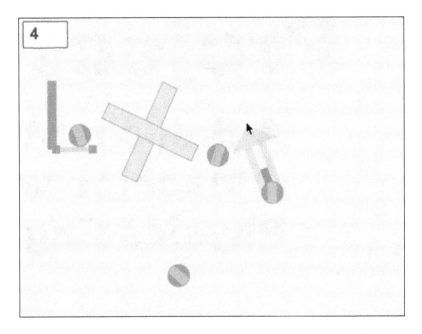

Why is it awesome?

When we build games without a physics engine, we create our own game loop and reposition each game object in every frame. For instance, if we move a character to the right, we manage the position and movement speed ourselves.

Imagine that we are coding a ball-throwing logic now. We need to keep track of several variables. We have to calculate the x and y velocity based on the time and force applied. We also need to take the gravity into account; not to mention the different angles and materials we need to consider while calculating the bounce between the two objects.

Now, let's think of a physical world. We just defined how objects interact and all the collisions that happen automatically. It is similar to a real-world game; we focus on defining the rule and the world will handle everything else. Take basketball as an example. We define the height of the hoop, size of the ball, and distance of the three-point line. Then, the players just need to throw the ball. We never worry about the flying parabola and the bouncing on the board. Our space takes care of them by using the physics laws.

This is exactly what happens in the simulated physics world; it allows us to apply the physics properties to game objects. The objects are affected by the gravity and we can apply forces to them, making them collide with each other.

With the help of the physics engine, we can focus on defining the game-play rules and the relationship between the objects. Without the need to worry about collision and movement, we can save time to explore different game plays. We then elaborate and develop the setup further, as we like, among the prototypes.

We define the position of the hoop and the ball. Then, we apply an impulse force to the ball in the *x* and *y* dimensions. The engine will handle all the things in between. Finally, we get an event trigger if the ball passes through the hoop.

It is worth noting that some blockbuster games are also made with a physics engine. This includes games such as *Angry Birds*, *Cut the Rope*, and *Where's My Water*.

Your Hotshot objectives

We will divide the project into the following eight tasks:

- ▸ Creating the simulated physics world
- ▸ Shooting a ball
- ▸ Handling collision detection
- ▸ Defining levels
- ▸ Launching a bar with power
- ▸ Adding a cross obstacle
- ▸ Visualizing graphics
- ▸ Choosing a level

Mission checklist

Similar to the previous project, we create a project folder that contains the `index.html` file and the `scripts` and `styles` folders. Inside the `scripts` folder, we create three files: `physics.js`, `view.js`, and `game.js`.

The `physics.js` file is the most important file in this project. It contains all the logic related to the physics world including creating level objects, spawning dynamic balls, applying force to the objects, and handling collision.

The `view.js` file is a helper for the view logic including the scoreboard and the ball-shooting indicator.

The `game.js` file, as usual, is the entry point of the game. It also manages the levels and coordinates between the physics world and view.

Preparing the vendor files

We also need a `vendors` folder that holds the third-party libraries. This includes the CreateJS suite—EaselJS, MovieClip, TweenJS, PreloadJS—and Box2D.

Box2D is the physics engine that we are going to use in this project. We need to download the engine code from `https://code.google.com/p/box2dweb/`. It is a port version from ActionScript to JavaScript.

We need the `Box2dWeb-2.1.a.3.min.js` file or its nonminified version for debugging. We put this file in the `vendors` folder.

Box2D is an open source physics-simulation engine that was created by Erin Catto. It was originally written in C++. Later, it was ported to ActionScript because of the popularity of Flash games, and then it was ported to JavaScript. There are different versions of ports. The one we are using is called **Box2DWeb**, which was ported from ActionScript's version Box2D 2.1. Using an old version may cause issues. Also, it will be difficult to find help online because most developers have switched to 2.1.

Creating a simulated physics world

Our first task is to create a simulated physics world and put two objects inside it.

Prepare for lift off

In the `index.html` file, the core part is the `game` section. We have two `canvas` elements in this game. The `debug-canvas` element is for the Box2D engine and `canvas` is for the CreateJS library:

```
<section id="game" class="row">
    <canvas id="debug-canvas" width="480" height="360"></canvas>
    <canvas id="canvas" width="480" height="360"></canvas>
</section>
```

We prepare a dedicated file for all the physics-related logic. We prepare the `physics.js` file with the following code:

```
;(function(game, cjs, b2d){
  // code here later
}).call(this, game, createjs, Box2D);
```

Engage thrusters

The following steps create the physics world as the foundation of the game:

1. The Box2D classes are put in different modules. We will need to reference some common classes as we go along. We use the following code to create an alias for these Box2D classes:

```
// alias
var b2Vec2 = Box2D.Common.Math.b2Vec2
, b2AABB = Box2D.Collision.b2AABB
, b2BodyDef = Box2D.Dynamics.b2BodyDef
, b2Body = Box2D.Dynamics.b2Body
, b2FixtureDef = Box2D.Dynamics.b2FixtureDef
, b2Fixture = Box2D.Dynamics.b2Fixture
, b2World = Box2D.Dynamics.b2World
, b2MassData = Box2D.Collision.Shapes.b2MassData
, b2PolygonShape = Box2D.Collision.Shapes.b2PolygonShape
, b2CircleShape = Box2D.Collision.Shapes.b2CircleShape
, b2DebugDraw = Box2D.Dynamics.b2DebugDraw
, b2MouseJointDef = Box2D.Dynamics.Joints.b2MouseJointDef
, b2RevoluteJointDef = Box2D.Dynamics.Joints.b2RevoluteJointDef
;
```

2. We prepare a variable that states how many pixels define 1 meter in the physics world. We also define a Boolean to determine if we need to draw the debug draw:

```
var pxPerMeter = 30; // 30 pixels = 1 meter. Box3D uses meters and
we use pixels.
var shouldDrawDebug = false;
```

3. All the physics methods will be put into the game.physics object. We create this literal object before we code our logics:

```
var physics = game.physics = {};
```

4. The first method in the physics object creates the world:

```
physics.createWorld = function() {
  var gravity = new b2Vec2(0, 9.8);
  this.world = new b2World(gravity, /*allow sleep= */ true);

  // create two temoporary bodies
  var bodyDef = new b2BodyDef;
  var fixDef = new b2FixtureDef;

  bodyDef.type = b2Body.b2_staticBody;
  bodyDef.position.x = 100/pxPerMeter;
```

```
      bodyDef.position.y = 100/pxPerMeter;

      fixDef.shape = new b2PolygonShape();
      fixDef.shape.SetAsBox(20/pxPerMeter, 20/pxPerMeter);

      this.world.CreateBody(bodyDef).CreateFixture(fixDef);

      bodyDef.type = b2Body.b2_dynamicBody;
      bodyDef.position.x = 200/pxPerMeter;
      bodyDef.position.y = 100/pxPerMeter;

      this.world.CreateBody(bodyDef).CreateFixture(fixDef);
      // end of temporary code
   }
```

5. The `update` method is the game loop's tick event for the physics engine.
    It calculates the world step and refreshes debug draw. The world step
    upgrades the physics world. We'll discuss it later:

```
physics.update = function() {
   this.world.Step(1/60, 10, 10);
   if (shouldDrawDebug) {
     this.world.DrawDebugData();
   }
   this.world.ClearForces();
};
```

6. Before we can refresh the debug draw, we need to set it up. We pass a canvas
    reference to the Box2D debug draw instance and configure the drawing settings:

```
physics.showDebugDraw = function() {
   shouldDrawDebug = true;

   //set up debug draw
   var debugDraw = new b2DebugDraw();
   debugDraw.SetSprite(document.getElementById("debug-canvas").
getContext("2d"));
   debugDraw.SetDrawScale(pxPerMeter);
   debugDraw.SetFillAlpha(0.3);
   debugDraw.SetLineThickness(1.0);
   debugDraw.SetFlags(b2DebugDraw.e_shapeBit | b2DebugDraw.e_
jointBit);
   this.world.SetDebugDraw(debugDraw);
};
```

7. Let's move to the `game.js` file. We define the game-starting logic that sets up the EaselJS stage and Ticker. It creates the world and sets up the debug draw. The `tick` method calls the `physics.update` method:

```
;(function(game, cjs){
  game.start = function() {
    cjs.EventDispatcher.initialize(game); // allow the game object
to listen and dispatch custom events.

    game.canvas = document.getElementById('canvas');

    game.stage = new cjs.Stage(game.canvas);

    cjs.Ticker.setFPS(60);
    cjs.Ticker.addEventListener('tick', game.stage); // add game.
stage to ticker make the stage.update call automatically.
    cjs.Ticker.addEventListener('tick', game.tick); // gameloop

    game.physics.createWorld();
    game.physics.showDebugDraw();
  };

  game.tick = function(){
    if (cjs.Ticker.getPaused()) { return; } // run when not paused

    game.physics.update();

  };

  game.start();
}).call(this, game, createjs);
```

After these steps, we should have a result as shown in the following screenshot. It is a physics world with two bodies. One body stays in position and the other one falls to the bottom.

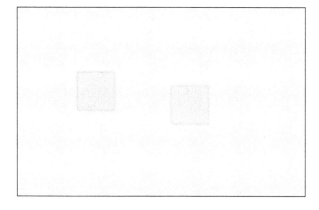

Objective complete – mini debriefing

We have defined our first physical world with one static object and one dynamic object that falls to the bottom.

A static object is an object that is not affected by gravity and any other forces. On the other hand, a dynamic object is affected by all the forces.

Defining gravity

In reality, we have gravity on every planet. It's the same in the Box2D world. We need to define gravity for the world. This is a ball-shooting game, so we will follow the rules of gravity on Earth. We use 0 for the x-axis and 9.8 for the y-axis.

It is worth noting that we do not need to use the 9.8 value. For instance, we can set a smaller gravity value to simulate other planets in space—maybe even the moon; or, we can set the gravity to zero to create a top-down view of the ice hockey game, where we apply force to the puck and benefit from the collision.

Debug draw

The physics engine focuses purely on the mathematical calculation. It doesn't care about how the world will be presented finally, but it does provide a visual method in order to make the debugging easier.

This debug draw is very useful before we use our graphics to represent the world.

We won't use the debug draw in production. Actually, we can decide how we want to visualize this physics world. So far in this book, we have learned two ways to visualize the game. The first way is by using the DOM objects and the second one is by using the canvas drawing method. We will visualize the world with our graphics in later tasks.

Understanding body definition and fixture definition

In order to define objects in the physics world, we need two definitions: a body definition and fixture definition.

The body is in charge of the physical properties, such as its position in the world, taking and applying force, moving speed, and the angular speed when rotating.

We use fixtures to handle the shape of the object. The fixture definition also defines the properties on how the object interacts with others while colliding, such as friction and restitution.

Defining shapes

Shapes are defined in a fixture. The two most common shapes in Box2D are rectangle and circle. We define a rectangle with the `SetAsBox` function by providing half of its width and height. Also, the circle shape is defined by the radius.

It is worth noting that the position of the body is at the center of the shape. It is different from EaselJS in that the default origin point is set at the top-left corner.

Pixels per meter

When we define the dimension and location of the body, we use **meter** as a unit. That's because Box2D uses **metric** for calculation to make the physics behavior realistic.

But we usually calculate in pixels on the screen. So, we need to convert between pixels on the screen and meters in the physics world. That's why we need the `pxPerMeter` variable here. The value of this variable might change from project to project.

The update method

In the game tick, we update the physics world.

The first thing we need to do is take the world to the next step. Box2D calculates objects based on steps. It is the same as we see in the physical world when a second is passed. If a ball is falling, at any fixed time, the ball is static with the property of the falling velocity. In the next millisecond, or nanosecond, the ball falls to a new position. This is exactly how steps work in the Box2D world. In every single step, the objects are static with their physics properties. When we go a step further, Box2D takes the properties into consideration and applies them to the objects.

This step takes three arguments. The first argument is the time passed since the last step. Normally, it follows the frame-per-second parameter that we set for the game. The second and the third arguments are the iteration of velocity and position. This is the maximum iterations Box2D tries when resolving a collision. Usually, we set them to a low value.

The reason we clear the force is because the force will be applied indefinitely if we do not clear it. That means the object keeps receiving the force on each frame until we clear it. Normally, clearing forces on every frame will make the objects more manageable.

Classified intel

We often need to represent a 2D vector in the physics world. Box2D uses `b2vec` for this purpose. Similar to the `b2vec` function, we use quite a lot of Box2D functions and classes. They are modularized into namespaces. We need to alias the most common classes to make our code shorter.

When you need to seek help on Box2D, the original C++ Box2D website or even the documentation of the Flash edition helps a lot. You can learn from there and apply the JavaScript syntax in Box2DWeb from the following URLs:

- `http://www.box2d.org/manual.html`
- `http://www.box2dflash.org/docs/2.1a/`

Shooting the ball

In this task, we create a hoop and allow the player to throw the ball by clicking the mouse button. The ball may or may not pass through the hoop based on the throwing angle and power.

Prepare for lift off

We remove the two bodies that were created in the first task. Those two bodies were just an experiment and we don't need them anymore.

Engage thrusters

In the following steps, we will create the core part of this project—shooting the ball:

1. We will create a hoop and spawn a ball in the physics world. We create a function for these two tasks:

```
physics.createLevel = function() {
  this.createHoop();

  // the first ball
  this.spawnBall();
};
```

2. We are going to spawn many balls. We define the following method for this task. In this task, we hardcode the position, ball size, and fixture properties. The ball is spawned as a static object until the player throws the ball out:

```
physics.spawnBall = function() {
  var positionX = 300;
  var positionY = 200;
  var radius = 13;

  var bodyDef = new b2BodyDef;

  var fixDef = new b2FixtureDef;
```

```
   fixDef.density = 0.6;
   fixDef.friction = 0.8;
   fixDef.restitution = 0.1;

   bodyDef.type = b2Body.b2_staticBody;

   bodyDef.position.x = positionX/pxPerMeter;
   bodyDef.position.y = positionY/pxPerMeter;

   fixDef.shape = new b2CircleShape(radius/pxPerMeter);

   this.ball = this.world.CreateBody(bodyDef);
   this.ball.CreateFixture(fixDef);

};
```

3. We will need to get the ball position to calculate the throwing angle. We define the following method to get the ball position and convert it into screen coordinates:

```
physics.ballPosition = function(){
  var pos = this.ball.GetPosition();
  return {
    x: pos.x * pxPerMeter,
    y: pos.y * pxPerMeter
  };
};
```

4. By using the cursor and ball position, we can calculate the angle. This is the Math function that returns the angle, which will be explained later:

```
physics.launchAngle = function(stageX, stageY) {
  var ballPos = this.ballPosition();

  var diffX = stageX - ballPos.x;
  var diffY = stageY - ballPos.y;

  // Quadrant
  var degreeAddition = 0; // Quadrant I
  if (diffX < 0 && diffY > 0) {
    degreeAddition = Math.PI; // Quadrant II
  } else if (diffX < 0 && diffY < 0) {
    degreeAddition = Math.PI; // Quadrant III
  } else if (diffX > 0 && diffY < 0) {
    degreeAddition = Math.PI * 2; // Quadrant IV
  }
```

```
        var theta = Math.atan(diffY / diffX) + degreeAddition;
        return theta;
    };
```

5. We have prepared the `Math` methods and can finally throw the ball with the following method:

```
physics.shootBall = function(stageX, stageY, ticksDiff) {
    this.ball.SetType(b2Body.b2_dynamicBody);

    var theta = this.launchAngle(stageX, stageY);

    var r = Math.log(ticksDiff) * 50; // power

    var resultX = r * Math.cos(theta);
    var resultY = r * Math.sin(theta);

    this.ball.ApplyTorque(30); // rotate it

    // shoot the ball
    this.ball.ApplyImpulse(new b2Vec2(resultX/pxPerMeter, resultY/
pxPerMeter), this.ball.GetWorldCenter());

    this.ball = undefined;
};
```

6. We need a target for the throwing action. So, we create the hoop with the following code. A hoop is constructed using a board and two squares:

```
physics.createHoop = function() {
    var hoopX = 50;
    var hoopY = 100;

    var bodyDef = new b2BodyDef;
    var fixDef = new b2FixtureDef;

    // default fixture
    fixDef.density = 1.0;
    fixDef.friction = 0.5;
    fixDef.restitution = 0.2;

    // hoop
    bodyDef.type = b2Body.b2_staticBody;
    bodyDef.position.x = hoopX/pxPerMeter;
    bodyDef.position.y = hoopY/pxPerMeter;
    bodyDef.angle = 0;
```

```
fixDef.shape = new b2PolygonShape();
fixDef.shape.SetAsBox(5/pxPerMeter, 5/pxPerMeter);

var body = this.world.CreateBody(bodyDef);
body.CreateFixture(fixDef);

bodyDef.type = b2Body.b2_staticBody;
bodyDef.position.x = (hoopX+45)/pxPerMeter;
bodyDef.position.y = hoopY/pxPerMeter;
bodyDef.angle = 0;

fixDef.shape = new b2PolygonShape();
fixDef.shape.SetAsBox(5/pxPerMeter, 5/pxPerMeter);

body = this.world.CreateBody(bodyDef);
body.CreateFixture(fixDef);


// hoop board dimension: 10x80 (5x40 in half value)
bodyDef.type = b2Body.b2_staticBody;
bodyDef.position.x = (hoopX-5)/pxPerMeter;
bodyDef.position.y = (hoopY-40)/pxPerMeter;
bodyDef.angle = 0;

fixDef.shape = new b2PolygonShape();
fixDef.shape.SetAsBox(5/pxPerMeter, 40/pxPerMeter);
fixDef.restitution = 0.05;

var board = this.world.CreateBody(bodyDef);
board.CreateFixture(fixDef);
};
```

7. Now, we can initialize the world by calling the `createLevel` method. At the same time, we should remove the creation of two test objects that we added in the last task:

```
game.physics.createLevel();
```

8. In the `game.js` file, we handle the `mousedown` and `mouseup` events to get the position of the cursor and the duration for which the mouse button was kept pressed. The cursor's position determines the angle and the duration determines the power:

```
isPlaying = true;

game.tickWhenDown = 0;
game.tickWhenUp = 0;
```

```
game.stage.on('stagemousedown', function(e){
  if (!isPlaying) { return; }
  game.tickWhenDown = cjs.Ticker.getTicks();
});

game.stage.on('stagemouseup', function(e){
  if (!isPlaying) { return; }
  game.tickWhenUp = cjs.Ticker.getTicks();
  ticksDiff = game.tickWhenUp - game.tickWhenDown;

  game.physics.shootBall(e.stageX, e.stageY, ticksDiff);

  setTimeout(game.spawnBall, 500);
});
```

9. Finally, we spawn another ball after the last ball is thrown:

```
game.spawnBall = function() {
  game.physics.spawnBall();
};
```

After performing these steps, we should get the result as shown in the following screenshot. We can click anywhere on the screen; once the mouse button is released, the ball is thrown towards the position of the cursor. When the angle and power is right, the ball is thrown into the hoop.

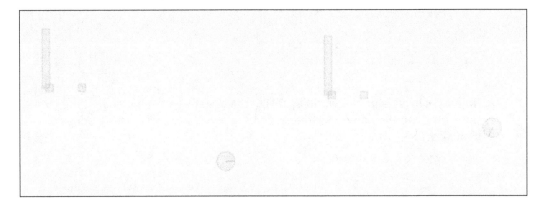

Objective complete – mini debriefing

Thanks to the physics engine, we only have to define the position of the objects, throwing angle, and power to create the entire ball-throwing logic. The engine automatically calculates the path of the throw and the bounce of the ball.

Shooting the ball

We change the state of the ball from static to dynamic before applying some force to it. Forces only affect dynamic bodies.

Once we know any two points in the screen, we can calculate the rotation angle. This is done using the geometry formula. The following figure shows the relationship between the edges of the triangle and angles between them:

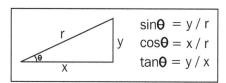

$$\sin\theta = y / r$$
$$\cos\theta = x / r$$
$$\tan\theta = y / x$$

The calculated angle is correct only if it is in the first quadrant. We determine the quadrant of the mouse cursor by referencing the ball's position as the original point. The following figure shows the four quadrants:

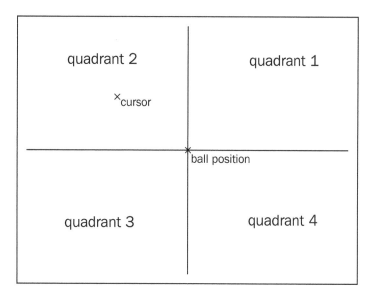

According to math, we need to add additional degrees to the calculated result if the cursor is not in the first quadrant. The degrees to be added, depending on the quadrant, are shown as follows:

- ▶ Quadrant 1: Add 0
- ▶ Quadrant 2 and 3: Add 180 (PI)
- ▶ Quadrant 4: Add 360 (*PI * 2*)

After we get the angle, we need the value of the power. The power is based on the time duration of the mouse button being pressed.

The less amount of time the mouse button is being pressed, the less power is applied to the ball. The longer the mouse button is pressed, the more power is applied. You may find that the power will be hard to control if we use a linear scale. It is very difficult to find the right timing. Either the power is too little to be noticeable or too much that the ball flies directly out of the screen. The duration is too sensitive.

We use the logarithm to solve this problem. The logarithm makes the shooting power much smoother. Imagine when we click on the mouse. It is not very different if we keep it pressed for 500 milliseconds or 1 second. But the value indeed has doubled. That's why the timing is difficult. The power of force is determined in the millisecond scale. Now with the logarithm, the value is determined by the exponential of the duration. **100 milliseconds** may mean that the value is **1** and **1 second** may mean that the value is **2**. It is still more powerful when kept pressed for longer. But the value difference is not that sensitive anymore. The following figure shows how the logarithm decreases the sensitivity:

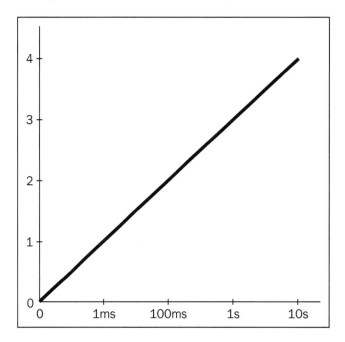

After we have the angle and power, we decompose the vector into x-axis and y-axis vectors using a geometry formula. This is the impulse force that we apply to the ball.

Applying the force

There are two ways to apply force in Box2D: `ApplyForce` and `ApplyImpulse`.

In Box2D, force is often consistently applied to a body for a while. For example, we speed up a car by applying force. We use impulse, for instance, to apply a one-time force. Throwing a ball is more like an impulse than a constant force.

Explaining the construction of the physics world

The hoop is constructed using three static bodies—a board and two squares, as illustrated in the following figure:

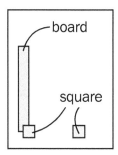

Classified intel

In the real world, when basketball players throw the ball, they spin the ball as shown in the following figure:

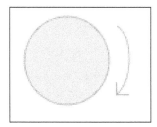

We make the ball spin by applying torque to it while the ball is thrown.

Handling collision detection

In this task, we detect if the ball passes through the hoop and we reward the player with scores. We will also create a world boundary and remove balls that are out of bounds.

Prepare for lift off

The detection is done by placing a sensor between the hoop squares. The following figure shows how the sensor is placed:

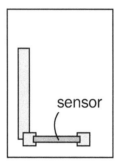

For the boundary, it will be a long body that is placed at the bottom of the world, as shown in the following figure:

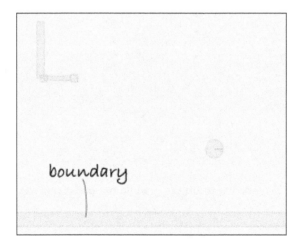

Engage thrusters

Let's add the sensor and handle the collision in the following steps:

1. First, we append the `createHoop` method to create a body between the two little hoop squares. We set it as a sensor so that the balls can pass through it:

```
physics.createHoop = function() {
  // existing hoop code goes here.

  // hoop sensor
  bodyDef.type = b2Body.b2_staticBody;
  bodyDef.position.x = (hoopX+20)/pxPerMeter;
  bodyDef.position.y = hoopY/pxPerMeter;
  bodyDef.angle = 0;

  fixDef.isSensor = true;
  fixDef.shape = new b2PolygonShape();
  fixDef.shape.SetAsBox(20/pxPerMeter, 3/pxPerMeter);

  body = this.world.CreateBody(bodyDef);
  body.CreateFixture(fixDef);
};
```

2. Then, we set up the contact listener in the following method definition. It registers out its own `beginContact` method to the Box2D engine:

```
physics.setupContactListener = function() {
  // contact
  var contactListener = new Box2D.Dynamics.b2ContactListener;
  contactListener.BeginContact = function(contact, manifold) {
     if (contact.GetFixtureA().IsSensor() || contact.GetFixtureB().
IsSensor()) {
        game.increaseScore();
     }
  };
  this.world.SetContactListener(contactListener);
};
```

3. Besides detection collision between the hoop and ball, we will also detect the collision between the balls and world boundary. We remove the balls that hit the boundary. To remove bodies in the physics world, we first need to store the reference of the bodies that we are going to remove. So, we define an array in the physics object:

```
physics.bodiesToRemove = [];
```

4. Next, we code the following method to create a large body as a boundary:

```
physics.createWorldBoundary = function() {
  var bodyDef = new b2BodyDef;
  var fixDef = new b2FixtureDef;

  bodyDef.type = b2Body.b2_staticBody;
  bodyDef.position.x = -800/pxPerMeter;
  bodyDef.position.y = 300/pxPerMeter;
  bodyDef.angle = 0;

  fixDef.shape = new b2PolygonShape();
  fixDef.shape.SetAsBox(2000/pxPerMeter, 10/pxPerMeter);

  body = this.world.CreateBody(bodyDef);
  body.CreateFixture(fixDef);

  body.SetUserData({isBoundary:true}); // distinguish this object
from others.
};
```

5. It's time to invoke our two new methods:

```
physics.createLevel = function() {

  this.createWorldBoundary();

  this.setupContactListener();

  // existing code goes here
};
```

6. In the contact-handling method, we add checking between the balls and boundary. We add those ball bodies to the list:

```
physics.setupContactListener = function() {
  // contact
  var contactListener = new Box2D.Dynamics.b2ContactListener;
  contactListener.BeginContact = function(contact, manifold) {
    if (contact.GetFixtureA().IsSensor() || contact.GetFixtureB().
IsSensor()) {
      game.increaseScore();
    }

    // world boundary.
    var userDataA = contact.GetFixtureA().GetBody().GetUserData();
```

```
        var userDataB = contact.GetFixtureB().GetBody().GetUserData();
        if (userDataA !== null && userDataA.isBoundary ||
            userDataB !== null && userDataB.isBoundary) {

          // which one is boundary?
          var boundary = contact.GetFixtureA().GetBody();
          var body = contact.GetFixtureB().GetBody();

          if (userDataB !== null && userDataB.isBoundary) {
            boundary = contact.GetFixtureB().GetBody();
            body = contact.GetFixtureA().GetBody();
          }

          physics.bodiesToRemove.push(body);

        }
      };
    this.world.SetContactListener(contactListener);
  };
```

7. Remember the array for body removal? We now use it in the `update` function.
   We iterate the list and destroy each body in that array:

```
physics.update = function() {

  // existing code goes here.

  // remove bodies
  for (var i=0, len=this.bodiesToRemove.length; i<len; i++) {
    var body = this.bodiesToRemove[i];
    var sprite = body.GetUserData();
    if (sprite) {
      sprite.parent.removeChild(sprite);
    }
    this.world.DestroyBody(body);
  }
  this.bodiesToRemove.length = 0;
};
```

8. We can now move to the `game.js` file where we init the game score:

```
game.score = 0;
```

9. We define the following method to increase the game score:

```
game.increaseScore = function() {
  game.score += 1;
  console.log(game.score); // out to console until we display it
in interface.
};
```

Objective complete – mini debriefing

A sensor fixture allows a body to pass through it. We may not be able to see the sensor, but the contact listener tells us when a fixture collides with the sensor.

Contact listener

The contact is made with `ContactListener`. Box2D informs us that there is contact between the two fixtures. In the `BeginContact` function, we get the two fixtures that collide with each other. We need to check which bodies they are and code our custom logic. By using `GetBody` on the fixture, we can get the body. With the `GetUserData` method, we have access to the custom data that we set to the body. We can only determine what action is to be taken after knowing which objects collide.

 The `BeginContact` function provides the two contacting fixtures: `fixtureA` and `fixtureB`. We guarantee to obtain the two fixtures when the contact occurs, but the order of the fixtures is not guaranteed.

The contact listener, by default, is triggered by every body's collision. We need to filter the result and only focus on what we are interested in. Here, we are interested in two collision pairs: the ball/hoop and balls/boundary pairs.

There are more controls on the object's contacts. The following URL explains the anatomy of a Box2D collision. The post targets the C++ edition but the same concept also works in the JavaScript version: `http://www.iforce2d.net/b2dtut/collision-anatomy`.

User data

The Box2D engine knows that eventually we need to attach our own data to each body. That's why it provides a User data on each object. We can use the `SetUserData` or `GetUserData` methods to access custom data. We set an object in the boundary so that we can identify it from other bodies when we handle the collision. Otherwise, we cannot tell which bodies cause the collisions.

 In JavaScript, we can attach properties to any object. The reason the `SetUserData` and `GetUserData` methods exist is because these methods were ported from strictly typed OOP languages—C++ and ActionScript. These languages require a dedicated user data property to be predefined in the class body and expose a get/setter function for the programmer to use.

Classified intel

You may notice that we have placed the boundary much higher than the designed place. That's for our debugging approach. By putting the boundary inside the sight, we can see that the balls are removed once they collide with the boundary. After we confirm that the balls-removal logic works, we can place the boundary at a lower level and make it invisible to the players.

Object removal

Destroying bodies within a physics step may cause issues in the Box2D engine. That's why we always destroy bodies after each step is completely calculated. In the `update` method, we execute the object removal code after the `step` function.

Defining levels

In this task, we define multiple levels that contain different combinations of obstacles.

Prepare for lift off

We have successfully put bodies in the physics world in the previous tasks. In this task, we would like to extract the body placement into an easier definition, so that we can massively define a series of levels.

In these levels, we define the position of the hoop and ball. We also define how obstacles are placed in each level.

We define the levels in a new file called `level.js`. Let's include it in HTML:

```
<script src="scripts/level.js"></script>
```

Engage thrusters

We will now work on the newly created `level.js` file:

1. In the `level.js` file, we define the balls and levels data. Most of the data defines the physics properties:

```
game.balls = {
  'slow ball': {
    className: 'SlowBall',
    radius: 13,
    density: 0.6,
    friction: 0.8,
    restitution: 0.1
```

```
      },
      'bouncy ball': {
        className: 'BouncyBall',
        radius: 10,
        density: 1.1,
        friction: 0.8,
        restitution: 0.4
      }
    };
    game.levels = [
      {
        hoopPosition: {x:50, y:150},
        ballName: 'slow ball',
        ballPosition: {x:350, y:250},
        ballRandomRange: {x:60, y:60},
        obstacles: []
      },
      {
        hoopPosition: {x:50, y:200},
        ballName: 'bouncy ball',
        ballPosition: {x:300, y:250},
        ballRandomRange: {x:80, y:80},
        obstacles: [
          {
            type: 'rect',
            graphicName: 'BrownSquare',
            position: {x: 150, y: 160},
            dimension: {width: 10, height:10},
            angle: 45
          }
        ]
      },
      {
        hoopPosition: {x:50, y:160},
        ballName: 'slow ball',
        ballPosition: {x:350, y:250},
        ballRandomRange: {x:80, y:80},
        obstacles: [
          {
            type: 'rect',
            graphicName: 'BrownSquare',
            position: {x: 200, y: 160},
            dimension: {width: 10, height:10},
            angle: 0
```

```
            },
            {
                type: 'rect',
                graphicName: 'BrownSquare',
                position: {x: 200, y: 120},
                dimension: {width: 10, height:10},
                angle: 0
            },
        ]
    }
];
game.currentLevel = game.levels[0]; // default the 1st level.
```

2. In the `physics.js` file, when we create the physics world, we load the level and use it to create the obstacle and hoop:

```
physics.createLevel = function() {

    var level = game.currentLevel;
    this.createObstacles(level);
    this.createHoop(level);

    // existing code goes here.
};
```

3. When creating the hoop, we use the level definition for the position of the hoop:

```
physics.createHoop = function(level) {
    var hoopX = level.hoopPosition.x;
    var hoopY = level.hoopPosition.y;

    // existing code goes here.
}
```

4. Similar to the hoop, we use the level definition for the ball spawning position. The difference is that we add a random range to the ball so it is not exactly the same position on every shot:

```
physics.spawnBall = function() {
    var level = game.currentLevel;
    var ball = game.balls[level.ballName];

    var positionX = level.ballPosition.x + Math.random()*level.
ballRandomRange.x - level.ballRandomRange.x/2;
    var positionY = level.ballPosition.y + Math.random()*level.
ballRandomRange.y - level.ballRandomRange.y/2;
    var radius = ball.radius;
```

```
    var fixDef = new b2FixtureDef;
    fixDef.density = ball.density;
    fixDef.friction = ball.friction;
    fixDef.restitution = ball.restitution;

    // existing code goes here.
}
```

5. Instead of hardcoding the obstacle, we iterate the obstacles' list from the level definition and create the obstacle:

```
physics.createObstacles = function(level) {
  var bodyDef = new b2BodyDef;
  var fixDef = new b2FixtureDef;

  // default fixture
  fixDef.density = 1.0;
  fixDef.friction = 0.5;
  fixDef.restitution = 0.2;

  // obstacles
  var body;
  for(var i=0, len=level.obstacles.length; i<len; i++) {
    var o = level.obstacles[i];

    bodyDef.type = b2Body.b2_staticBody;
    bodyDef.position.x = o.position.x/pxPerMeter;
    bodyDef.position.y = o.position.y/pxPerMeter;

    bodyDef.angle = o.angle;

    if (o.type === 'rect') {
      fixDef.shape = new b2PolygonShape();
      fixDef.shape.SetAsBox(o.dimension.width/pxPerMeter,
o.dimension.height/pxPerMeter);
      body = this.world.CreateBody(bodyDef);
      body.CreateFixture(fixDef);
    }
  }
};
```

The following screenshot shows the game that now loads a level with a 45-degree-rotated square obstacle:

Objective complete – mini debriefing

We have placed the obstacles in different levels. Now, we can play different levels by providing the level number in the code.

Building the level

We used literal objects to represent levels. While we construct the world with the createLevel method, we use the level definition to create the hoop, balls, and obstacles.

We didn't use much size variation here for the obstacles because we will need graphics to represent them later. Having too many dimensions makes the graphics preparation more difficult.

Besides placement, we define different types of balls by setting different values for the radius, density, restitution, and friction.

With a combination of these four variables, we can create a wide range of different types of balls. The radius affects the difficulty of hitting the hoop because of the size. The density affects the mass and amount of power that a player needs to apply. The restitution and friction defines how bouncy the ball should be. Then, in each level, we define which ball type is used. Visually, we will use different colors for different kinds of balls. We will work on the visual graphics in the later tasks.

Classified intel

The restitution defines how bouncy an object is when it interacts with another object. This value is usually between 0 and 1. The bounciness is decided by the restitution values of two colliding objects. Specifically, Box2D sets the restitution value to the maximum value of both the colliding objects. In such a mechanism, we define the hoop board to have a small restitution value. The bounciness result will be determined by the ball, which will have different values that are higher than the restitution of the board.

Designing the physics world

Defining the object placement purely in code can be quite difficult sometimes. We need to align the objects in code with our imagination. By using a visual editor, we can make the design process easier.

I usually take the following approach. I launch any graphical editor and set the dimension to match the game canvas. Next, I put a similar rectangle in the art board to get the position value. Then, I can easily grab the position value from the art board and put the value in the code.

After this, I place the position's value in the code with the Box2D body type.

If you need a more advanced physics editor for a complex scene, there are several visual editors on the Web. The following are some of them:

▸ The Box2D editor (`https://code.google.com/p/box2d-editor/`)

▸ The Physics editor (`https://www.codeandweb.com/physicseditor`)

▸ The RUBE editor (`https://www.iforce2d.net/rube/`)

Adding a launch bar with power

The player doesn't know how much power needs to be applied to the ball. This will lead to confusion. We can improve this by displaying a power indicator when shooting the ball.

Prepare for lift off

We will create the hierarchy directly from Flash. The following screenshot shows the symbol hierarchy:

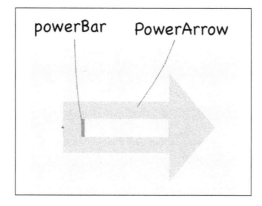

Then, we export these graphics into a JS file that we can use directly in the CreateJS library. Or, you can find the file from the code bundle.

We create another new file, `view.js`. We will place the logic to control the assets there. Specifically, we control the power indicator graphics inside this file.

We will need to include the new files into the HTML before we move on:

```
<script src="scripts/assets.js"></script>
<script src="scripts/view.js"></script>
```

Engage thrusters

Let's execute the following steps to create the power indicator:

1. First, we set up a new file called `view.js`. Inside the file, we initialize the power indicator graphics and define methods that show/hide it, rotate it, and also update the length of the power bar:

```
var game = this.game || (this.game={});
var createjs = createjs || {};

;(function(game, cjs){
  game.view = game.view || {};

  game.view.initPowerIndicator = function() {
    this.power = new lib.PowerArrow();
    game.stage.addChild(this.power);
    this.power.visible = false; // we hide it upon init.
  };
```

```
          game.view.showPowerIndicator = function(x, y) {
            this.power.visible = true;
            this.power.x = x;
            this.power.y = y;
          };
          game.view.hidePowerIndicator = function() {
            this.power.visible = false;
          };
          game.view.rotatePowerIndicator = function(rotation) {
            this.power.rotation = rotation;
          };
          game.view.updatePowerBar = function(value) {
            this.power.powerBar.scaleY = Math.min(30, value); // maximum
      30 scaleY
          };
      }).call(this, game, createjs);
```

2. Then, we move to the `game.js` file. When the game starts, we initialize the power indicator:

```
    game.view.initPowerIndicator();
```

3. We use the cursor's position to calculate the ball-throwing angle. We listen to the `mousedown` event on the `canvas` tag:

```
    game.stage.on('stagemousedown', function(e){
      if (!isPlaying) { return; }
      var position = game.physics.ballPosition();
      game.view.showPowerIndicator(position.x, position.y);

      var rotation = game.physics.launchAngle(e.stageX, e.stageY);
      game.view.rotatePowerIndicator(rotation * 180 / Math.PI); //
    convert to degree

      game.tickWhenDown = cjs.Ticker.getTicks();
      game.view.updatePowerBar(0);
    });
    game.stage.on('stagemousemove', function(e){
      if (!isPlaying) { return; }
      var rotation = game.physics.launchAngle(e.stageX, e.stageY);
      game.view.rotatePowerIndicator(rotation * 180 / Math.PI); //
    convert to degree
    });
```

```
game.stage.on('stagemouseup', function(e){
    if (!isPlaying) { return; }
    game.view.hidePowerIndicator();
    game.tickWhenUp = cjs.Ticker.getTicks();
    ticksDiff = game.tickWhenUp - game.tickWhenDown;

    game.physics.shootBall(e.stageX, e.stageY, ticksDiff);

    setTimeout(game.spawnBall, 500);
});
```

4. We need to update the power indicator to reflect the power value. We need to do this inside the `tick` function:

```
game.tick = function(){
    // existing code goes here.
    // launch power preview
    var ticksDiff = cjs.Ticker.getTicks() - game.tickWhenDown;
    game.view.updatePowerBar(ticksDiff);
};
```

Let's test the game in the browser. When we press and hold the mouse button, the power arrow indicator displays the power bar growing until we release the mouse. If we move the mouse, the arrow always points from the ball to where the cursor is. The following screenshot shows this effect:

Objective complete – mini debriefing

In Flash, we create a symbol named `PowerArrow`. This is the symbol name that we can use with `new lib.PowerArrow()` to create an instance of these graphics. It contains a small red rectangular symbol. We name the instance of this rectangle `powerBar`. The following screenshot shows the instance of the **PowerBar** symbol to be named `powerBar`:

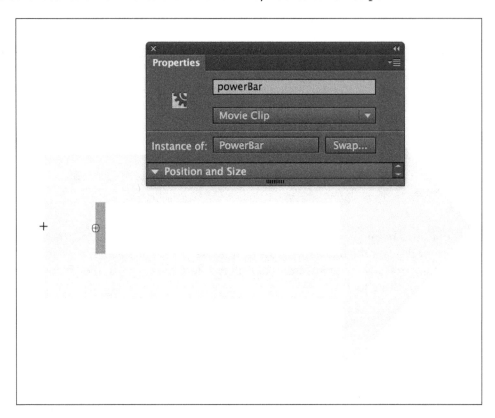

Then, we can access these graphics directly inside the `PowerArrow` instance:

```
var graphic = new PowerArrow();
graphics.powerBar; // we have access to the powerBar from PowerArrow
instance.
```

We place the registration point at the bottom of the arrow. This allows us to rotate the arrow nicely. The following screenshot shows how the arrow rotates:

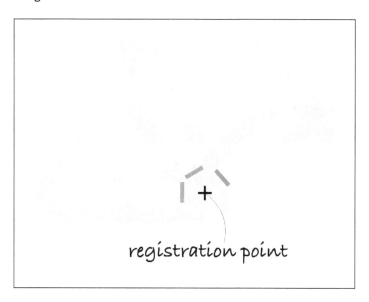

Classified intel

We used Flash to create and export the graphics hierarchy. Thanks to the high-level integration between Adobe Flash and the CreateJS library, we can design the graphics structure and outlook in Flash and then directly use them in the code. In case we don't have Flash, we can create the same effect without the need of Flash by using several techniques. I'll describe some of them later in the project.

If we are creating this approach in the EaselJS library, we programmatically create a red rectangular shape and add it to the container that contains the arrow graphics. Then, we set the registration point of this container to the same position as we showed in the previous screenshot.

If we are creating these graphics with DOM and CSS, we can create the graphics structure in DOM. Then, we position and rotate the arrow by setting the transform-origin point to the DOM.

You can find more information about using CSS transform-origin at `http://css-tricks.com/almanac/properties/t/transform-origin/`.

Adding a cross obstacle

We should be used to the static body by now. It is time to add more types of obstacles to the physics world.

In this task, we add a cross obstacle with motor spinning.

Engage thrusters

Let's execute the following steps to create a spinning cross in the world:

1. First, we define a new method that creates a cross. It is a long method. A cross is constructed with two fixtures in one body and then a static body with a revolute joint to spin the cross:

```
physics.createCross = function(obstacle) {
  var bodyDef = new b2BodyDef;
  var fixDef = new b2FixtureDef;

  // default fixture
  fixDef.density = 0.2;
  fixDef.friction = 0.5;
  fixDef.restitution = 0.2;

  bodyDef.type = b2Body.b2_dynamicBody;
  bodyDef.position.x = obstacle.position.x/pxPerMeter;
  bodyDef.position.y = obstacle.position.y/pxPerMeter;
  fixDef.shape = new b2PolygonShape();
  fixDef.shape.SetAsBox(obstacle.length/pxPerMeter, obstacle.
width/pxPerMeter);
  var cross = this.world.CreateBody(bodyDef);
  cross.CreateFixture(fixDef);
  fixDef.shape.SetAsBox(obstacle.width/pxPerMeter, obstacle.
length/pxPerMeter);
  cross.CreateFixture(fixDef);

  // a circle as the spinning joint
  bodyDef.type = b2Body.b2_staticBody;
  fixDef.shape = new b2CircleShape(10/pxPerMeter);
  var circle = this.world.CreateBody(bodyDef);
  circle.CreateFixture(fixDef);

  var revoluteJointDef = new b2RevoluteJointDef;
  revoluteJointDef.bodyA = cross;
```

```
        revoluteJointDef.bodyB = circle;
        revoluteJointDef.collideConnected = false;

        revoluteJointDef.maxMotorTorque = obstacle.maxTorque;
        revoluteJointDef.motorSpeed = obstacle.motorSpeed;
        revoluteJointDef.enableMotor = obstacle.enableMotor;

        this.world.CreateJoint(revoluteJointDef);
    };
```

2. Then, we update the level creation code to take care of the new cross obstacle:

```
if (o.type === 'rect') {
  // existing rect obstacle code goes here.
} else if (o.type === 'cross') {
  this.createCross(o);
}
```

3. We define a new level with our new cross obstacle. Let's add the following level definition into the levels array:

```
game.levels = [
  {
    hoopPosition: {x:50, y:160},
    ballName: 'slow ball',
    ballPosition: {x:350, y:250},
    ballRandomRange: {x:80, y:80},
    obstacles: [
      {
        type: 'cross',
        graphicName: 'Cross',
        position: {x: 165, y: 140},
        length: 60,
        width: 10,
        enableMotor: true,
        maxTorque: 25,
        motorSpeed: 3.0
      },
    ]
  },
  // existing levels definition goes here.
];
```

The following screenshot shows the creation of the new cross obstruction:

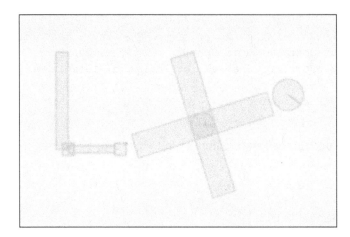

Objective complete – mini debriefing

There are several steps to create the spinning cross. First, we create the cross body with two fixtures attached to it. One object can be composed of several parts. This is the same as the fact that we can have multiple fixtures attached to one body. We have two rectangular-shaped fixtures to composite the cross body.

The cross is a dynamic body, so it can be affected by the balls motion. But it will also fall because of the gravity. So, we create another static body by using a joint and a static body. We can attach the dynamic cross to the static one. Different kinds of joints represent different types of relationships. For example, here we use a revolute joint to limit the cross to rotation. We also make it spin automatically by enabling the motor on the joint.

Then, we extract the variables into the level definition.

Classified intel

There are different types of joints. The following are some common joints when developing games:

- The revolute joint
- The distance joint
- The prismatic joint
- The pulley joint

You can find some joints examples in a web article by Allan Bishop at
`http://blog.allanbishop.com/box2d-2-1a-tutorial-part-2-joints/`.

Visualizing the graphics

So far, we have been using debug draw. In this task, we replace it with our own visualize method. We are still using the canvas, but we make use of CreateJS to manage the display objects.

Prepare for lift off

We want to ensure that the graphics are ready. The following screenshot shows the graphics we have prepared:

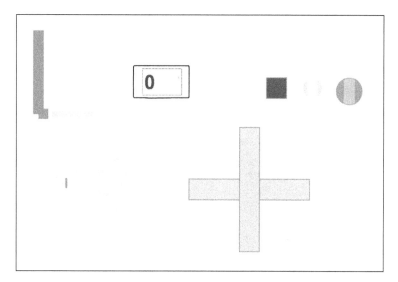

Engage thrusters

Let's start visualizing the game with our graphics:

1. In the view.js file, we create the following method that attaches a sprite graphic to the body:

```
game.view.addSpriteToBody = function(body, spriteName, index) {
  var sprite = new lib[spriteName]();
  sprite.x = -99;
  if (index !== undefined) {
    game.stage.addChildAt(sprite, index);
  } else {
    game.stage.addChild(sprite);
  }
  body.SetUserData(sprite);
};
```

2. Let's move to the `physics.js` file. On all the bodies, we use the method we just created to attach sprites. The first one is the rectangle shape obstacle:

```
if (o.type === 'rect') {
  // existing code goes here.
  game.view.addSpriteToBody(body, o.graphicName);
} else if (o.type === 'cross') {
  // existing code goes here.
}
```

3. Then we add the cross graphics to the spinning cross obstacle:

```
physics.createCross = function(obstacle) {
  // existing code goes here.
  game.view.addSpriteToBody(cross, obstacle.graphicName);
}
```

4. Then, we move to the hoop creation code. The hoop is constructed with the board and squares. We need to add three sprites to this code:

```
physics.createHoop = function(level) {
  // existing left square body code goes here.
  game.view.addSpriteToBody(body, 'HoopSquare');

  // existing right square body code goes here.
  game.view.addSpriteToBody(body, 'HoopSquare');

  // existing hoop board code goes here.
  game.view.addSpriteToBody(board, 'HoopBoard');

  // existing hoop sensor code goes here.
  game.view.addSpriteToBody(body, 'HoopSensor', 0);

};
```

5. Then, we add the ball graphics. The graphics are based on the type of the ball:

```
physics.spawnBall = function() {
  // existing ball code goes here
  game.view.addSpriteToBody(this.ball, ball.className);
};
```

6. Attaching the graphics to the body is just the first step. We need to update the graphics position and rotation based on the bodies' new properties:

```
physics.update = function() {
  // existing code goes here.
```

```
    // draw sprites
    var body = this.world.GetBodyList();
    while (body) {
      var sprite = body.GetUserData();

      if (sprite) {
        var position = body.GetWorldCenter();
        sprite.x = position.x * pxPerMeter;
        sprite.y = position.y * pxPerMeter;
        sprite.rotation = body.GetAngle() * 180 / Math.PI; // rad to
    degree
      }

      body = body.GetNext();
    }
    // existing bodies removal code goes here.
  };
```

The following screenshot shows the result of representing the physics bodies with our graphics:

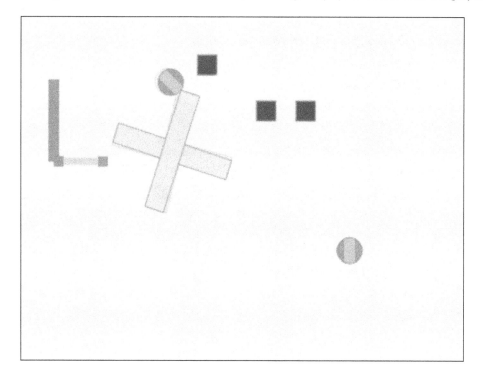

Objective complete – mini debriefing

We set the custom data object when we created the boundary. In this task, we use the custom data to store the reference of the graphics sprites.

We use `SetUserData` to assign the sprite to a body.

We iterate through all the bodies on every frame and use `GetUserData` to get the reference of the sprite.

Then, we update the sprites position and rotation based on the body's physics properties.

When visualizing, as Box2D uses the center point to position the body, we can set the registration point of the graphics to the center too. This makes the graphic placement a lot easier.

Adding the addChildAt display object to a specific z-index when adding a child

When we add the display object, we can also decide the z-index by specifying the index in the display list. By default, the z-order is decided by the order of calling the `addChild` method. If we want to add a sprite to a specific z-index, we can use the `addChildAt` method where the second parameter takes the z-index.

Classified intel

It is our choice to choose how to visualize the physics world. We can use canvas and the EaselJS library or we can even use the DOM elements with the CSS transform.

I have made a physics game with the CSS transform for its position and rotation. Thanks to the 3D acceleration, it runs at 60 frames-per-second even on an iPhone.

We have used Flash exporting to CreateJS vector drawing code. We can alternatively export all the graphics into separate files instead of using the Flash vector exporting option.

Visualizing the spinning cross

We have limited the dimensions of the obstacles. That's because it will be challenging to have too many dimensions when we use graphics to represent them.

For any dynamic dimensions, we will need to use the EaselJS vector drawing.

9-slice scaling

If we want to scale a bitmap graphic nonproportionally on the graphics, we can apply a technique called 9-slice scaling.

9-slice is not present in EaselJS by default. But there is a patch by Josh Tynjala for this purpose. Applying the code patch from the following URL makes bitmap scaling work in a more flexible way: `https://github.com/CreateJS/EaselJS/pull/281`.

 In case the pull request is removed, the mentioned class is copied into the following gist: `https://gist.github.com/makzan/b1bb3ee6764ef316ce92`.

If we use HTML and CSS to visualize the physics world, we can use the border-image property for 9-slice scaling. The following URL shows how this property works:

`http://css-tricks.com/understanding-border-image/`

An online generator allows us to visually configure and generate the border image code:

`http://border-image.com/`

 I have even created a coins falling machine game with Box2D using DOM and CSS to visualize all the graphics. By making use of the `translate` and `rotate` functions from the transform property, I can make the game run smoothly even on mobile devices. You may try the game at the following URL:

`http://42games.net/html5/ChickenRainHTML5/`

Choosing a level

In this task, we create a scene that lets the player choose which level they want to play.

Prepare for lift off

We have defined many levels with different types of obstacles. The following figure shows the structure of the LevelSelection symbol:

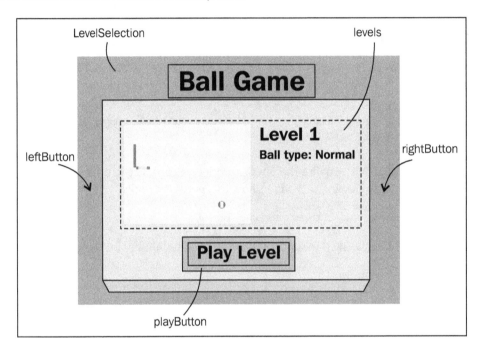

We also create a ScoreBoard symbol that contains a text field:

Engage thrusters

We have prepared the graphics. Let's work on the code to add the level-choosing logic:

1. This is something related to the view, so we will put the code in the `view.js` file. The graphics are already defined and exported. We create the following method to show `scoreBoard` in the game scene. The `scoreboard` symbol shows the player's score:

```
game.view.showScoreBoard = function(){
  this.scoreBoard = new lib.ScoreBoard();
  this.scoreBoard.x = 10;
  this.scoreBoard.y = 10;
  game.stage.addChild(this.scoreBoard);
};
```

2. We create the following function to update the text with the latest score:

```
game.view.updateScore = function() {
  this.scoreBoard.textField.text = game.score + '';
};
```

3. The level selection interface is a little bit longer. We detect the click on the left and right arrows:

```
// level selection
var levelSelection = new lib.LevelSelection();
game.stage.addChild(levelSelection);
levelSelection.levels.stop();

levelSelection.rightButton.on('click', function(){
  var next = levelSelection.levels.currentFrame + 1;
  levelSelection.levels.gotoAndStop(next);
});
levelSelection.leftButton.on('click', function(){
  var prev = levelSelection.levels.currentFrame - 1;
  levelSelection.levels.gotoAndStop(prev);
});
```

4. Now, we only start the physics world after a level is selected. We update the game start method to put the world level creation logic inside the click event handler of the play button. We also need an `isPlaying` Boolean to control the game flow:

```
// start the game play
var isPlaying = false;
levelSelection.playButton.on('click', function() {
  levelSelection.parent.removeChild(levelSelection);
```

```
        // game.physics.showDebugDraw();

        game.score = 0;

        game.currentLevel = game.levels[levelSelection.levels.
    currentFrame];

        game.physics.createLevel();

        game.view.showScoreBoard();

        isPlaying = true;
    });
```

5. Whenever we increase the score, we request the view to update the scoreboard:

```
game.increaseScore = function() {
    // existing code goes here.
    game.view.updateScore();
};
```

6. We have used some image files in this task, but we need to load them before we can use them. We define the following load function. Actually, it is the same one from the last task. We just reuse it:

```
game.load = function() {
    // load bitmap assets before starting the game
    var loader = new createjs.LoadQueue(false);
    loader.addEventListener("fileload", function(e){
        if (e.item.type === "image") { images[e.item.id] = e.result; }
    // assign to images object for assets.js to use
    });
    loader.addEventListener("complete", game.start);
    loader.loadManifest(lib.properties.manifest);
};
```

7. Finally, we replace the game.start() calling with the game.load() method:

```
game.load();
```

Objective complete – mini debriefing

We have improved the game flow by showing the player a level selection screen.

Choosing a level

We show an interface to let the player choose which level to play. In each level selection, we show the preview image and which ball is used in the level. The ball parameter includes the ball size, mass, and bounce. These different parameters make each level unique and the player needs a different strategy to shoot the ball.

We show the ball type on each level. This is useful for the player because the ball type affects the playing strategy.

Classified intel

The levels are the six frame symbols that are defined in Adobe Flash. We can use the `gotoAndStop` method to display each frame. The following screenshot shows the Flash environment with the six frames defined:

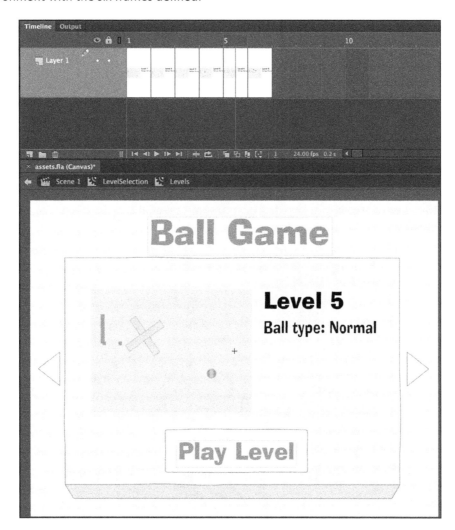

As an alternative to Flash, we can create the six images in order to choose a level and show them in a sequence when the player clicks on the left and right buttons. Or, we can place the six images on a timeline if we want to make use of the `gotoAndStop` method.

Clearing all bodies to start the game all over

In future developments, we may need to clear the world and start the game all over. We can use the following method to clear all the bodies in the Box2D world:

```
physics.clearWorld = function() {
  var body = this.world.GetBodyList();
  while (body) {
    var sprite = body.GetUserData();
    if (sprite) {
      sprite.parent.removeChild(sprite);
    }
    var b = body;
    body = body.GetNext();
    this.world.DestroyBody(b);
  }
};
```

Mission accomplished

We created a physical game in this project. The player is presented with a level selection screen. Then, he/she needs to try his/her best to shoot the ball into the hoop. The following screenshot shows each state of the game:

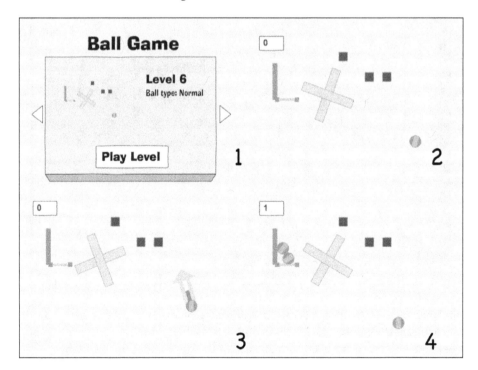

Hotshot challenges

We have created a ball-shooting game. Before we publish the game, we can still improve it in many ways.

We can make the game more addictive by introducing an advanced scoring calculation. When the player hits the target many times in a row, we reward more points for the combo effect.

We can define a special item that the player can buy or collect in the game. Here are some suggestions for the special effect. The player may apply an effect that makes the hoop wider so it is easier to hit the target. Or the ball can be less bouncy, which also makes it easier for the ball thrown to arrive at the hoop, or you can add an item that doubles the scores on each hit.

We can also add more types of obstacle to the game. For example, we can add a prismatic joint that moves an obstacle left and right.

Project 8

Creating a Sushi Shop Game with Device Scaling

We are going to create a game that serves sushi to customers. We'll design it in a way that it can be played on desktops, tablets, and mobile phones. Once this is done, we'll deploy it on the Internet and fine-tune it for touch devices.

Mission briefing

This is a time-management game where the player first opens a sushi stand. Then, there are customers who come and request a dish of sushi, and the player clicks on the ingredients to make the sushi based on the recipe that we will define in this game. Customers get angry and leave when the player fails to serve them, so they need to manage the timing and order of each sushi request.

Moreover, the game will be responsive to the size of the browser's window. The game displays well on narrow screens such as those present in mobile devices and wide screens such as those present in desktops.

The following screenshot shows the gameplay of our sushi game. First the player selects the ingredients to make the sushi on the right-hand side and then clicks on the customers to serve them.

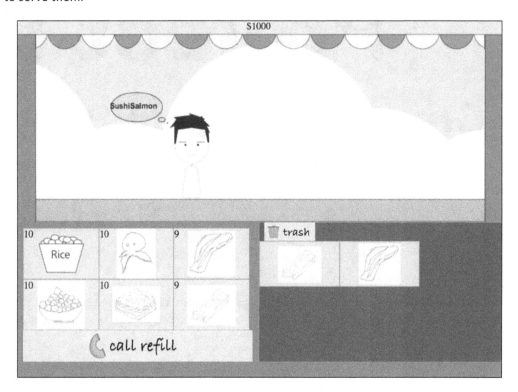

Why is it awesome?

This game makes use of what we have learned in this book. We separate the game into data, view, and controller. The view is in both the canvas and the DOM element. It combines the ease of a DOM-based control with CSS and the process of creating animations via the CreateJS suite. By using several CSS techniques, we make the game responsive to different screen sizes.

We will also learn how to deploy the project for the public to play. This includes *minifying* the code and publishing the code online. We also fine-tune the game for touch and mobile devices. Finally, we will learn how to use web audio in a browser and add sound effects to our game.

You can visit the `http://makzan.net/html5-games/sushi-shop/` to play the example game in order to have a better understanding of what we will build in this project.

Your Hotshot objectives

We will go through the following eight tasks to complete the project:

- ▶ Creating a responsive layout
- ▶ Decorating the game
- ▶ Making the sushi
- ▶ Creating a customer queue
- ▶ Refilling sushi ingredients
- ▶ Adding sound effects
- ▶ Distributing the game
- ▶ Making the game mobile friendly

Mission checklist

The project's folder structure is similar to what we covered in the previous projects. We have the `index.html` file as the entry point, the `Styles` folder for CSS files, the `Images` folder for graphic assets, the `Vendors` folder for third-party libraries, and the `Scripts` folder for all logic files. We will also add an `audio` folder for sound effect files.

SoundJS

In this project, we add an audio library that will help us play sound effects. It is called `SoundJS` and it is part of the `CreateJS` suite. We can download it from the CreateJS website or from the code bundle of this book.

The HTML file will import the logic files in the following order:

```
<script src="vendors/easeljs-0.7.1.min.js"></script>
<script src="vendors/tweenjs-0.5.1.min.js"></script>
<script src="vendors/movieclip-0.7.1.min.js"></script>
<script src="vendors/preloadjs-0.4.1.min.js"></script>
<script src='scripts/assets.js'></script>
<script src='scripts/helpers.js'></script>
<script src='scripts/view.js'></script>
<script src='scripts/data.js'></script>
<script src='scripts/customer.js'></script>
<script src='scripts/game.js'></script>
```

 Note that during development, we separate logic into many files; however, in production, we try to merge them all into one file. We will discuss this later when distributing the game.

Making the responsive layout

We are going to create the skeleton of the layout in this task that will fit into different screen sizes.

Prepare for lift off

The majority of the layout changes come in three screen sizes. They are narrow screen, medium screen, and wide screen. As illustrated in the following figure, the screen includes the customer view, cash indicator, ingredients, refilling button, sushi boards, and recipe. The following layout is for a wide screen where the main game view is to the left and the static recipes section is to the right. When the screen is narrower than this, we put the static recipes at the bottom to make more space for the game.

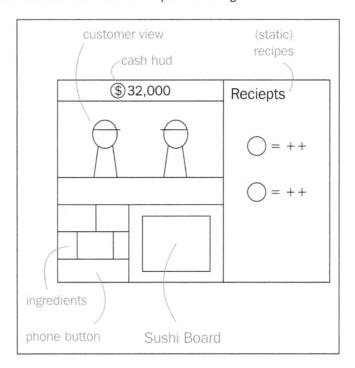

When the screen is large enough, we put the game on the left-hand side and the recipe to the right. When the screen is narrower, we rearrange the recipe from the right to the bottom. Putting the recipe section right below the game creates more game space for the player to play. When the game is displayed on a small mobile screen, we further downscale the game and squeeze the customer view. In CSS, it is known as media queries. Media queries apply rules based on media properties such as the width of the screen and its height.

Engage thrusters

Let's work on the HTML and CSS to create the layout's skeleton:

1. First, in the `index.html` file, we define the following DOM nodes for the game elements. The structure defines how the nodes are grouped:

```html
...
<div id="game">
  <div id="status-bar">$23,000</div>
  <div id="customer-view">
    <canvas id="canvas" width="100" height="100">
    </canvas>
  </div>
  <div id="dishes"></div>
  <div id="sushi-area">
    <div id="ingredients">
      <div class="ingredient" data-type='rice'>10</div>
      <div class="ingredient"
        data-type='octopus'>10</div>
      <div class="ingredient" data-type='salmon'>10</div>
      <div class="ingredient" data-type=
        'salmon-roe'>10</div>
      <div class="ingredient"
        data-type='seaweed'>10</div>
      <div class="ingredient" data-type='egg'>10</div>
      <div id="phone"></div>
    </div>
    <div id="sushi-board">
      <a id="delete-sushi-btn">Delete</a>
      <div id="others"></div>
      <div id="rices"></div>
      <div id="seaweeds"></div>
    </div>
  </div>
</div>
<div id="recipes">
  <h1>Sushi Recipes</h1>
  <p><img src="images/recipe.png" alt="recipe"></p>
</div>
...
```

2. Most of the layout-changing logic code is present in CSS. We have the following styles for the layout:

```css
/* Main layout */
/* By default, the game is 100% width and the recipes is at the
bottom of the game */
```

```css
#game {
  width: 100%;
  float: left;
}
#recipes {
  float: right;
  width: 100%;
  background: #ACACAC;
}

/* layout inside #game element */
/* from top to bottom: status, customer view, sushi*/
#status-bar {
  background: #D8D8D8;
  border-bottom: 1px solid #979797;
  width: 100%;
  height: 25px;
  line-height: 25px;
  text-align: center;
}

#customer-view {
  width: 100%;
  height: 300px;
}
#sushi-area {
  background: #9D7335;
  width: 100%;
  height: 250px;
}

/* sushi-board and ingredients are inside sushi area */
/* sushi board on the right of ingredients buttons */
#sushi-board {
  background: #913030;
  border: 1px solid #979797;
  width: 50%;
  height: 90%;
  float: right;
}

/* ingredients buttons on the left of sushi board */
#ingredients {
  width: 50%;
```

```
    float: left;
    padding: 10px;
    overflow: auto;
}

/* individual ingredient inside the ingredients section*/
.ingredient {
    width: 33%;
    height: 33%;
    background: #D8D8D8;
    border: 1px solid #979797;
    float: left;
}

/* phone button after the individual ingredient*/
#phone {
    width: 100%;
    height: 20%;
    background: #D8D8D8;
    float: left;
}
```

3. The ingredients buttons and the sushi board is laid towards the left and right
    respectively. Each of these occupies 50 percent of space in the wide screen
    view. When the screen is less than 501 pixels, we change the ratio to make
    the ingredients buttons' width to 70 percent. This makes it easier to select
    the buttons in a small screen view:

```
/* mobile portrait view */
@media screen and (max-width: 500px) {
    #ingredients {
        width: 70%;
    }
    #sushi-board {
        width: 30%;
    }
}
```

4. The screen space will be too small to display all the game elements when they
    are displayed on a mobile device in landscape orientation. In the following media
    query code that applies rules to a landscape mobile screen, we further squeeze
    the height of the interface and put the money status bar to the top-left corner:

```
/* mobile landscape view */
@media screen and (max-device-width: 550px) and (orientation :
landscape) {
```

```css
#status-bar {
  float: left;
  width: auto;
  padding-left: 3px;
  padding-right: 3px;
  border-right: 1px solid #979797;
}
#customer-view { /*reduce the height of customer view*/
  height: 100px;
}
#sushi-area { /*reduce the height of sushi area*/
  height: 200px;
}
}
```

5. In contrast, when the screen is wide enough, we use the following styles to put the entire game on the left-hand side and the recipe section to the right:

```css
/* wide screen */
@media screen and (min-width: 800px) {
  #game {
    width: 60%;
  }
  #recipes {
    width: 40%;
  }
}
```

6. Although most of the resizing is done in CSS, we need JavaScript to change the canvas's size. It is because the size of the canvas isn't a style. The canvas's dimension is the data that we need to set with the JavaScript API. In the `view.js` file, we set up the resize logic to change the canvas's width and height based on its parent's dimension. After resizing the canvas of the customer view, we also reposition the customers inside the view to ensure they are displayed correctly:

```javascript
game.view = {};

game.view.init = function() {
  initCustomerView();
  initDOMElements();
  initResizeHandler();
};
function initResizeHandler() {
  var customerView = document.getElementById
    ('customer-view');
```

```
var resizeCanvas = function() {
  game.canvas.width = customerView.offsetWidth;
  game.canvas.height = customerView.offsetHeight;
};
resizeCanvas();

// register the resize event.
window.onresize = function(){
  resizeCanvas();
  repositionCustomer();
};

function repositionCustomer() {
  // todo
}
repositionCustomer();
}
```

Objective complete – mini debriefing

We have created a skeleton that the game components resize or reposition according to the game's screen.

The elements use percentages to make the size flexible enough to fit different screen sizes. When the layout changes dramatically, we reposition the elements with media queries. A media query lets us define rules that only applies to the selectors when the media type matches. For example, we can apply rules to the screen size that's larger or smaller than a certain value. In this task, we defined two break points, 500 pixels and 800 pixels, to determine whether the game is being displayed in a narrow, medium, or wide screen.

We also need to define a mobile landscape query because the screen's height isn't large enough to display all the game elements while in the mobile device.

Classified intel

We have set the canvas's size at the resize event. It is worth knowing that setting the width or height of the canvas will clear all the drawings and reset the canvas. That's not a problem for us because EaselJS redraws the display list on every tick. This is why you may see that some other example code on the Internet clears the canvas by calling `canvas.width = canvas.width`.

Decorating the game

Before moving to the core game logic, we decorate the game's layout with graphics.

Prepare for lift off

The required graphics assets are shown in the following screenshot. Let's put the image files into the `images` folder:

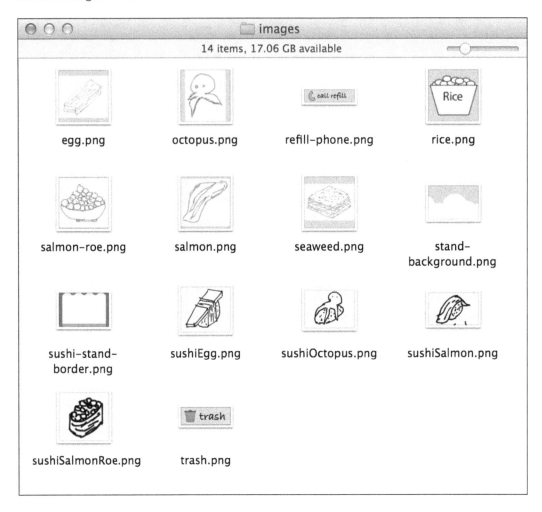

Engage thrusters

In these steps, we add the graphics to beautify our DOM elements:

1. First, we add the background and border image to the customer view:

```
#customer-view {
  background: url(../images/stand-background.png) center
    center no-repeat;
  background-size: cover;
  border-style: solid;
  border-width: 26px 32px 42px 32px;
  border-image: url(../images/sushi-stand-border.png) 26
    32 42 32 repeat;
}
```

2. The border's width affects the canvas's size. In the `view.js` file, we add the following function to get the border width style from the computed style:

```
var getBorderWidths = function(element) {
// get computed style.
var style = getComputedStyle(element);

  // return the 4 values as object.
  return {
    top: parseInt(style.borderTopWidth),
    right: parseInt(style.borderRightWidth),
    bottom: parseInt(style.borderBottomWidth),
    left: parseInt(style.borderLeftWidth)
  };
};
```

3. After we define the `getBorderWidths` function, we need to modify the `resizeCanvas` method to adjust with the border's width based on the values:

```
var resizeCanvas = function() {
  var w = getBorderWidths(customerView);
  game.canvas.width = customerView.offsetWidth - w.left -
    w.right;
  game.canvas.height = customerView.offsetHeight - w.top
    - w.bottom;
};
```

4. We then define graphics for the phone button:

```
#phone {
  background: #D8D8D8 url(../images/refill-phone.png)
    center center no-repeat;
  background-size: contain;
}
```

5. We also define the trash button that discards our sushi:

```
#delete-sushi-btn {
  display: block;
  width: 100px;
  height: 30px;
  background: url(../images/trash.png) center center
    no-repeat;
  background-size: contain;
}
```

6. Next, we define the ingredient's graphics:

```
.ingredient {
  background-position: center center;
  background-repeat: no-repeat;
  background-size: contain;
}
.ingredient[data-type='rice'] {
  background-image: url(../images/rice.png);
}
.ingredient[data-type='egg'] {
  background-image: url(../images/egg.png);
}
.ingredient[data-type='octopus'] {
  background-image: url(../images/octopus.png);
}
.ingredient[data-type='salmon'] {
  background-image: url(../images/salmon.png);
}
.ingredient[data-type='salmon-roe'] {
  background-image: url(../images/salmon-roe.png);
}
.ingredient[data-type='seaweed'] {
  background-image: url(../images/seaweed.png);
}
```

7. We then add the sushi graphics to the sushi classes:

```css
.sushi {
  width: 100%;
  min-height: 100px;
  background-position: center center;
  background-repeat: no-repeat;
  background-size: contain;
}
.sushiSalmonRoe {
  background-image: url(../images/sushiSalmonRoe.png);
}
.sushiSalmon {
  background-image: url(../images/sushiSalmon.png);
}
.sushiEgg {
  background-image: url(../images/sushiEgg.png);
}
.sushiOctopus {
  background-image: url(../images/sushiOctopus.png);
}
```

Objective complete – mini debriefing

We have decorated our game's layout with graphics. Let's take a look at the CSS properties we used in this task.

Background-size – cover and contain

The `background-size` property specifies the size of the background image. We can use numeric values or the `cover` and `contain` keywords.

We used `background-size: cover` for the customer view, but we used `background-size: contain` for the buttons. The cover will scale the background image and fill the DOM element with the image. When the aspect ratio is not the same between the element and the image, the image is scaled and cropped. In contrast, the `contain` value scales the image to fit inside the element. When the aspect ratio is not the same, there would be an empty space on the side.

The key difference is that the cover image would be cropped in order to fill the element, while the `contain` value would always show the entire image and leave an empty space.

The background image of the customer view is a sky that can be cropped without worrying about losing any important information. On the other hand, the ingredients' graphics are important and we don't want any part of it being cropped because of the element resizing. That's why we used the `contain` value instead of the `cover` value for `background-size` of the buttons.

Using border-image to decorate the customer view

We used `border-image` to decorate the customer view. The benefit of `border-image` is that it takes care of resizing. It is a 9-slice scaling in style sheet. This property takes the image URL and the 9-slice setting as a value. The following figure shows how the corners keep the dimension and the edges scaled when the DOM element dimension is changed. There are several repeating options available when the edge scales; they are `stretch`, `repeat`, and `round`.

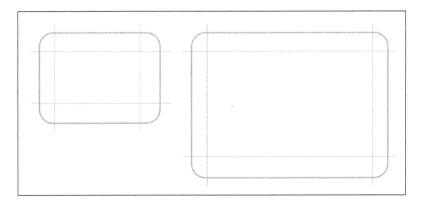

Mozilla Developer Network provides a detailed usage on the `border-image` property:

`https://developer.mozilla.org/en-US/docs/Web/CSS/border-image`

However, it is still difficult to set the slice offset without any visual feedback. The online tool, `http://border-image.com/`, would help in generating the code from the image visually. The following screenshot shows the tool that lets a user drag the offset with both the slider controls and guidelines loaded on the image. Once the dragging is done, we can copy the CSS code generated at the bottom text area. The border of the code area is exactly the preview of the code. We encourage you to check out that website and play with the `border-image` property to understand how to use this property better.

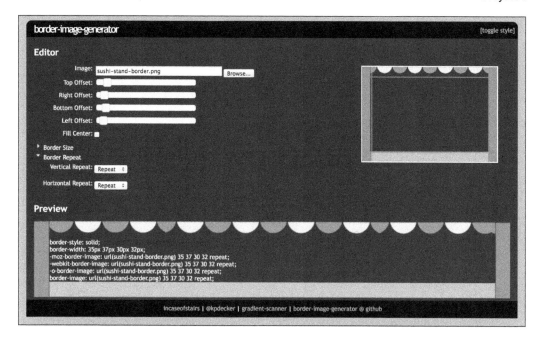

Making the sushi

In this task, we add the logic to composite the sushi by selecting the ingredients.

Prepare for lift off

The following figure shows the recipes of the sushi:

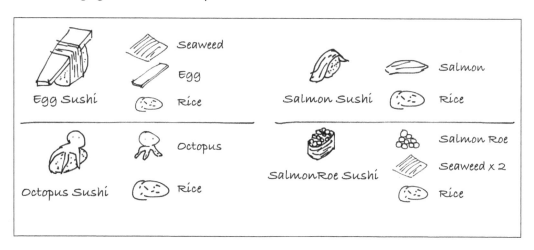

Engage thrusters

Follow the given steps to create the sushi:

1. We need a function to compare two given arrays. The array is in one dimension only so we don't need any deep comparison. Put the following comparing function in the `helpers.js` file:

    ```
    game.helper.arrayIsEqual = function(array1, array2) {
      if (array1.length !== array2.length) {
        return false;
      }
      for (var i = 0, len=array1.length; i < len; i++) {
        if (array1[i] !== array2[i]) {
          return false;
        }
      }
      return true;
    };
    ```

2. Then we need another helper function that clears all the children nodes inside a given DOM element. Defining the following function inside the `helpers.js` file helps us to keep a cleaner code base:

    ```
    game.helper.clearChildren = function(node) {
      while (node.lastChild) {
        node.removeChild(node.lastChild);
      }
    };
    ```

3. We use three layers to represent the ingredients in the sushi board. We define the method that clears all the nodes inside the three layers defined as follows:

    ```
    game.view.clearAllIngredients = function() {
     game.helper.clearChildren(others);
     game.helper.clearChildren(rices);
     game.helper.clearChildren(seaweeds);
    };
    ```

4. In the `data.js` file, we store the selected ingredients in a list of array:

    ```
    game.sushiOnHand = [];
    ```

5. We define a function to quickly clear all the ingredients on hand if the player needs to trash the sushi for selecting the wrong ingredients as given in the following code:

```
game.trashSushi = function() {
  game.sushiOnHand.length = 0; // clear it
  game.view.clearAllIngredients();
};
```

6. Let's move back to the `view.js` file. There are some mouse interaction events for the DOM user interface. The following internal function inside the `view.js` file sets up the DOM elements for the clicking events:

```
function initDOMElements() {
  var ingredients =
    document.querySelectorAll('.ingredient');
  for (var i=0, len=ingredients.length; i<len; i++) {
    var element = ingredients[i];
    element.onclick = ingredientOnClick;
  };

  // trash button
  var deleteButton = document.getElementById
    ('delete-sushi-btn');
  deleteButton.onclick = function(){
    game.trashSushi();
  };

  // logic of clicking the ingredients
  // reference of 3 layers in sushi board
  // for the ingredientOnClick function to use
  var others = document.getElementById('others');
  var rices = document.getElementById('rices');
  var seaweeds = document.getElementById('seaweeds');

  var ingredientOnClick = function() {
    var type = this.dataset.type;

    // DATA
    game.sushiOnHand.push(type);
    game.sushiOnHand = game.sushiOnHand.sort();

    addIngredientToScreen(type);
  };
};
```

7. We then code the long `addIngredientToScreen` method that displays the added ingredient on the screen:

```
var addIngredientToScreen = function(type) {
  var isEqualToAnySushi = false;
  var sushiName = '';
  // loop all receipes
  for (var key in game.receipes) {
    if (game.receipes.hasOwnProperty(key)) {
      isEqualToAnySushi =
        game.helper.arrayIsEqual(game.sushiOnHand,
        game.receipes[key]);
      sushiName = key;
      if (isEqualToAnySushi) {
        break; // must break the loop to keep the current equal
one.
      }
    }
  }

  // UI
  // show ingredients or final sushi image?
  if (isEqualToAnySushi) {
    // show one sushi image instead of individual ingredient.
    game.view.clearAllIngredients();

    var sushi = document.createElement('div');
    sushi.classList.add(sushiName, 'sushi');
    others.appendChild(sushi);
  } else {
    // clone the individual ingredient to sushi board.
    var node =
      ingredientsNode.querySelector
      (".ingredient[data-type="+ type +"]").cloneNode();
    if (type === 'rice') {
      rices.appendChild(node);
    } else if (type === 'seaweed') {
      seaweeds.appendChild(node);
    } else {
      others.appendChild(node);
    }
  }
};
```

Objective complete – mini debriefing

The sushi is composited by ingredients. This is similar to the color quest composition in *Project 1, Building a CSS Quest Game*.

We store the ingredients in the form of data called `sushiOnHand` to compare logic. At the same time, the DOM element of the selected ingredients is displayed on the sushi board.

We need to check whether the two arrays are equal. Our arrays are in simple one dimension. We created a helper that checks whether both the arrays contain the same elements.

 It's worth noting that the `arrayIsEqual` function only focuses on comparing the given arrays. Therefore, it should not care about sorting them. On the other hand, we ensure that the arrays of ingredients are always sorted.

When the ingredient is clicked, we put the clone ingredient's DOM node into the sushi board. When the combination of the ingredient matches any sushi, we replace the cloned ingredients with one sushi image.

Sometimes a player may need to trash the things on the sushi board because of a wrong combination. We trash and empty the sushi board in both the data and view. We reset the data array by setting the length to 0. The clearing of the three ingredient layers is done by removing all the nodes inside.

Classified intel

We cloned the ingredient node into the sushi board to composite the sushi. We used three layers to help order the ingredients in a better way. The three layers are seaweed, rice, and others. A recap on the HTML layout of the three layers is given in the following code:

```
<div id="sushi-board">
  <a id="delete-sushi-btn"></a>
  <div id="others"></div>
  <div id="rices"></div>
  <div id="seaweeds"></div>
</div>
```

Creating a customer queue

We have created a way to make sushi. Now it's time to serve the customer. We create the customer queue in this task.

Prepare for lift off

The customer graphics is generated from Adobe Flash. It contains two frames: normal and angry. The following figure shows the two states of the customer:

The reason why we use a canvas for the customer view is because with it we can optionally add animation to both the frames. For example, an angry sprite can be an animated movie clip that animates an angry bubble.

The customer asset is generated in the `assets.js` file from Flash and can be found in the code bundle. The bundle also includes the source of the Flash document to easily modify the graphics.

Engage thrusters

Let's work on the following steps to add the customer and queue logic to our game:

1. In the `view.js` file, we define a function to set up the customer view:

```
function initCustomerView() {
  // Canvas
  game.canvas = document.getElementById('canvas');

  game.stage = new cjs.Stage(game.canvas);

  cjs.Ticker.setFPS(60);

  // add game.stage to ticker to make the stage update
automatically.
  cjs.Ticker.addEventListener('tick', game.stage);
  cjs.Ticker.addEventListener('tick', game.tick);

  game.view.queueLeft = new cjs.Container();
  game.stage.addChild(game.view.queueLeft);

  game.view.queueRight = new cjs.Container();
  game.stage.addChild(game.view.queueRight);
}
```

2. Then, we create a `Customer` class in a dedicated file called `customer.js`. The constructor takes two parameters, namely, style number and queue choice:

```
function Customer(number, leftOrRight) {
  cjs.Container.call(this); // super call Container.

  this.number = number;

  // randomize a sushi
  this.wants = randomWants() ;

  // has eaten the sushi and leaving?
  this.hasEaten = false;

  // queued or was shown in front of the queue?
  this.hasShownUp = false;

  // how much time was wasted in waiting?
  this.hasWaitForTicks = 0;
```

```
    // queue index, 0 for left and 1 for right queue.
    this.queueIndex = 0;
    if (leftOrRight === 'right') this.queueIndex = 1;
    this.on('tick', this.tick);
}


// customer extends createJS Container.
Customer.prototype =
    Object.create(cjs.Container.prototype);
```

3. The `randomWants` function is an internal function that generates a random sushi request:

```
// customer's helper functions
function randomWants() {
    options = ['sushiSalmonRoe', 'sushiOctopus', 'sushiSalmon',
    'sushiEgg'];

    var index = Math.floor(Math.random() * options.length);
    return options[index];
}
```

4. In each tick, we check the waiting time of the customer. When the customer waits for too long, it changes its own state to angry:

```
Customer.prototype.tick = function() {
    this.hasWaitForTicks += 1;
    if (this.hasWaitForTicks === 300) { // turns angry
        this.graphics.gotoAndStop('angry');
    }
    if (this.hasWaitForTicks> 500) { // waited too long
        this.remove();
    }
    if (this.hasEaten) {
        this.remove();
    }
};
```

5. When we remove a customer, we remove it from two places. They are the queue array and the EaselJS display list:

```
Customer.prototype.remove = function() {
    // remove customer
    this.parent.removeChild(this);
    game.removeFromQueue(this.queueIndex);
};
```

6. A customer isn't displayed immediately when he or she is created. We only display the first customer in the queue. Therefore, the game tick function in the `game.js` file will display the customer in front of the sushi stand. We define the following method to display the customer:

```
Customer.prototype.showUp = function() {
    this.graphics = new lib['Customer'+this.number]();
    this.graphics.gotoAndStop('normal'); // normal state at first
    this.graphics.on('click', customerOnClick.bind(this));
    this.addChild(this.graphics);

    // bubble that shows what sushi the customer wants.
    var bubble = new lib.Bubble();
    bubble.x = -40;
    bubble.y = -120;
    this.addChild(bubble);

    // set the type
    bubble.sushiType.gotoAndStop(this.wants);

    this.hasShownUp = true; // mark the flag
};
```

7. Make sure to export the `Customer` definition to the game scope for other logic to access it:

```
game.Customer = Customer;
```

8. When a customer is clicked on, we send the sushi in hand to the customer. If the sushi in hand matches the sushi request, the customer leaves happily:

```
function customerOnClick() {
    // check if is what customer wants
    var isEqual =
        game.helper.arrayIsEqual(game.sushiOnHand,
        game.receipes[this.wants]);
    if (isEqual) {
        this.hasEaten = true;
    }
    game.trashSushi();
}
```

9. Let's move to queue management. We define two arrays to store customer queues:

```
game.queues = [];
game.queues[0] = [];
game.queues[1] = [];
```

10. We need to remove the first array element once the customer is served and he or she leaves the queue:

```
game.removeFromQueue = function(index) {
 game.queues[index].shift();
};
```

11. We create a timer interval to generate a new customer and put him/her in the queue:

```
game.tick = function() {
  var durationForNewCustomer = 500;
  if (cjs.Ticker.getTicks() % durationForNewCustomer ===
    0) {
    game.summonNewCustomer();
    // queue 0
    var customer = game.queues[0][0];
    if (customer && !customer.hasShownUp) {
      customer.showUp();
    }
    // queue 1
    var customer = game.queues[1][0];
    if (customer && !customer.hasShownUp) {
      customer.showUp();
    }
  }
};
```

12. Now, we need a logic code to summon a new customer:

```
game.summonNewCustomer = function() {
  // left or right?
  var leftOrRight = 'left';
  var queueIndex = 0;
  if (Math.random() >= 0.5) {
   leftOrRight = 'right';
   queueIndex = 1;
  }
  var customer = new game.Customer(1, leftOrRight);
  game.queues[queueIndex].push(customer);

  if (leftOrRight === 'left') {
    game.view.queueLeft.addChild(customer);
  } else {
    game.view.queueRight.addChild(customer);
  }
};
```

13. When the canvas is resized, we reposition the two customer queues with the following method:

```
// 0.35 and 0.8 positions shows both queues in better spacing.
var leftPos = 0.35;
var rightPos = 0.8;
function repositionCustomer() {
  game.view.queueLeft.x = game.canvas.width * leftPos;
  game.view.queueLeft.y = game.canvas.height;
  game.view.queueRight.x = game.canvas.width * rightPos;
  game.view.queueRight.y = game.canvas.height;
}
```

Objective complete – mini debriefing

The following figure explains how the customer view is represented in both data and view. In view, we only see two customers at the most. However, in data, we generate more customers and put them in queues. Once the customer at the first position is served, we move the second one to the front of the shop, and display the customer in the view.

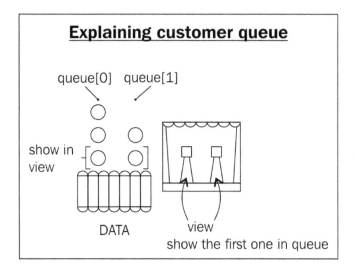

The following figure shows how we put two containers in the customer view. The queues in view are containers with their position defined. The benefit is that we don't need to handle the position of the customer. We just need to add the customer sprite into the correct queue container.

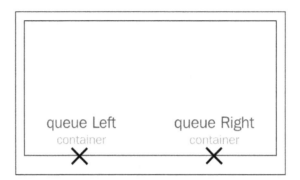

Resizing the canvas

First, we listen for the element resize event. Then, we reposition customers based on the new game dimension. Since all customer sprites are added to either the left or right queue container, we only need to reposition these two containers. The left queue is 35 percent from the left edge and the right queue is 80 percent from the left edge.

Refilling sushi ingredients

In this task, we will control the ingredients' amounts and refill. We will also introduce a currency.

Engage thrusters

In these steps, we will polish the game with a cash mechanism:

1. We store the cash value in the data.js file:

```
game.cash = 1000;
```

2. In the view.js file, we define a corresponding refresh method:

```
var cashNode = document.getElementById('status-bar');
game.view.refreshCash = function(){
  cashNode.textContent = '$' + game.cash;
}
```

3. We ensure that the cash DOM node shows the cash correctly by refreshing it when the game starts:

```
game.view.refreshCash();
```

4. In the `data.js` file, we define how many pieces of each ingredient need to be set up. Initially, the number is set to 10:

```
game.amount = [];
game.amount['rice'] = 10;
game.amount['octopus'] = 10;
game.amount['salmon'] = 10;
game.amount['salmon-roe'] = 10;
game.amount['seaweed'] = 10;
game.amount['egg'] = 10;
```

5. We add a method to increase the amount of total ingredients:

```
game.increaseAmount = function() {
  for(var key in game.amount) {
    if (game.amount.hasOwnProperty(key)) {
      game.amount[key] += 10;
      game.view.refreshAmount(key);
    }
  }
};
```

6. We also need the following logic to refresh the user interface for an ingredient's amount:

```
// individual ingredient node.
var ingredientsNode = document.getElementById('ingredients');

game.view.refreshAmount = function(type) {
  ingredientsNode.querySelector(".ingredient[data-type=
    "+ type +"]").textContent = game.amount[type];
};
```

7. Then, we register the click event for the phone button. It reduces the cash and increases the ingredients' stock:

```
// phone call to refill ingredients
var phoneBtn = document.getElementById('phone');
phoneBtn.onclick = function() {
  var needCash = 600;
  if (game.cash>= needCash) {
    game.increaseAmount();
```

```
        game.cash -= needCash;
        game.view.refreshCash();
    }
};
```

8. When any ingredient button is clicked on, we reduce the amount of the ingredient:

```
if (game.amount[type] > 0) {
  game.amount[type] -= 1;
  game.view.refreshAmount(type);
} else {
  return;   // EXIT function if not enough amount.
}
```

9. Finally, let's move to the `customer.js` file. When the customer finishes eating the sushi, we reward the player with money by adding the following code to the customer-leaving condition:

```
if (isEqual) {
...
  // Existing code goes here
  game.cash += 120;
  game.view.refreshCash();
}
```

Objective complete – mini debriefing

We have created a cash flow and controlled the flow of the number of ingredients. A player makes sushi to earn money and uses the money to refill ingredients. We used an array to control the amount so that we can use the for-loop to control the entire amount at once.

The code is clear because we have separated the logic into different responsibilities. We put the button events in the view component and the number of ingredients and cash control into the data part. This makes our code easy to read and maintain.

Classified intel

We displayed the cash amount without formatting. There are code snippets or libraries to format numbers if you want to display the cash in the accounting format with a comma separating the thousands. The following are two number-formatting libraries worth checking out:

▶ **accounting.js**: http://josscrowcroft.github.io/accounting.js/

▶ **Numeral.js**: http://numeraljs.com

Adding sound effects

In this task, we will add sound effects to the game.

Prepare for lift off

We want to ensure that the SoundJS library is ready in the `vendors` folder. If the file is missing, we can find it in the CreateJS website or the code bundle.

We also need to have the following sound effects files prepared in the `audio` folder. There are sound effects to start the game, click on a button, trash sushi, and earn money.

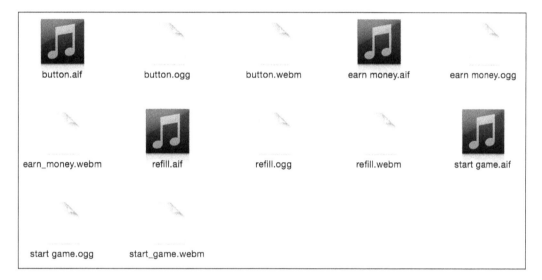

Engage thrusters

In the following steps, we will add sound effects to our game:

1. Let's begin by loading the audio file. We add the following sound-loading code into the `game.js` file:

```
game.load = function() {
  // begin loading content (only sounds to load)
  var assetsPath = "audio/";
manifest = [
      {id:"button", src:"button.ogg"},
      {id:"refill", src:"refill.ogg"},
      {id:"earn-money", src:"earn money.ogg"},
      {id:"start-game", src:"start game.ogg"}
  ];
```

```
    cjs.Sound.alternateExtensions = ['aif', 'webm'];
    preload = new cjs.LoadQueue(true, assetsPath);
    preload.installPlugin(cjs.Sound);
    preload.addEventListener("complete", game.start);
    preload.loadManifest(manifest);
};
```

2. Before we have any preloader, we start the game directly in the `game.js` file. Now we load the game; the loader will start the game only after all the assets are loaded. We replace the `game.start()` method's execution with `game.load()` inside the `game.js` file.

3. When the game starts, we play the sound:

```
game.start = function() {
    ...
    // existing code goes here.
    cjs.Sound.play("start-game");
};
```

4. When the trash button or the ingredients buttons are clicked, we play the following button sound:

```
cjs.Sound.play("button");
```

5. We play the "money-earning" sound when we successfully serve the customer:

```
if (isEqual) {
cjs.Sound.play("earn-money");
    // existing code goes here.
    ...
}
```

6. When we refill the ingredients, we play the refill sound:

```
cjs.Sound.play("refill");
```

Objective complete – mini debriefing

We have added sound effects to our game. Just as we used to preload the images, we need to preload the audio files. Therefore, we use PreloadJS to load the audio assets. We start the game after all the assets are loaded.

We can use the `<audio>` HTML tag to play the audio. However, an audio library, such as SoundJS, would provide easier controls and fallbacks in a different technology when web audio is not available.

We simply play sounds in this task. We can do more with SoundJS, such as controlling the volumes. The following URL contains the documentation of the SoundJS library with detailed discussion on its usage:

```
http://www.createjs.com/#!/SoundJS/documentation
```

Classified intel

We need several file formats of the audio file because different browsers support different formats. With the help of the SoundJS library, we provide three to four formats, and the library will choose the one that can be played in the browser.

The following table shows the audio format support available at the time of writing this book:

Browsers	Ogg	WAV	AIFF	WebM
Google Chrome	Yes	Yes	No	Yes
Mozilla Firefox	Yes	Yes	No	Yes
Apple Safari	Yes	Yes	Yes	No
Internet Explorer	No	No	No	No

Actually, browser compatibility is more complicated than what is shown in the preceding table. The support is different for different browser versions. The mobile version of browsers makes things more complicated. I recommend checking the browser support online while working on a new project. It is because the browser upgrade may add or remove support for certain audio formats. The following URL contains a good article on the latest web audio:

```
https://developer.mozilla.org/en-US/docs/HTML/Supported_media_formats
```

Note that the MP3 format is not really free to use. The patent of MP3 makes serving MP3 files to individuals cost a huge license fee. So, please use MP3 cautiously and only as the last choice. The following URL is one among the many articles that discuss the issues you get using MP3 and web audio:

```
https://www.scirra.com/blog/64/why-you-shouldnt-
use-mp3-in-your-html5-games
```

Distributing the game

The game is playable and fits in different screens. We are now ready to make the game public.

Prepare for lift off

YUI from Yahoo is a commonly used compressor. It can be installed and used locally as a standalone program. We can also use preprocessor tools such as the ones we mentioned in *Project 6*, *Space Defenders*, which come with the YUI-compressing option inside the tools. However, in this task, we make it simple by using an online compressor.

Engage thrusters

Let's work on the following steps to deploy our game on the Internet:

1. We concatenate and compress the logic and the styling of files using a compressor. In this task, we use an online tool. The `http://gpbmike.github.io/refresh-sf/` URL contains the **Online JavaScript/CSS Compressor** tool.

2. Select all the JavaScript files and drag them onto the text field of the compressor website.

3. Click on the **Compress JavaScript** button and the tool generates the compressed code into the text area of the result.

4. Then, we can get the file and put it into the project by clicking on the **Save** button.

5. Make sure we update the `index.html` file to include the compressed code instead of the development code.

6. We will repeat the same steps for the CSS file. Let's upload the CSS file; choose CSS as the file type and compress the code. We save the compressed CSS code and update the `index.html` file to link to the minified CSS file.

7. We are ready to upload the game to the server. We use a simple way that uses an online static file-hosting service. Go to the `http://getforge.com` URL of the Forge online service and create a free account of the service, which allows one static public site.

8. Compress the website and upload the website to the Forge service by dragging the ZIP file directly to the browser. The following screenshot shows the service with our HTML5 game uploaded:

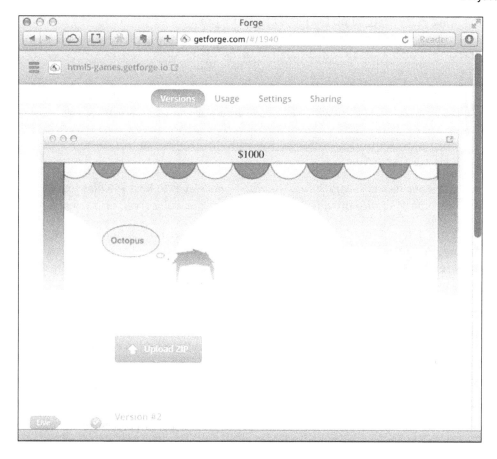

9. After uploading the game, we can choose a URL that links to the website. For example, the URL I chose was `http://html5-games.getforge.io/`

Objective complete – mini debriefing

We have completed the steps that convert the code from the development stage into the production-ready stage. We also uploaded the game online so that we can send it to others to play.

Concatenate and minify the code

At the development stage, we separate the logic code into small chunks. This divides the code into different parts for different purposes. During production, we trim all the unnecessary characters such as spaces, newline characters, and comments. YUI is one of these compressors. You can check out their official page at `http://yui.github.io/yuicompressor/` for detailed usage.

The following essay from Yahoo Developer Network provides an insight on why we need to minify our code: `https://developer.yahoo.com/blogs/ydnfiveblog/high-performance-sites-rule-10-minify-javascript-7208.html`

> It's worth noting that in practice, we use preprocessor tools with the compressor plugin included and installed. So, sometimes we do not directly execute the YUI compressor program.

Hosting a static website

We can host static files in several ways. The traditional way is to host the files from a hosting service. This type of service provides us with access to the web server, for example, Apache.

Static files are different for files with server-side logic, such as PHP or Ruby on Rails. A server-side language requires a server to execute the logic before sending back data to a client-side web browser. Serving static files from the server only requires the server to get the file and send the content directly back to the client.

Therefore, there are different approaches besides using a traditional hosting service. We can use Dropbox to serve static files. We can use Amazon Simple Storage Service, also known as S3, to serve the files. We can even use a **Platfrom as a service (PaaS)** offering, such as *Heroku*, for quick deployment of HTML5 games. There are even some web services that provide easy static file hosting, such as the one we used in this task.

We used the service called `GetForge`. I used it as a demo because it is one of the easiest ways to publish files online without going through a long setup process. As mentioned, we have plenty of options, and you can use the most comfortable one.

Classified intel

There are other distribution channels available to publish the game. An HTML5 game can run anywhere where a modern web browser is installed. In the Mac and iOS development kits, there is a web browser component called `WebView`. We have a similar web view component for Android and Windows platform too. These native components allow us to run HTML5 games inside a native application.

For example, we can package the game into a Mac app by using Xcode, Apple's development tool, with `WebView`. Alternatively, we can use a project called `Node-Webkit` that embeds a chromium browser engine into an executable application.

For mobile distribution, we can use the native SDK or a service called Adobe PhoneGap Build (`https://build.phonegap.com/`). The service builds your HTML5 game into several mobile platforms, including iOS and Android.

Making the game mobile friendly

Making a game work on a mobile platform is not only about the screen resolution, but also about changing from a mouse cursor input to touches and a lot of performance tuning. In this task, we make the game work better on mobile phones by providing touch screen support.

Prepare for lift off

When we publish the game on the Web, we can have several settings to enhance the experience when playing on a mobile touch device. We add the following launch screen and app icon to the images folder:

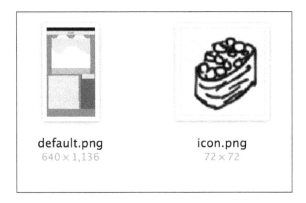

default.png
640 × 1,136

icon.png
72 × 72

We need another library to help improve the clicking events on a DOM element in mobile devices. It eliminates a clicking delay that is added by the mobile platform. We will discuss the delay later. Download the `fastclick.js` file from `https://github.com/ftlabs/fastclick` and add it to the `vendors` folder. Make sure we import this file in the `index.html` file.

Engage thrusters

1. First, we enable the touch event for the customer view:

    ```
    cjs.Touch.enable(game.stage, /*single touch=*/ true,
      /*allow default=*/ true);
    ```

2. Add the following `meta` tags to the `index.html` file. It tells the mobile device to use the real screen resolution to display the content. Otherwise, the mobile device will try to simulate the screen width of a desktop:

    ```
    <meta name="viewport" content="width=device-width,
      initial-scale=1.0, minimum-scale=1.0,
      maximum-scale=1.0, minimal-ui">
    ```

You can refer to the following article on how the viewport affects the rendering of a web page: `https://developer.mozilla.org/en/docs/Mozilla/Mobile/Viewport_meta_tag`.

3. Then, we have several iOS-only setups. The following tag allows iOS to recognize the game as a mobile web app:

```
<meta name="apple-mobile-web-app-capable" content="yes">
```

4. Then, we configure the app icon:

```
<link rel="apple-touch-icon" href="images/icon.png">
```

5. When the web page is installed in the home screen as a web app, it shows a launching screen upon startup. We can define the launching screen with the following `meta` tag placed in the head section:

```
<link rel="apple-touch-startup-image"
  href="images/default.png">
```

6. The mobile screen is too small, so we need to rearrange the customer graphics and the sushi bubble graphics. We add the following code to the `showUp` method of the customer:

```
Customer.prototype.showUp = function() {
...
  // existing code goes here.

  // scale down if in small screen
  if (game.stage.canvas.width<= 320){
    this.scaleX = this.scaleY = 0.6;
  }
  if (game.stage.canvas.height<= 150) {
    bubble.x = -40;
    bubble.y = -50;
    bubble.scaleX = bubble.scaleY = 1.5;
    this.scaleX = this.scaleY = 0.5;
  };
};
```

Let's put the code online and test the app on a mobile device as shown in the following screenshot:

Now, if we play the game in iOS and bookmark the game as the home screen, we will see that the system uses the icon file as shown in the following screenshot:

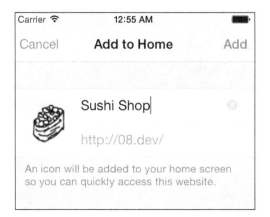

 Most of the time, we may require a development server to test the game on a mobile. If it is a mobile simulator, we can test with localhost. If we use a real device to test, we will need to access it via the local network. Some apps help to make this progress easier. Xip.io and CodeKit are two easy options to create a server for the project folder and get access to it via mobile devices under LAN.

Objective complete – mini debriefing

On the following screenshot, you will see that the customer view is squeezed into a very small area. We need to scale down the customer sprite and put the sushi bubble on the side to fit into the view. We don't want the player to scroll up and down to play the game because it would ruin the experience.

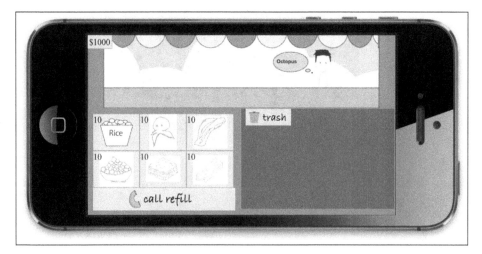

Enable the touch event

In EaselJS, we use `cjs.Touch.enable` to enable the touch event. The first argument is related to the game stage. The second argument defines a single touch or multiple touches. The third argument determines whether the default browser's touch event is preserved or not. If the default behavior is disabled, the user cannot scroll down the page by dragging on the game stage.

There is a delay of 300 ms on a click event in a mobile device. This delay is good for normal web browsing as the reader will not accidently missclick on the links that may be present on the web page. However, in the game, we need to get rid of the delay to make the UI feel responsive to the player's action.

We can eliminate the delay by using the `touchstart` and `touchend` event. We can change the click event to a touch event ourselves, or we can use the `fastclick` library. Using the library is easier because it automatically detects the original click event and changes that may appear while using the touch event without any modification to the code.

An iOS mobile web app

When the `apple-mobile-web-app-capable` meta tag is used, iOS treats the web page as a web app. A web app would show up as a native app in the multi-task switching screen. The following screenshot shows how our web app sits besides the native **Settings** app:

The following URL shows the complete code to configure the web app for different iOS devices:

`https://gist.github.com/makzan/6124d8d8ea1eb08c32e7`

Classified intel

There are several tags in the `<head>` section to set up the web app. The viewport tags can have several options.

Please use `maximum-scale` with caution. On the Web, we usually don't want to restrict the scaling of a page. Some users may need to zoom in to the content to read it in an easier fashion. Content accessibility has a higher priority than visual scale controlling. However, when we distribute the content as an app, we want to disable the scaling, so we set both the maximum and minimum scale to `1.0`.

Mobile app distribution

Another way to publish the game would be by distributing the game as a mobile app. All we need to do is use a mobile web view to present the HTML inside a native mobile application. Alternatively, we can use Adobe PhoneGap Build for this purpose. In some games, we can use a native renderer, such as CocoonJS from Luide, to boost the rendering performance while distributing the game to the mobile App Store.

Offline cache

We can even take the mobile web game further by making it work offline. This is done using a technique called application cache manifest. You can read a detailed explanation on it on the following Mozilla Developer Network page:

`http://developer.mozilla.org/en/docs/HTML/Using_the_application_cache`

Take an online game, *PieGuy*, as an example. Try to use an iOS mobile device by following the ensuing steps:

1. Go to `http://mrgan.com/pieguy`.
2. Bookmark the game as the home screen.
3. Open the game once for the system to load the asset files.
4. Restart the game and get into the offline mode, such as the airplane mode.
5. Open the game from the home screen and the game still works.

Mission accomplished

We've built a game that works in different environments. Here, clients walk in and order sushi, and the player then selects the ingredients to make the correct sushi to earn money. We also added sounds to the game. Finally, we published the game on the Web that a player can install on their iOS home screen as a mobile web app. The following is the screenshot of our game running on a tablet:

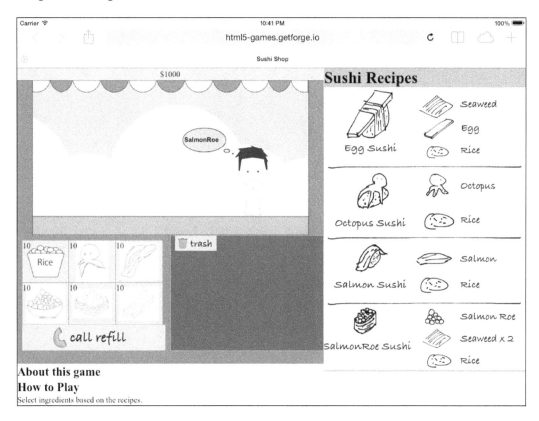

A Hotshot challenge

We have learned how to publish our HTML5 games on the Web and make it mobile friendly. Now, how about we revise the seven games we created and publish them?

Index

U

update method 258
updateTilesPosition function 100
user interface, isometric city game
  designing 156-162
  tween-based cloud animation 163
user interface, tower defense game
  Adobe Flash 212, 213
  background layer 211
  effect layer 212
  foundation, building 207-210
  head-up display (HUD) 212
  major layer 212
  setting up 206

V

vendor folder
  preparing 256
view classes
  building 186
view.js file 255
view object, runway 97

About Packt Publishing

Packt, pronounced 'packed', published its first book "*Mastering phpMyAdmin for Effective MySQL Management*" in April 2004 and subsequently continued to specialize in publishing highly focused books on specific technologies and solutions.

Our books and publications share the experiences of your fellow IT professionals in adapting and customizing today's systems, applications, and frameworks. Our solution based books give you the knowledge and power to customize the software and technologies you're using to get the job done. Packt books are more specific and less general than the IT books you have seen in the past. Our unique business model allows us to bring you more focused information, giving you more of what you need to know, and less of what you don't.

Packt is a modern, yet unique publishing company, which focuses on producing quality, cutting-edge books for communities of developers, administrators, and newbies alike. For more information, please visit our website: www.packtpub.com.

Writing for Packt

We welcome all inquiries from people who are interested in authoring. Book proposals should be sent to author@packtpub.com. If your book idea is still at an early stage and you would like to discuss it first before writing a formal book proposal, contact us; one of our commissioning editors will get in touch with you.

We're not just looking for published authors; if you have strong technical skills but no writing experience, our experienced editors can help you develop a writing career, or simply get some additional reward for your expertise.

HTML5 Game Development with ImpactJS

ISBN: 978-1-84969-456-8   Paperback: 304 pages

A step-by-step guide to developing your own 2D games

1. A practical hands-on approach to teach you how to build your own game from scratch.

2. Learn to incorporate game physics.

3. How to monetize and deploy to the web and mobile platforms.

Learn HTML5 by Creating Fun Games

ISBN: 978-1-84969-602-9   Paperback: 374 pages

Learn one of the most popular markup languages by creating simple yet fun games

1. Learn the basics of this emerging technology and have fun doing it.

2. Unleash the new and exciting features and APIs of HTML5.

3. Create responsive games that can be played on a browser and on a mobile device.

Please check **www.PacktPub.com** for information on our titles

www.ingramcontent.com/pod-product-compliance
Lightning Source LLC
LaVergne TN
LVHW062303060326
832902LV00013B/2029